THE BIG BOOK OF SAILING

THE SAILORS, THE SHIPS, AND THE SEA

EDITED BY
FRANK GRUBE AND GERHARD RICHTER

PHOTOGRAPHS BY
SVANTE DOMIZLAFF AND
HARALD MERTES

BARRON'S
Woodbury, New York · London · Toronto · Sydney

First English language edition published in 1979 by Barron's Educational Series, Inc.
©1978 Hoffmann und Campe Verlag

All inquiries should be addressed to:
Barron's Educational Series, Inc.
113 Crossways Park Drive
Woodbury, New York 11797

Library of Congress Catalog Card No. 79-11549
International Standard Book No. 0-8120-5324-9
Library of Congress Cataloging in Publication Data
Main entry under title:

The Big book of sailing.

   Translation of Das grosse Buch vom Segeln—Manner, yachten, und die See.
   1. Sailing—Addresses, essays, lectures. 2. Yacht racing—Addresses,
essays, lectures. I. Grube, Frank, 1946- II. Richter, Gerhard, 1945-
GV811.G7413   797.1'4   79-11549
ISBN 0-8120-5324-9

PRINTED IN JAPAN

THE BIG BOOK OF
SAILING

CONTENTS

VI THE LONELY MEN AND THE SEA

VII AND THE SEA IS SO FAR

VIII SAILING TO HELL AND BACK

IX APPENDIX

The nature of sailing reflects the nature of the sea. The wind rules over the water, setting waves and swells in motion. The sea remains at rest until the wind moves it. The sailing vessel was our response to this force that sweeps across the surface of the sea.

The sailing ship is a natural configuration, shaped by a given natural environment and created to fit into that environment. It forms an organic unity with its surroundings, with wind and water. The same winds that churn the sea send huge sailing boats weighing thousands of tons slicing through the waves, and the men who take their helms enter into this magnificent interplay of natural forces, thus becoming part of nature themselves. The sailor is constantly subject to the dictates of nature, and a remarkably high level of sailing skill can develop from his intimate knowledge of wind and sea. An adept and experienced skipper can even sail a small, well-built yacht in such a way that it will steer itself and automatically hold to the desired course without anyone at the helm. This is true not only for short periods of time but for days and weeks on end.

Ernst Alexander Römer

The traveler who looks down on the Atlantic from the window of a jet airliner or surveys the sea from the deck of a luxury liner has a completely different relationship to nature than someone who rides the swells of the trackless seas in a 30-foot yacht and has only himself or his fellow crewmen to depend on. The sailor becomes one with his vessel, just as the rider becomes one with his horse.

Ever since steam and diesel engines conquered the seas, our daily lives have become increasingly dominated by technology and more and more remote from nature. But at the same time, the sea, with its seemingly endless expanses, has taken on an ever-greater fascination. It is difficult, of course, in an age when giant tankers run aground on reefs and sand bars, shatter like glass, and cover the sea with a deadly blanket of oil, to recall to memory the many stories of adventure and romance that our ancestors have passed down to us. But the many yachts and yawls that continue to ply the Seven Seas today still convey to us a feeling for those earlier days when clipper ships, driven by the wind alone, their rigging obedient to the muscle power of their crews, crossed the seas under full sail, transporting men and goods from one harbor to another. Despite technology, despite the steam and diesel engine, the sailing ship is still alive and well. Rousseau's cry of "back to nature!" was never more popular.

The winds have blown from the beginning of time, and man has always made use of them. He invented, constructed, and tested those woven surfaces that then, as sails, carried men and their ships across uncharted waters to distant new worlds. Curiosity sent men out to sea; nostalgia brought them home again. Many were claimed by the foaming waves. But despite all danger, men have continued to go to sea and try their mettle against the elements that have shaped the course of the world from time immemorial.

Anyone who wants to know the age of the earth need only look at a stormy sea. The gray of this immense surface, the lines the wind cuts in the face of the waves, the huge masses of churning foam tossed about like the white hair of an old man all make the sea in a storm appear ancient, drab, lusterless, and bleak, as if it had been created before the first light ever dawned.

Joseph Conrad

Is it just the age of the earth that is reflected in the sea? Are not we ourselves reflected in the still waters of the doldrums or of a momentary calm? Is it not perhaps the search for the meaning of existence that draws us to the sea? On the ocean's surface, we confront the earth—and it confronts us—face to face. Until very recent times, entire nations have lived from the force of the wind in sails. The wind has spelled the difference between victory and defeat in war. Countries and continents have been discovered and conquered by the sail. But now the oceans have fallen victim to our calculations of profit and loss. They have been cut down, shrunk, reduced to economic terms. Tall-masted ships have passed into mythology. But thanks to a high standard of living and sufficient leisure time, almost anyone today can relive the romance of the sea that, according to many who experienced the last days of the sailing vessels, was purely a product of writers' imaginations.

Here, as in so many areas, the Anglo-Saxon countries led the way. As early as the late eighteenth century sailing was—for a select elite, at any rate—a sport rather than a job. These amateur sailors established clubs and their yachts, which were deliberately designed for speed, began to differ more and more from their utilitarian ancestors. Races were held, and inventive minds created faster and faster boats with better and better sailing qualities. Incredible sums in pounds and dollars were invested in the hulls of these proud yachts.

New ideas swept away concepts of beauty that had dominated shipbuilding for generations. Where once the richly decorated and luxuriously equipped ship had been considered beautiful, it was now the fast, narrow-keeled yacht that took the prize. But a yacht had to be more than just fast. It had to be able to sail close to the wind; it had to be stable; and it had to skim across the water like an aquaplane. If it is true that beauty is a product of functionality, then the modern yacht is one of the most beautiful things that humans have ever created.

When the great era of the sailing ship had come to an end and the period of the coal- and oil-fired giants dawned, what had been a vocation became an avocation, a passion, a high art. It is true there are no more uncharted patches on the maps of our earth, but the search for adventure and the attraction of nature unsullied by man continue to draw men to the sea. There is nothing modern technology will ever invent that can stifle men's love for wind and sea.

It was this love that moved a crew of sail-crazed amateurs to produce this book. No windjammer ever put out to sea without its full contingent of sailors before the mast, and without all the mates, swabs, and skippers who have helped us, this book would never have seen the light of day. They led us through a labyrinth of halyards, blocks, stays, and knots, and we want to thank everyone who has helped us put together these pages in praise of sea and sail. We are particularly grateful to Svante Domizlaff, Harald Mertes, and Alexander Rost.

Frank Grube   Gerhard Richter

Sea Fever

I must go down to the seas again, to the lonely sea and the sky,
And all I ask is a tall ship and a star to steer her by,
And the wheel's kick and the wind's song and the white sail's shaking,
And a gray mist on the sea's face and a gray dawn breaking.

I must go down to the seas again, for the call of the running tide
Is a wild call and a clear call that may not be denied;
And all I ask is a windy day with the white clouds flying,
And the flung spray and the blown spume, and the sea gulls crying.

I must go down to the seas again, to the vagrant gypsy life.
To the gull's way and the whale's way where the wind's like a whetted knife;
And all I ask is a merry yarn from a laughing fellow rover,
And quiet sleep and a sweet dream when the long trick's over.

John Masefield

I
REFLECTIONS OF THE SEA

The sailing and racing of yachts has developed a class of fore-and-aft sailors, men born and bred to the sea, fishing in winter and yachting in summer; men to whom the handling of that particular rig presents no mystery. It is their striving for victory that has elevated the sailing of pleasure craft to the dignity of a fine art in that special sense. As I have said, I know nothing of racing and but little of fore-and-aft rig; but the advantages of such a rig are obvious, especially for purposes of pleasure, whether in cruising or racing. It requires less effort in handling; the trimming of the sail-planes to the wind can be done with speed and accuracy; the unbroken spread of the sail-area is of infinite advantage; and the greatest possible amount of canvas can be displayed upon the least possible quantity of spars. Lightness and concentrated power are the great qualities of fore-and-aft rig.

A fleet of fore-and-afters at anchor has its own slender graciousness. The setting of their sails resembles more than anything else the unfolding of a bird's wings; the facility of their evolutions is a pleasure to the eye. They are birds of the sea, whose swimming is like flying, and resembles more a natural function than the handling of man-invented appliances. The fore-and-aft rig in its simplicity and the beauty of its aspect under every angle of vision is, I believe, unapproachable. A schooner, yawl, or cutter in charge of a capable man seems to handle herself as if endowed with the power of reasoning and the gift of swift execution. One laughs with sheer pleasure at a smart piece of manœuvring, as at a manifestation of a living creature's quick wit and graceful precision.

Of those three varieties of fore-and-aft rig, the cutter—the racing rig *par excellence*—is of an appearance the most imposing, from the fact that practically all her canvas is in one piece. The enormous mainsail of a cutter, as she draws slowly past a point of land or the end of a jetty under your admiring gaze, invests her with an air of lofty and silent majesty. At anchor a schooner looks better; she has an aspect of greater efficiency and a better balance to the eye, with her two masts distributed over the hull with a swaggering rake aft. The yawl rig one comes in time to love. It is, I should think, the easiest of all to manage.

For racing, a cutter; for a long pleasure voyage, a schooner; for cruising in home waters, the yawl; and the handling of them all is indeed a fine art. It requires not only the knowledge of the general principles of sailing, but a particular acquaintance with the character of the craft. All vessels are handled in the same way as far as theory goes, just as you may deal with all men on broad and rigid principles. But if you want that success in life which comes from the affection and confidence of your fellows, then with no two men, however similar they may appear in their nature, will you deal in the same way. There may be a rule of conduct; there is no rule of human fellowship. To deal with men is as fine an art as it is to deal with ships. Both men and ships live in an unstable element, are subject to subtle and powerful influences, and want to have their merits understood rather than their faults found out.

It is not what your ship will *not* do that you want to know to get on terms of successful partnership with her; it is, rather, that you ought to have a precise knowledge of what she will do for you when called upon to put forth what is in her by a sympathetic touch. At first sight the difference does not seem great in either line of dealing with the difficult problem of limitations. But the difference is great. The difference lies in the spirit in which the problem is approached. After all, the art of handling ships is finer, perhaps, than the art of handling men.

And, like all fine arts, it must be based upon a broad, solid sincerity, which, like a law of Nature, rules an infinity of different phenomena. Your endeavor must be singleminded. You would talk differently to a coal-heaver and to a professor. But is this duplicity? I deny it. The truth consists in the genuineness of the feeling, in the genuine recognition of the two men, so similar and so different, as your two partners in the hazard of life. Obviously, a humbug, thinking only of winning his little race, would stand a chance of profiting by his artifices. Men, professors or coal-heavers, are easily deceived; they even have an extraordinary knack of lending themselves to deception, a sort of curious and inexplicable propensity to allow themselves to be led by the nose with their eyes open. But a ship is a creature which we have brought into the world, as it were on purpose to keep us up to the mark. In her handling a ship will not put up with a mere pretender, as, for

instance, the public will do with Mr. X, the popular statesman, Mr. Y, the popular scientist, or Mr. Z, the popular—what shall we say?—anything from a teacher of high morality to a bagman—who have won their little race. But I would like (though not accustomed to betting) to wager a large sum that not one of the few first-rate skippers of racing yachts has ever been a humbug. It would have been too difficult. The difficulty arises from the fact that one does not deal with ships in a mob, but with a ship as an individual. So we may have to do with men. But in each of us there lurks some particle of the mob spirit, of the mob temperament. No matter how earnestly we strive against each other, we remain brothers on the lowest side of our intellect and in the instability of our feelings. With ships it is not so. Much as they are to us they are nothing to each other. Those sensitive creatures have no ears for our blandishments. It takes something more than words to cajole them to do our will, to cover us with glory. Luckily, too, or else there would have been more shoddy reputations for first-rate seamanship. Ships have no ears, I repeat, though, indeed, I think I have known ships who really seemed to have had eyes, or else I cannot understand on what ground a certain 1000-ton barque of my acquaintance on one particular occasion refused to answer her helm, thereby saving a frightful smash to two ships and to a very good man's reputation. I knew her intimately for two years, and in no other instance either before or since have I known her to do that thing. The man she had served so well (guessing, perhaps, at the depths of his affection for her) I have known much longer, and in bare justice to him I must say that this confidence-shattering experience (though so fortunate) only augmented his trust in her. Yes, our ships have no ears, and thus they cannot be deceived. I would illustrate my idea of fidelity as between man and ship, between the master and his art, by a statement which, though it might appear shockingly sophisticated, is really very simple. I would say that a racing-yacht skipper who thought of nothing else but the glory of winning the race would never attain to any eminence of reputation. The genuine masters of their craft—I say this confidently from my experience of ships—have thought of nothing but of doing their very best by the vessel under their charge. To forget one's self, to surrender all personal feeling in the service of that fine art, is the only way for a seaman to the faithful discharge of his trust.

Such is the service of a fine art and of ships that sail the sea. And therein I think I can lay my finger upon the difference between the seamen of yesterday, who are still with us, and the seamen of to-morrow, already entered upon the possession of their inheritance. History repeats itself, but the special call of an art which has passed away is never reproduced. It is as utterly gone out of the world as the song of a destroyed wild bird. Nothing will awaken the same response of pleasurable emotion or conscientious endeavour. And the sailing of any vessel afloat is an art whose fine form seems already receding from us on its way to the overshadowed Valley of Oblivion. The taking of a modern steamship about the world (though one would not minimize its responsibilities) has not the same quality of intimacy with nature, which, after all, is an indispensable condition to the building up of an art. It is less personal and a more exact calling; less arduous, but also less gratifying in the lack of close communion between the artist and the medium of his art. It is, in short, less a matter of love. Its effects are measured exactly in time and space as no effect of an art can be. It is an occupation which a man not desperately subject to sea-sickness can be imagined to follow with content, without enthusiasm, with industry, without affection. Punctuality is its watchword. The incertitude which attends closely every artistic endeavour is absent from its regulated enterprise. It has no great moments of self-confidence, or moments not less great of doubt and heart-searching. It is an industry which, like other industries, has its romance, its honour, and its rewards, its bitter anxieties and its hours of ease. But such sea-going has not the artistic quality of a single-handed struggle with something much greater than yourself; it is not the laborious, absorbing practice of an art whose ultimate result remains on the knees of the gods. It is not an individual, temperamental achievement, but simply the skilled use of a captured force, merely another step forward upon the way of universal conquest.

Joseph Conrad

12

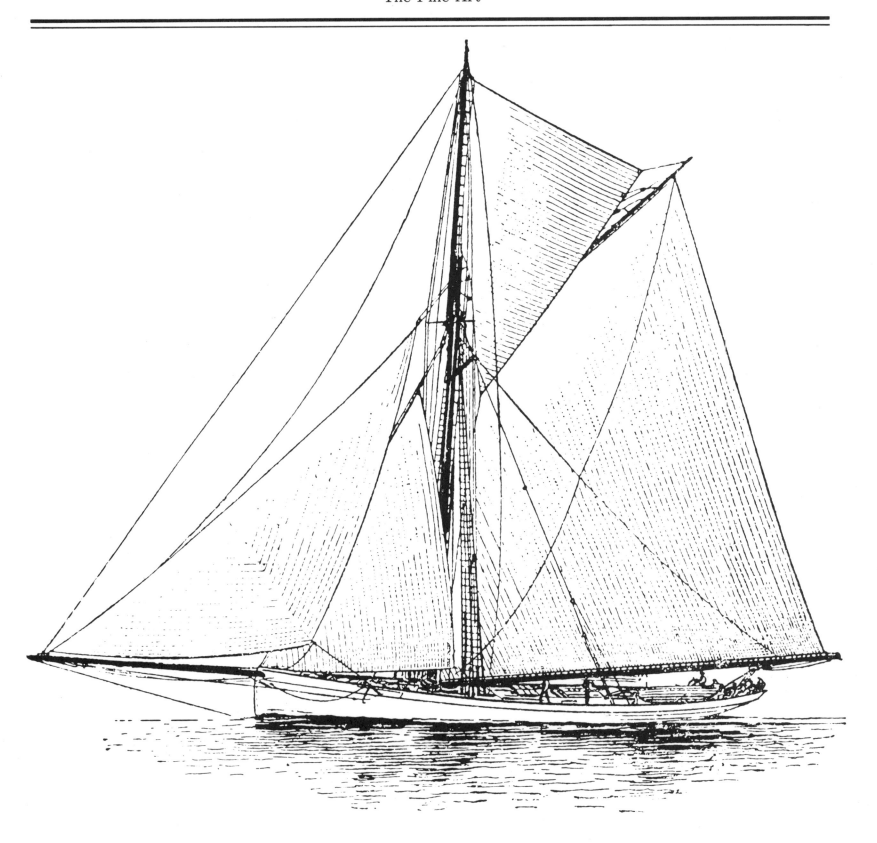

In the story of the Creation, the earth, the heavens, and the waters were the first things called into being. Everything else stemmed from these three. And this is how it felt to us one evening as a light breeze came up out of the east-northeast. Both sky and air became physically perceptible. Gray patches of sea rose into view, and, as a natural consequence, men moved into action. The motor fell silent, and the monotony of its steady throbbing came to an end. New sounds fell on our ears, irregular sounds, natural sounds. The rigging creaked and the water began to whisper past the bow. Our ship drew its first slow breaths like a man given up for drowned, whose heart and lungs begin to pump faintly again. The boat came alive under out feet, and as we picked up speed we seemed to experience anew the creation of this infinitely varied world. And the morning and the evening were the first day, a day of new expectations, new hopes, and a new existence.

Poor deprived landlubbers have no idea how delicious a narrow ship's bunk is. I was dog-tired and with a rare sense of well being, I rolled and turned in my berth a few times until I had curled up under my covers and settled into my accustomed on-board sleeping position. The blue glow of a clear summer evening seeped through the skylight and outlined the familiar objects of the cabin, a retreat that always conveyed an atmosphere of peace and safety, even in the stormiest hours. The gentle swaying of the ship gradually lulled me into the dreamland of sleep.

It would be interesting to record the motions of a ship with some kind of sensitive instrument. They are incredibly varied yet retain a basic uniformity. They are monotonous yet as unpredictable as the countless rhythmic variations of the willful sea. What is it that allows a man, luxuriating in the pleasures of his bunk, to peer into the depths of those demonic times when life originated? Some inkling of primordial impressions lets us regain a realm of irreality in which none of our senses had awakened and we felt nothing but physical closeness and the rhythm of our own blood, a realm in which all living beings sense their origin. It is no coincidence that the rocking cradle is the oldest known means we have for quieting a newborn child. Even before light and sound are able to work their comforting magic on an infant, the rocking of a cradle or of a mother's arms can dispel the disharmony of new impressions and restore, in spirit at least, the new citizen of this world to the peace and quiet of that unknown realm he has just left behind. It seems as though the sea is the ultimate source of all being.

A child surely has closer contact with that other world of its origin than an adult does. For the adult, that contact has been obliterated by the flood of impressions he has experienced in his short stay on this earth. This is why the child yearns for the rocking of the sea and the soft swayings of its cradle, hoping to recover its lost state of utter contentment. No one knows where we come from, and no one knows where we are going. But of all the visual images our world presents to us, the sea strikes us as the primordial mother of all life and as a symbol of all beginning.

If happiness is too great, we cannot enjoy it. The desire to fully enjoy these hours in a bunk drifting through the world drives away sleep. Although the exhausted body relaxes, the mind falls helpless victim to the spell of one train of thought after another. With painful logic, these thoughts lead on to new problems. Inquiries into the meaning and value of life awaken a consciousness that we are inextricably involved, willing or not, in the life of the world; and this insight tempts us to relinquish our critical faculties. Faced with the danger of going under in the massive movements of the universe, we feel our fear increase. The sea engulfs the dry land and swallows up the stars, just as it did before the first day of the Creation. Beyond time and space, the heart, enveloped in the glassy waters, takes ever-deeper breaths. The eye no longer sees, the ear no longer hears. Only the heart listens for its own beat and for the whispering of minute, indestructible cells that tell a story billions of years old in the language of the world's rhythms.

Ocean sailing arises from a need for adventure and, as a sport, it arises from the human need for play. In their games, children imitate the adult activities they admire. They play storekeeper or Indian chief, Davy Crockett or trolley car conductor, indulging in all the variations their childish fantasy can invent. If we give a child the imaginary task of being a stagecoach driver or Davy Crockett and invest his play with an element of adult reality, if, for example, we let a child actually take the reins in his hands and be in charge of the horses or ask him to join in the search for a lost object in such a way that he can imagine himself a woodsman searching for a lost party or a sheriff pursuing a band of rustlers, then his interest in this "real" activity will be increased a hundredfold. He will feel an immense pride in fulfilling a task in the adult world as well as a pleasure comparable only to that of the artist who succeeds in translating the stirrings of his imagination into a finished work. The appeal of ocean sailing is of a similar nature. At first, the amateur sailor only plays at being a professional sailor. But the sea does not distinguish between professionals and amateurs, and gradually the amateur's play becomes serious business. The child's spirit, which is always alive in any kind of sport, experiences tremendous satisfaction when actions born of the playful impulse to imitate are not only important but can also spell the difference between life and death. The amateur sailor feels great pride—a pride that usually goes unexpressed—when he calculates his position perfectly, when his signals conform strictly to regulations, and when his ship cleaves to its course as precisely as a professional's would.

The delight of deepwater sailing is that we play at being adults. We act as if we had the genuine duties of professional seamen to perform, and our play takes on an inner seriousness in light of the fact that we are indeed seafarers with real reponsibilities to fulfill.

All night long we run under full sail and a

15

genoa jib. The darkness of the night closing in around us makes the little world of our ship seem even smaller. Our running lights send their warning beams out ahead of us. The stern lamp throws a small circle of light on our wake and on the white, ceaselessly spinning line of the log trailing behind us. Below deck all is darkness except in the navigator's station, where a small lamp lights up the table with the charts and log book.

The helmsman's perceptions of the world around him are limited to the faintly illuminated compass dial before him. All he sees is how the mark on the compass housing persistently attempts to wander to one side or the other, and he tries to counteract these movements.

The watch captain paces back and forth carrying the heavy night binoculars with him, or he settles down next to the helmsman for a nocturnal chat. The safety of the vessel is entrusted to the crew member who is watch captain. The faith the rest of the crew have in his sense of responsibility lets them sleep soundly.

It is a strange feeling for the man on deck to know that his comrades sleeping in the bunks below are dependent on his reliability. The slightest lapse of attention on his part can bring disaster. On the open sea, danger is not so omnipresent, but in the coastal waters that yachts frequent most, the watch is a serious affair indeed. This psychic stress contributes to the maturing process and the great educational value that deepwater sailing offers impressionable young people. No other sport provides this particular challenge because in no other sport are such constant demands made on alertness, nor are the consequences of inattention so grave.

On a yacht, every individual puts his life in the hands of his fellow crew members. On land, there is much talk of esprit de corps, and much fuss is made over declarations of loyalty. Verbiage of this kind is superfluous at sea, and, for a crew that shares a common fate, comradeship is taken for granted. While a sailor is standing watch on deck he is completely absorbed by his duties. When he is relieved at the appointed hour, he sheds the tensions and responsibility of the watch and entrusts to his follower not only the watch but also his own life and perhaps the lives of his wife and children as well. The total confidence that one sailor has in the reliability of another always amazes the observer. I have often noted how a crewman coming off watch will go below deck without a care in the world. It hardly seems possible that he has just endured hours of unrelieved stress, watching constantly to prevent an accidental jibe or struggling to keep the yacht from running off course and playing havoc with the navigator's dead reckoning. But once he has been relieved of his post, none of these worries concerns him in the least. He passes them on to the next man, who will now watch over the welfare of ship and crew as devotedly as his predecessor has. Perhaps nothing else reflects the ethic of the sea as vividly as this total mutual confidence among sailors.

A rush of thoughts comes to the sailor as he and his fellows stand in respectful silence before the majesty of the night sea. He is

16

stripped of all ambition and material concerns and gives himself up to a higher consciousness. Images from the past and dreams of the future stream past his mind's eye. They arise from the knowledge that, standing there on the planking of the deck, he embodies a shared idea that has created and still keeps alive an organic community in the midst of the sea.

The deepest feelings rarely take the form of words. Sailors hardly ever talk about personal allegiance, but I would imagine that almost every seaman on a night watch has thought about it at one time or another.

"Sleep well, my friends," he has said to himself, "I'll watch over your well-being just as you have watched over mine."

We raised anchor at four in the morning. Wind Force 3, clear skies. In the afternoon we were sailing between the myriad rocky islets off Mariehamn. A fine, misty rain was falling, making everything loom much larger before the eye. The masts of several large yachts seemed to reach beyond sight. I had forgotten that Mariehamn has become a refuge for the most majestic sailing ships from almost all parts of the world.

In the hazy air, the ever more shadowy outlines of one ship after another pass by like a procession of ghostly giants. Like a ghost fleet indeed, unreal as in a dream, they all swing in the same direction on their heavy anchor chains. Not a movement disturbs the stony silence on board them. It is hard to imagine the life that filled those decks only a few years ago, and the spell that locks them in silence now will not be broken again until the starting signal for the Grain Race from Australia to England releases a stir of hectic activity among the sails of these vessels.

They are not steamships that pick their way along narrow channels; they are not streetcars that stop at every corner; and they are not fashionable floating hotels that regard their time at sea only as an unavoidable disruption in the conduct of their business on land.

These are genuine children of the trackless waters. They need the wide horizons of the open sea to live. For them, even the English Channel is oppressively narrow. Once they put out to sea, they will not be underway for only hours or days but for months at a time, sailing in a single movement from Finland to Australia.

Even in their home port they do not lie at dockside where the dust and refuse of the land can reach them. Instead, they lie pensively at anchor in the pale white light of the northern summer sky, waiting until their times comes and the small tugs carefully lead these giant swans, one after another, out past the reefs.

They are much too proud and their wingspans much too broad to make their way themselves between the islands and cliffs. For this, they avail themselves of the slavish work of the tugs. They tolerate the presence of these lowly vessels when they have need of their services, but once they reach the open water, the stark lines of their masts and spars fill with the natural curves of white sails; and without looking back, they sweep out into the limitless sea where the servant tugs, with their towropes, never dare to follow.

17

No other human creation so perfectly unites functionality and prosaic utility with a sense of organic nature and romantic beauty. The sailboat was invented and constructed by man, but it belongs nonetheless to an order of living beings that have developed naturally over the centuries and that have their own qualities, eccentricities, and demands. The sailor never thinks of his craft as constructed of inanimate materials.

When we saw those yachts at Mariehamn, they were lying motionless and lifeless on the gray water. The naked angles of their rigging were reminiscent of the rigidity the body assumes when the dreaming soul has temporarily left it behind. Ten, twenty, and more of these ghost ships rose up before us and disappeared again in the fog.

Days later. At every encounter with foul weather, I am astounded again by what a good boat can endure. When a gleaming, swirling, threatening wave enters the circle of light cast by the running lights and bears down in one powerful sweep on the ceaselessly laboring ship, anyone would expect bulwark, strakes, and superstructures to splinter into pieces. But the boat usually rides with the wave and adapts itself to it so that the attack is robbed of its force and the mountain of water slides harmlessly under the keel. Woe to the man who thinks he can oppose nature head on! It is a disastrous error to prize heroic defiance above rational judgment and to celebrate unjustified triumphs in cases where nature was kind enough to let stupidity go unpunished.

Romantics do not like to see idealistic images destroyed, but appearances have no value at sea. It is all the same to the sea and stars whether a man is proud, arrogant, or courageous. If he is a match for the forces he encounters, then all is well. If he is not, then fate will take him, and he will disappear in violence and destruction.

It is easy to lose heart in the darkness of the night. The increasing violence of the seas makes me nervous, and I listen anxiously to the voices of the wind in the rigging. Will our sails be able to withstand the forces? How much longer should I wait until I take in sail, and what course should I take? The sea determines what I can and cannot do. My task is simply to recognize nature's will and act accordingly.

How foolish ideas of conquest are. Recognize nature's will and act accordingly—that is the great wisdom one learns at sea. How foolish to talk of a battle with the elements. We are at their mercy, and we have to obey them if we are to survive. Our most satisfying victories are gains in knowledge and adaptability.

I have to choose the size and set of my sails in accordance with the strength and direction of the wind. The waves determine how I handle the helm. If the forces I encounter become too strong to let me hold to my course, I have to give it up and either scud before the wind or heave to. When the wind and sea rise to the fullness of their power, all I can hope for is minimal safety in aimless drifting. Even the largest steamers, including the sturdiest vessels naval architecture and technology have been able to create, have to take the limits of their capabilities into account. If they forget these limits, they will perish. What meaning does a word like *courage* or the concept of a heroic gesture have in this sobering context?

How satisfying it is when the movements of the boat are in harmony with the wind and sea. How blissful it is to experience the safety and security that come with being in step with the rhythms of nature. A shimmering star breaks through the tattered clouds above us. It stands aloof in the heavens, totally indifferent to whether the sailor perishes through his own inadequacies or manages to survive a little while longer.

The roar of the sea and the organ tones of the wind surround us. The turnbuckles are equipped with small holes in which marline-spikes are inserted for taking up or easing off tension on the stays. The wind plays on these holes as if it were playing a woodwind instrument. The tones swell and die down, alternating between a sharp *fortissimo* and a low whisper, depending on the angle and force of the individual gusts that produce them. We often hear the rush of an approaching gust from far off and feel it coming closer and closer, yet every time we are astounded by the speed and force with which it strikes. The stays and the shrouds on the weather side, taut as piano strings, sing under its touch. The loose blocks on the mast rattle fiercely, and the sea claws at the bow press deeply into the water.

There must be a law of nature that assures the futility of all efforts that seek to put an end to conflict among human beings. It seems as though nature fears that a reduction of torment would be accompanied by a reduction in vital energy. Why is it that those prophets who try to bring about peace are always misunderstood, viciously persecuted, and crucified?

At sea, time loses its meaning. It is of value to a sailor only as a measuring stick he uses to schedule his watches and order his log book by. But the meaning of time is lost in the vastness of the sea. We never know whether hours or minutes have gone by. The sun sets, and we are amazed by that event. The night gives way to dawn, and we think, "Is it day already?"

The day dawned gray and drizzly. A dismal morning shed a sobering light on the melancholy of darkness. Total darkness is more congenial than a half light that creates an aura of ugliness.

On shore, wind and weather lose their force and live on, like a great *symphonia maris*, only in the sailor's dreams. The howling and whistling still ring in his ears. Sky and sea mingle and dissolve in the chaos of the first day of the Creation. The sea breathes deeply, its vast breast rising and falling, swelling to the bursting point and then sinking again; and we are reminded of how a violent storm of feeling can possess our own breasts, forcing us to gasp for breath and bringing us to the edge of unconsciousness.

The massive waves roll ceaselessly toward us across vast distances. Our own sense of being rises and sinks between dizzying heights and dreary depths. The air throbs with the pounding notes of a roaring ground bass. We try to escape this realm of rolling mountains,

19

try to shake off this vision of gigantic masses of water, seen as in a delirium of fever; but the rise and fall of the waves grows louder and louder until our own will is extinguished and the blood pulses through exhausted limbs in time with the heaving and sinking of the sea's breast.

Above the swelling movement of the bass the strings play swift, nervous runs, trying to assert their voices, but the crest of a mighty wave obliterates their self-important claims. Shrill flutes and plaintive bassoons shriek to a high *fortissimo* until their ride on the back of a wave ends in the hushed rustling of the foam. In this lull, small, distinct voices come alive. A single oboe intones a tentative melody that seeks refuge in the unpeopled silence, hoping to run its joyous and carefree course to its end. A single violin dances arabesques around a calm center. But then a crescendo announces a new rush of waves that comes closer and closer until the entire orchestra is once again playing at full volume.

On the broad slope of the wave, innumerable instruments vie with each other. We can breathe only in gasps; the roar becomes deafening. The shrieking and whimpering of the wind instruments are overpowered by a soundless tone too deep for our ears to hear, a tone we can perceive only with some inner sense, a tone like the last, indistinguishable sound that rises from the depths of a despairing soul. Shreds of foam snatch up this tone and fling it into the indifferent clouds scudding across a gray sky. Once again the flutes' piercing note stabs into nature's subsiding moan. Muffled drums rumble and die away. The oboe picks up its song in the momentary lull, recalling, after the achromatic flood that has just past, the line of a simple melody.

In endless succession the swells run under us and through us. Whole years and lifespans are compressed into minutes. There is no rest. The essence of seafaring is that you relinquish every last bit of solid footing. The only firm thing remaining to you is an idea, something as insubstantial as a compass needle.

The air trembles with the roar. You hear the timeless progress of a force that ignores you completely. Depleted, stripped down to the bare husk of yourself, you are left not even the awareness of your hopeless insignificance in the rhythm of the passing moments or of the passing eons. Yet all at once you hear through the gale and the roaring of the sea's heaving breast a new note. Like a great fanfare, a narrow beam of light breaks through the mass of clouds with ever-greater clarity. The dawn sky begins to glow; morning signals its arrival.

An ineffably lovely choir of gleaming trombones pierces through the orchestra and drowns out the torpid heavings of storm and sea. The light is blinding; the gates open; the majesty of the sun gleams over the water. The tones of the trombones become more powerful and authoritative. We are tossed about on the waves like a helpless wreck. Secret witnesses of this mighty event, we tremble in fear of being discovered in the rapidly growing light.

Hans Domizlaff

"A thin, silvery mist veiled the steady, majestic glow of a light that cast no shadows. This mist seemed to deprive the sky of its remoteness and the sea of its endlessness (Fig. 1). It was one of those days when the mighty ocean shows its amiable side, like a strong man in moments of closeness. At dawn we had seen a dark spot in the west that seemed to float high in the empty air behind a shimmering veil of faint, silvery blue mist. And this veil seemed to sway back and forth with us in the light breeze that slowly drove us forward (Fig. 2). The peace of the enchanting morning was so deep and undisturbed that we felt any loud word spoken on deck would dispel that unfathomable mystery that is born from the merging of sea and sky." *Joseph Conrad*

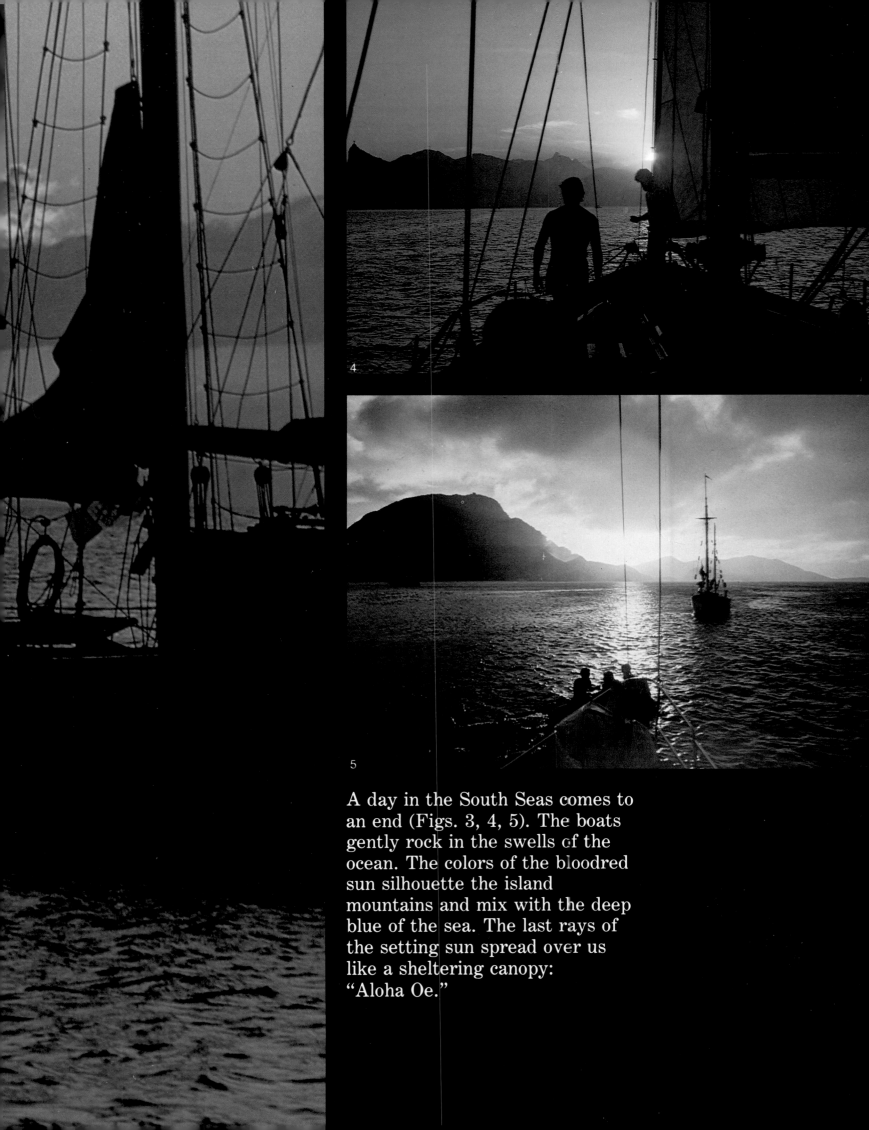

4

5

A day in the South Seas comes to
an end (Figs. 3, 4, 5). The boats
gently rock in the swells of the
ocean. The colors of the bloodred
sun silhouette the island
mountains and mix with the deep
blue of the sea. The last rays of
the setting sun spread over us
like a sheltering canopy:
"Aloha Oe."

There will always be men who will be drawn to the lonely reaches of the sea. There, where the ships ply their courses under full sail, a share of freedom and adventure can be found. Life at sea has a rhythm of its own: violent storms, spray, and rain give way to days of peace and relaxation. Sailing is a way of life for which there is no substitute (Fig. 6).

And for those who pit their skill and their boats against the power of the sea and race for thousands of miles in the hope of victory, sailing is a passion, a passion that can endure for 27,000 miles and more than 150 days. The first race of this kind was run in 1973. Seventeen yachts circled the globe in pursuit of victory. The winner was the 65-foot ketch *Sayula II*. When the same race was held again two years later, *Great Britain* won, and in the third competition held in 1977-78, *Flyer* took top honors. *Gauloises II* (Fig. 7) came in sixth.

A pilot cutter over fifty years old gets underway toward the polar ice (Fig. 8). The sun plays on the waves and sets the sea glistening in myriad colors. Then the first mountaintops loom in the distance over the horizon, ice floes are sighted (Fig. 12), and *Rundø* is soon surrounded by huge blocks of ice (Fig. 11). The skillful and experienced skipper of *Rundø* finds a path through this glittering barrier of greenish-white and bluish-white ice. The wide open sea is before us again, bordered by the bizarre coast of Greenland (Figs. 9, 10). The water and the air are blue, the color of purity and infinity, of peace and joy.

II
HOW
IT
STARTED

The top of a mast, pinlike in the distance, appears over the horizon, then there is a sail, rapidly becoming larger; a ship is in sight and approaching fast—unusually fast—and this means danger. The religious sailor, on board the ponderously moving East Indiaman, crosses himself. Muskets are loaded, cannon are made ready because a sail approaching fast means danger, greater danger than the dark clouds of a storm front looming on the horizon.

So it was for centuries: whoever sailed fast was suspect. Fast were the small privateers in the service of a government that only days before had declared war on the homeland of a lumbering merchantman, at sea for a month, who knew nothing of the conflict. Fast were the pirates, without countries. So too, the long ships of the Vikings, who had laid waste the coast of Britain, had been fast.

That speed, or pace—the modern, exciting term—later became an expression of more peaceful intentions. The Enlightenment, the revolutionary philosophical movement of the eighteenth century, with its penchant for the natural sciences (among them the new science of naval architecture), laid the foundations of the Technological Revolution of the nineteenth century. It awakened a gargantuan hunger for wares, and shipping achieved a rank in world transportation that to this day has been only partly overshadowed by air traffic. But economic success, sparked by the Technological Revolution, meant satisfying the hunger for wares faster than the competition could. Long before it became a slogan in American business offices, the motto on the seas was "Time is money."

The consequence of this motto, in terms of shipbuilding, was the clippers, the fast sailing ships. Although they carried little cargo, it was valuable and required speed—well-paying gold prospectors to California, gold from California, tea, contraband during the Civil War, opium on the smugglers' routes, and, in their waning years, grain and even slaves. Their hulls and sails could not deny a bit of the pirate heritage, but the clippers were the first merchantmen to sail in competition. The Tea Races—from the ports of China to the mouth of the Thames—did not only revolve around filling the cups of tea-thirsty Britons with fresh tea leaves and allowing the ordering merchant to make a tremendous killing on the Tea Exchange with a first offer. What made the Tea Races popular were the numerous bets made on them, just as people bet today in a football pool. The wager, therefore, was the strongest motivation for the then mostly Anglo-Saxon sports activities. This held true for the first purely amateur ocean race, held in 1866, in which three American yachts competed. Each of the three entrants had wagered $30,000. The sum of $60,000 was won by James Gordon Bennett, publisher of the *New York Herald*, who was the Commodore of the New York Yacht Club and the owner of *Henrietta*. With Bennett on board, *Henrietta* sailed to victory from Sandy Hook to the Needles at the western point of England's Isle of Wight in 13 days, 21 hours, 45 minutes.

The American yachts had generally the same

sharp hull shape the clippers had, and clippers and yachts were derived directly from a type of boat built strictly on the "time is money" principle—the American pilot cutter. Its construction was perfected after the end of the War of 1812. The American East Coast began to attract more and more of the mainstream of the sea traffic. Tricky estuaries and bays forced incoming ships to hire pilots and to pay them high wages. The pilots raced to each incoming vessel in their own little ships. Because business was booming, pilots could afford to pay the shipbuilders to develop increasingly faster "high flying" cutters for the dollar race. The first yachts in America were identical to these fast pilot cutters. Among them was *America*. With the first yacht, speed definitely lost its reputation as a sign of evil intentions. Today the soil, long since praised in poetry, is a symbol of peaceful seafaring.

One can say that the start of pleasure sailing marked the end of the long era of the unholy trinity of war, commerce, and piracy. The word *yacht*, possessing a number of meanings, had existed for centuries. In The Netherlands, *jaght* meant a hunter of smugglers and robbers; however, events before the middle of the nineteenth century were only the prelude to yachting history. England's King Charles II (who had the Greenwich Observatory built in 1675), for example, raced his brother, the Duke of York, on the lower Thames for a £100 bet; he had received *Mary*, a 49-foot yacht, with a crew of twenty, as a gift from the Dutch. Soon English shipwrights had offered the royal family and their entourage a total of twelve more pleasure boats. In 1720 the Water Club of Cork Harbour in Ireland was the first yachting association to be founded; the second was the Cumberland fleet in 1750 in England. Occasionally someone would try to see if his yacht was faster than someone else's. The Yacht Club, founded in 1815, had added the word *royal* to its name in 1820. In 1833, when it became the Royal Yacht Squadron, "whose head it was Her Majesty's pleasure to be," the rules of amateur sailing were formulated. Yachts began to be divided into racing classes, and rules were written for competition. How necessary these rules were was demonstrated in 1829, when the crew of Lord Belfast's *Louisa* went after a competitor's rigging with cutlasses. Racing rules and handicapping different sizes of yachts still present difficult problems for today's yachtsmen.

The sport now presented sailing in general in a new light. The peak of perfection was reached with the fast yachts designed by the British and the Americans (after 1900 also by the Germans and Australians)—both in model form and on the drawing board—and built by master craftsmen in the shipyards. The beauty of a ship was now perceived in a new way. Before, a beautiful ship had been a richly decorated one. An example was *Sovereign of the Seas*, which, in 1637, symbolized England's rule of the seas. She displayed the cumulative pomp of the baroque: fantastic coats-of-arms, mythological figures, allegorical shapes, and an abundance of carving. Antonius van Dyck, one of

Rubens' students and the court painter of Charles I, had designed the decorative details. The gilding of the hull alone cost more than £6,000, an immense sum at that time. The yachts of that period, designed for pleasure rather than competition, wallowed in golden splendor. However, the eye of the seaman was not fooled. The seaman's innermost desires were that a boat be fast and close-winded, stable and steady in a seaway. Imperative for such properties is the shape of the hull, or the lines, to use the expert's term. Because yachts do not have to carry freight or cannon, they can be totally without compromise. The designer need worry only about designing a fast hull. Today, unlike the seventeenth century, beauty and function go together. A fast boat is a pure and beautiful boat.

"Naval architect" and more recently, "yacht designer," are the professional titles used by most—predominantly Anglo-Saxon—yacht builders. It was not coincidence that they were far ahead of the architects of buildings in their search for functional beauty. Le Corbusier, who influenced the architecture of the twentieth century as few others have, was once enraptured by the "clean, clear, and healthy architecture" of shipbuilding. In it he saw the "liberation from choking styles" he had postulated in 1922. When he saw *Aquitania*, an ocean liner, he cried emphatically: "The same esthetics as that of your English pipes, your limousines!"; and scorning the "abode of the landlubbers" he celebrated the ocean steamer "of magnanimous and intimate effect" as "the first stage on the way to the realization of a world commensurate with the new spirit." Although fascinated by the new steamer, even Le Corbusier remained blind to the phenomenon of yachting.

Yet despite their exterior grace, a racing yacht of the early twentieth century had cluttered master's and guest's cabins with plush furniture and a marble fireplace, which for obvious reasons was never used. On the Krupps' *Germania*, the first great yacht hailed as German from masthead to keel, there was even a music room. But although the interiors remained neo-Gothic, neo-Renaissance, or pure hodgepodge in style, the shape of the yachts was modern. Long before the term *functionalism* became fashionable with architects, naval architects had found a true form. They solved their construction problems in different ways. Nathaniel Herreshoff built the cutter *Reliance*, 143 feet, 4 inches (43.48 meters), in 1903. No other yacht has ever carried as much sail—13,131 square feet (1,221 square meters), on a single mast. William Gardner designed *Atlantic*, 187 feet (57 meters), as a three-masted schooner. In the 1905 Transatlantic Race, she established a record of 12 days, 4 hours, 1 minute from the Sandy Hook lightship to the Lizard, a distance of over 3,013 miles. This record still stands. Sometimes naval architects overdid it: *Oona*, a yacht that attracted some attention in the 1880s, looked like a narrow ruler with a length of 46 feet (14 meters), she measured 5.5 feet (1.7 meters) on the beam. Britain's George Watson designed one of the first giant cutters for the Prince of Wales—122-foot *Britannia*, which challenged even the fastest American yachts between her launching in 1893 and 1936. This example was followed by Max Oertz, the first famous German designer, in his plans for Kaiser Wilhelm II's *Meteor*, the fourth yacht with that name. Whatever the differences and variations of yacht design, such clear, functional designs were seen nowhere on land.

It took a long time for factory technology to overcome its cast-iron stage and to at least begin to produce the same esthetics that the fast yachts had pioneered. The necessity for beauty, born from purpose, did not come to the sea by accident. Nature itself had proclaimed it. Wind and waves, and friction and lateral resistance, to mention the technical aspects, were the unescapable factors. *"Natura non facit saltus,"* the old philospher's maxim that nature does not progress in and thus does not tolerate deviations from her logic, was and still is the most important law in the building of yachts. Precious little can be achieved by trick and artifice. In other words, "no deviation" means but one thing: harmony. The old ground rule that a yacht with a strikingly harmonious profile is the fastest is still unassailable.

American naval historians consider the first American yacht to be *Onkahye*, launched in 1840 in New York. In any case, the push for high performance started with this yacht. Inventions that today seem mundane, such as the strong zinc-coated steel shrouds that made the tall clipper rig possible, were promptly put to use. Seamen, it is said, are conservative by trade. Designers, however, were and are innovative. The invention of the cold glue process led to the construction of light, strong, hollow wooden masts. W. Starling Burgess, the leading designer of his day, had the 164-foot mast of *Enterprise* built from two layers of aluminum, with a maximum diameter of only 22 inches (0.56 meters); 80,000 rivets linked the metal sheets. Hulls were built from composite materials—wood on steel frames first, later aluminum—as early as the nineteenth century. Today fiberglass keeps construction costs down. Herreshoff took a revolutionary step in 1883, when he moved all of the ballast, without which a ship cannot really sail, into a deep keel.

The concept of the modern racing yacht was realized with *Gloriana*, at first chidingly called a "funny boat" by her contemporaries, who soon came to admire her. The tall high aspect ratio rig, which enabled smaller boats to win the medals in the 1920 Olympics, was adapted for seagoing yachts. It was further improved with the introduction of nylon and Dacron sails in the 1940s and polyester sails in 1954. An Englishman, Thomas Ratsey, was the first to custom-tailor sails for every weather condition and every race strategy. He had grasped the laws of aerodynamics long before physicists knew how to formulate them. Riches accumulated during the days of industrial pioneering made possible almost any experiment in yachting. Even before World War I, when fullblooded yachts had become more and more expensive, America's millionaires united whenever a new defender

41

of the America's Cup was to be built. The era of the great yachts had begun in 1851, when the American schooner *America* defeated the yachts of the British Yacht Squadron, partly because she carried light, tightly woven cotton sails and because the mainsail was secured tightly to the boom, and not loosely, as had been the custom until then. The trophy she won, now known as the America's Cup, has stimulated high-performance yacht design as no other prize has. Although ocean races were also important, it was only a slight exaggeration to call the sailing of great yachts "the sport of kings"—including the banking, steel, railroad, and retail variety. However, the ships were sailed by professional, paid sailors and skippered by highly gifted, professional captains. The owner or owner-syndicates only paid the bills, perhaps sailed on board, and received the trophies. Only rarely were they on board as masters during the races. With the victory of the American yacht *Nina* in the 1928 Transatlantic Race, amateurs started to replace pros on the decks and at the helms of offshore yachts. This new era reached its peak with the 1931 Transatlantic Race, whose winner, *Dorade*, arrived in Portsmouth so early that the racing committee had to be roused from their beds. *Dorade*, the *Times* wrote, was the most wonderful little offshore yacht ever built. Olin Stephens had designed and sailed her. The most successful yacht designer of the twentieth century, he can safely be called the first scientist and the last artist of yacht building. Designing a pure ship has always been a stroke of genius and it still defies

scientific routine. The fact is that the lines of a hull cannot be completely captured in mathematical formulas, and one can philosophize and speculate about this as much as about the secrets of the atomic nucleus. Obviously, nature or truth, call it what you may, refuses to be robbed of its final veil. Sensibly enough, in yacht design this means that the right lines are a matter of the designer's intuition, born from his experience or his "feel." The last to depend entirely on intuition was British architect Charles E. Nicholson. His *Endeavour*, 131 feet (40 meters) long, failed to strip the Americans of the America's Cup by a hair in 1934; only errors in racing strategy kept the British from winning it. It was the last time in yacht construction—and probably in all of technology—that a genius could affirm himself on the basis of his "feel" alone, totally unassisted by instruments. The Americans were already solving the puzzles of hull design by conducting model tests in tanks; three years later, when they performed a multitude of experiments for their *Ranger*, the fastest yacht that ever sailed in the America's Cup, it became obvious that theoretical and model work proved itself. Today racing yachts are designed more by computers than on drawing boards. In order to sail faster and closer to the wind, the way privateers, pirates, smugglers, clippers, and pilot cutters did, seamanship has allied itself with science. Seamanship means nothing more than correct, seamanlike behavior and activity on board. One can argue endlessly over what science should or should not do, and in yachting, as in other fields, one can ask: how far should we push progress and follow its temptations. More and more yacht owners turn to nostalgia, sail old-timers, and have fun polishing brass. But those who wish to be in the forefront of yacht racing have to follow the course indicated in 1794 by Leonhard Euler, the Swiss mathematician, then at the Academy of Sciences in Berlin, who formulated a Theory of Shipbuilding. A fast yacht is created today with the help of complicated formulas and with materials that are produced from complex formulas. More than anything else, weight minimization and distribution are the guidelines for victory.

The ultimate yacht can only be imagined by crystal gazers. Perhaps it will use space-age technology in the maritime domain. The beginnings have already been made with the use of exquisite light and hard metals for flexible rigging and important gear. That quantum of magic, however, that was present in the first yacht, will never be expressed in numbers. And this gives the fast yacht—which made speed at sea honorable and whose development mirrors modern cultural history—a special status not limited to the technology of shipping and sailing. Today, as it sails filigreelike over the horizon into the view of the fascinated observer, it symbolizes optimism. Nothing on land can compare and there is certainly nothing better to be found there than a ship—in which lives the condensed heritage of the sailing ships and the hope for freedom from all constraints.

Alexander Rost

In December 1866, three American yachts sailed the first race ever from the United States to England on a dare. Rich men had hired crews and sailed across the Big Pond for the fun and glory of it. But in the summer of 1976 almost seventy German yachts, sailed exclusively by amateurs, crossed the Atlantic in both directions to participate in the Bicentennial celebrations. What happened in these 110 years? Who and what caused this explosive development? Let us have a look at the boats that crossed the Atlantic at the beginning and those that crossed at the end of those 110 years; the differences pinpoint two important stages of development—the transatlantic races of 1905 and 1936, both of which were sailed from west to east.

As early as 1866 the technical and industrial revolution had gathered a momentum that must have seemed both miraculous and a bit scary to its contemporaries; it remains impressive even today. Shipbuilding especially developed by leaps and bounds. Steam power established itself, iron and hybrid construction appeared, and electricity stood in the wings. Less spectacular things such as anchor-chains, forged anchors with iron shanks, and wire cables, to name only a few, soon were standard equipment on ships.

At this time sailing yachts emancipated themselves from the small utilitary vessels—the ballast moved from the interior of the boat to the keel; the impact of light construction and the tackle on boat speed was recognized; a few hollow masts and booms were on hand. The cotton sail started to affirm itself, primarily in the United States; it is less permeable and can be cut flatter than flax sailcloth. In *Watersport* magazine of 1887 we read:

It might be of interest to report something of the sails of the new American racing sloops and the way they are manufactured. The size of the immense cloth surfaces in the mainsail of modern racing yachts can hardly be appreciated by the public at large, who can only glimpse these sails from the decks of cruise steamers. The manufacture of these huge sails is extremely interesting. The cloth differs in many ways from the one used on ships. Even the fastest clippers do not use material of the quality considered mandatory on a yacht. The cloth for yacht sails is made from the best quality cotton. One sailcloth, made in Baltimore, exceeds all others in value.... The interested reader will barely grasp the difference in weight an extra fraction of an ounce per square foot can make for the whole sail. Sailors, though, who have to handle it, can tell you something about it: in humid weather or when the cloth gets wet it becomes as stiff and unmanageable as sheet iron. Aside from the thickness of the thread, the surface is very smooth because, apart from the stiff lay of the sails, the American puts great store on its smoothness, to cut wind resistance to a minimum.

The lines and sailplan of an American pilot schooner (Figs. 1, 2, and 3) afford us an idea of those yachts. How complicated the rigging was is apparent in Fig. 4, Rigging Plan of a Cutter. Looking at it one can understand why the yachts were sailed by professionals back then, especially since labor-saving devices such as winches were not in existence—only blocks and tackles. The three boats in the first race, *Henrietta*, *Vesta*, and *Fleetwing*, were two-masted schooners between 104 and 108 feet (32-33 meters) in length, all built in 1861. The navigation was done by compass, sextant, and chronometer, with the lead line and the hand log. No computers, but they in the guise of precalculated tables or pocket calculators, made life easy for the navigator. There were no radio facilities to relay messages or receive weather and time information. It was a rough-and-tumble race on the wild December seas.

The most significant Transatlantic Race was held in 1905. In second place, with an average speed of 9.53 knots—the winning *Atlantic*

logged 10.32 and average speeds in 1867 were between 9.15 and 9.25 knots—was the schooner *Hamburg* of the Hamburgische Seefahrt Verein. Her overall length was an even 160 feet, 9 inches (49 meters), 115 feet, 6 inches (35.2 meters) at the waterline, 23 feet (7.31 meters) beam; sail surface = 18,740 square feet (1,741 square meters). Not much had changed in the way of rigging, equipment, and sails since 1866, although there had been significant improvements. The masts were still solid wood though, with topmasts that were struck in heavy weather. The lines had been refined; steel and iron construction had gained wider acceptance. Even if those yachts were pleasing to the eye, no one would like to sail them today. The underbodies were significantly reduced; the detrimental effect of friction on large whetted surfaces had been recognized. Skippers and crews were hired hands, but, according to the rules, one amateur had to be aboard as a representative

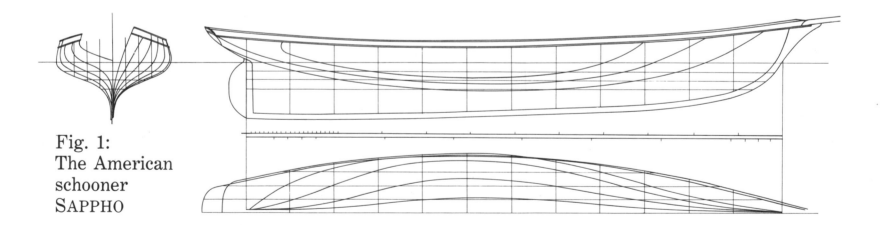

Fig. 1:
The American
schooner
SAPPHO

Fig. 2:
Sailplan of the
American schooner
WASHINGTON

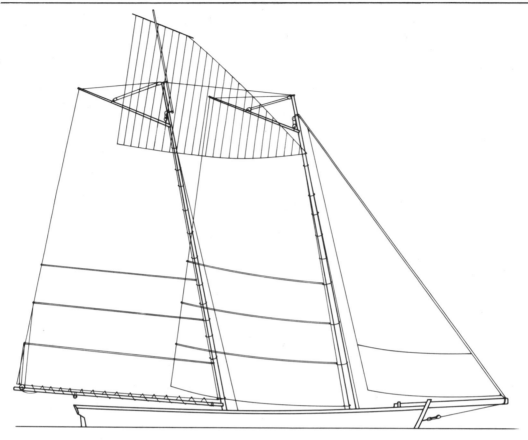

Fig. 3:
The American pilot schooner COOPER

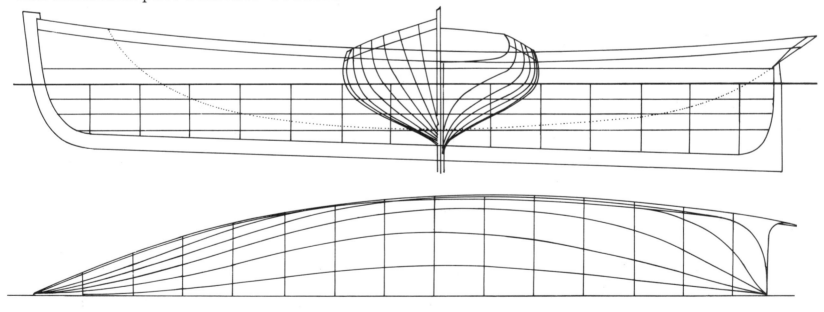

Fig. 4: Rigging plan

Standing Rig (rendered in continuous lines)

a Shrouds
b Dead-eye
c Spar halyard (fallreep)
d Stay
e Backstay
f Backstay kicking strap
g Topmast shroud, used as backstay
h Topmast shroud vang
i Topmast stay
k Bowsprit stay
l Bowsprit stay vang
m Bowsprit topping lift
o Trestle
p Futtock
q Stem
r Stern
s Rudder
t Mast cap
u Cross-tree
v Masttop
n Masthead ⎫
w Clew   ⎬ of sails
x Tack
y Peak
z Gaff throat ⎭

C Mast
D Main boom
E Topmast
F Jib boom
G Gaff
H topsail yard
J Spinnaker boom
K Mainsail
L Topsail
M Staysail
N Jib
O Stay jib
P Leech
Q Foot
R Luff
S Gaff leech

Running Rig (dotted lines)

1   Main topping lift
2   Main sheet
3   Reefing downhaul
4   Main outhaul
5   Main gaff purchase
6   Throat halyard
7   Peak halyard
8   Flag line
9   Topsail halyard
10 Topsail stripline
11 Topsail sheet
12 Topsail guy rope
13 Stay jib halyard
14 Stay jib sheet
15 Stay jib tack
16 Main jib halyard
17 Main jib sheet
18 Main jib outhaul
19 Staysail halyard
20 Staysail downhaul
21 Staysail tack
22 Staysail sheet
23 Spinnaker topping lift
24 Spinnaker guy
25 Spinnaker foreguy
26 Spinnaker outhaul

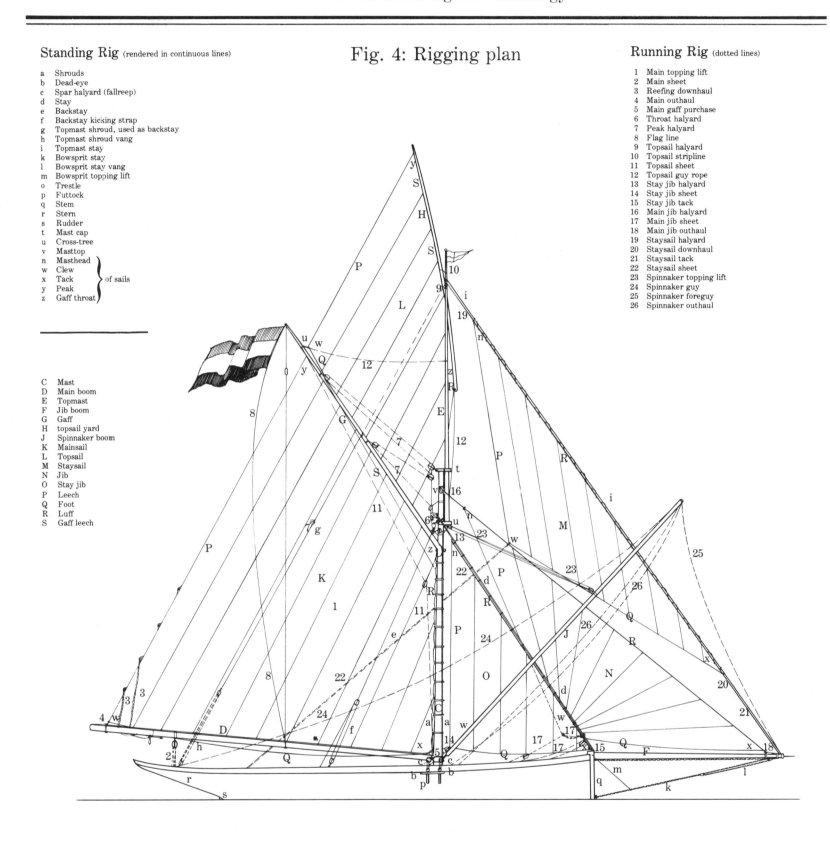

of the owner. On one of the boats he was the skipper. Thirty years later, the world, society, and life in general had radically changed; so had the yachtsman and his yacht. The boats participating in the 1936 Transatlantic Race had little in common with their predecessors of 1905. One example is the winner of the race, *Roland von Bremen* (Fig. 5), designed by Henry Gruber and built in 1936 by E. Burmester. Simultaneously, *Peter von Danzig* was being built along the same lines, only in iron, in the Danzig yards. Overall length was 59 feet, 5 inches (18.10 meters), length at the waterline was 42 feet (12.78 meters), beam was 13 feet, 5 inches (4.10 meters); with 1,474.6 square feet (137 square meters) of sail surface. *Roland* won the race with an average speed of 6.71 knots—not bad compared to the great boats of 1866 and 1905.

The lines had become stouter—even if not in comparison with today's wide hulls—showing their kinship with modern day-racing boats. Sailors had learned to sail vast distances with small boats and crews composed exclusively of amateurs. Some of the boats had paid hands to work and do maintenance. This was now possible because of the more manageable rigs that came with the smaller boats: the Marconi rig, hollow masts and booms, simpler fittings, and a more functional deck layout made work easier; also, winches were now available. The sails were cotton, the cordage natural fiber. There was more work than there is today since it was impossible to store wet sails. Zinc-coated wire cables were generally available but compared to today's stainless steel wire, needed considerable care. Most boats had radio transmitters and all had receivers; the radio direction finding equipment already introduced on larger vessels was too bulky for yachts. Most seagoing yachts had an auxiliary motor—outboard motors were not unusual on the smaller boats. By this time, most offshore boats adopted high-aspect radio rigs of the type used increasingly on racing yachts since 1910. At about the same time, the light hollow masts appeared, closely patterned after the wing of a gliding bird. They often assumed a whip shape that seems peculiar today. Under Manfred Curry's influence, the aerodynamics of sails became, especially in Germany, an intense preoccupation. Perhaps this was somewhat detrimental to the physics of the underbody, although as early as 1901 Max Oertz had indicated the similarity of the sail and the keel, comparing a close-hauled yacht to a gliding bird. Sails and lateral planes are comparable in their lift-creating functions to bird wings, although they are of unequal sizes, in the case of a yacht, owing to the density difference of their working media. To be sure, the early towing tests of sailing yachts brought many disappointments because the specific data of a yacht under sail were not yet completely understood.

Also, numerous apparently nonessential objects, important to everyday life aboard a small boat, had been improved by technical progress: cooking stoves, sanitary facilities, clothing, long-lasting provisions. A look at ads in old yachting magazines gives us some interesting clues. Often, happy-go-lucky

48

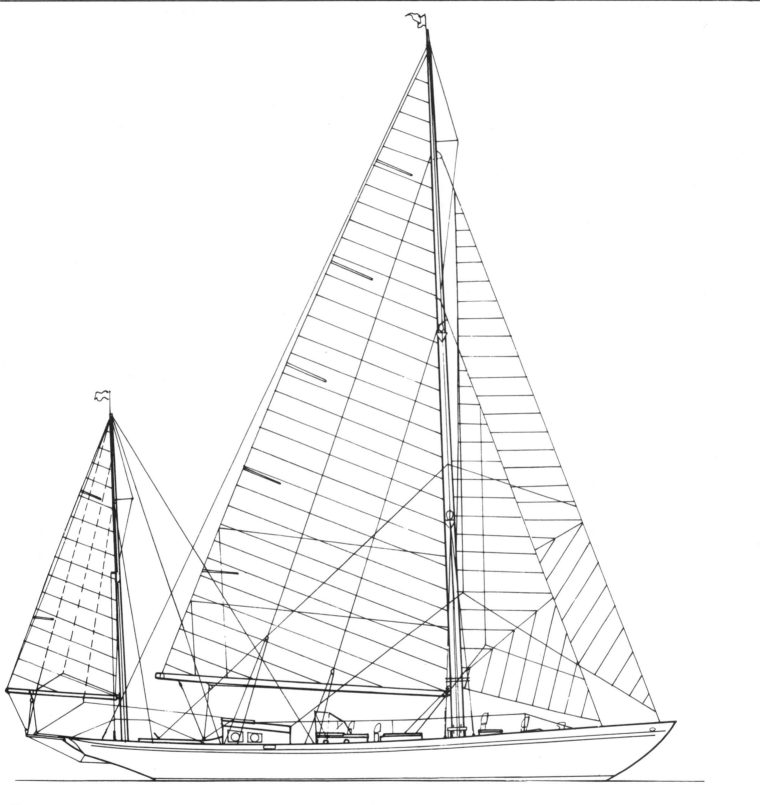

Fig. 5

ROLAND VON BREMEN

Fig. 6:
Line sketch of GLACER 34

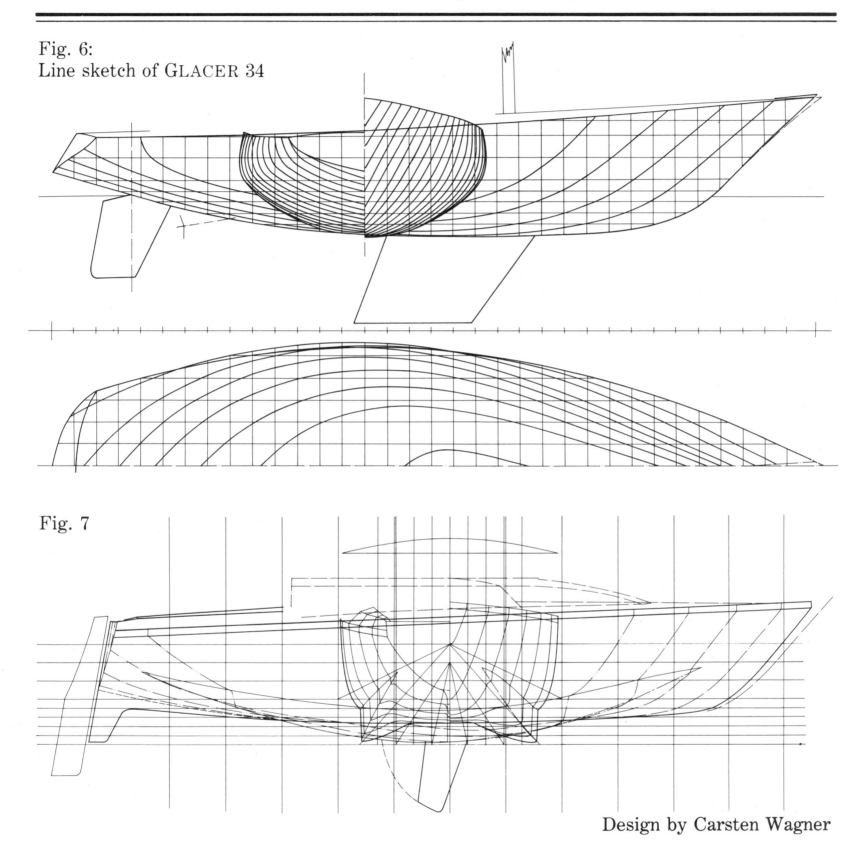

Fig. 7

Design by Carsten Wagner

sailors bore the cost and risk of the experiments. In these fast-moving times, the progress made in those seventy short years may seem slow, but one should not underestimate the headway made, especially if one considers how difficult it was to discard the old, long-proven ways.

World War II curtailed yacht construction, but not technological development. In light of the conditions existing at the time, it is not surprising that the Americans increased an already existing advantage. The technological development became a revolution, much like the changes in other areas of life. Along came new and improved construction materials combined with modern manufacturing methods—the premises of mass production: fiberglass and laminated and later glue-molded wood, used even for relatively large hulls. After the popular boat yacht made its appearance, the existing demand could not have been satisfied with wood as a construction material. Aluminum, used in boat building for the first time in 1895 by Max Oertz in Germany, became more seaworthy, and ways were discovered to weld these metals. Thus the riveting of aluminum which engendered molecular instability detrimental to material strength, became obsolete. Aluminum gained an increasing importance in the manufacture of masts and booms and has almost totally replaced the glued wooden mast today. An early precursor was the gigantic mast of *Enterprise*, defender of the 1930 America's Cup. It was 162 feet, 5 inches (49.5 meters) high, weighed 9 tons, and contained 80,000 rivets. The mast bore 8,073 square feet (750 square meters) of sail. For hull construction the difficult job of welding thin steel plates was mastered and even the brittle ferro-cement was adapted for sailing. Light construction became paramount; making the boat light on top increased the effect of the ballast keel, thus increasing the sail carrying capacity.

The striving for reduced weight was aimed not only at the hull, but also at the rigging and the sails. Today, the light weight, combined with flat, almost dinghylike hull shapes, makes surfing on waves—a state not unlike planing in following seas—possible even for ocean cruisers. This was nothing fundamentally new, since the racer had always known the value of light weight, but before the advent of more resistant materials, he had to accept a high risk of wear and destruction, something that cruising yachtsman could not afford to take. The new materials and procedures offered the offshore sailor sufficient safety even with reduced weight, and he did not hesitate to make use of them. The cruiser followed in his footsteps. The hull shape (Fig. 6), once soft and harmonious, became harsher: dinghylike hulls with flat bottoms, hard chines, a deep and narrow keel fin, the rudder separated from the keel fin and with or without a skeg, the sometimes considerable beam situated well aft, and the elongated bows. The new shapes may have given many an old salt the shivers, but then their performance must have seemed almost dizzying to them. The striving for maximum specific weight in the ballast led those who could afford it to pack spent

51

Fig. 8:
Details of a racing yacht

1 Coffee Grinder
2 Genoa sheet winches
3 Mainsheet winches
4 Spinnaker sheet winches
5 Genoa halyard winches
6 Spinnaker halyard winches
7 Winch for topping lift, mainsail reefing, and mainsail cunningham
8 Winch for downhaul and genoa cunningham
9 Crank pockets
10 Twin stay
11 Jib stay fittings
12 Front hatch
13 Spinnaker poles
14 Guy fair lead
15 Railing guide holes
16 Jib guide rail
17 9genoa guide rail
18 7genoa guide rail

19 Starcut (spinnaker) snatch block
20 Turning block for guy and genoa
21 Traveller shock cord
22 Turning block for spinnaker sheet
23 Hydraulic jack for backstay and boom
24 Rescue raft under helmsman's seat
25 Motor access hatch
26 Life jackets
27 Emergency steering
28 Radio direction finder
29 Backstay
30 Steering column and compass
31 Helmsman instrument panel
32 Central compass
33 Galley vent
34 Mainsheet and traveller
35 Boom vang
36 Crew's instrument panel
37 Hydraulic boom vang

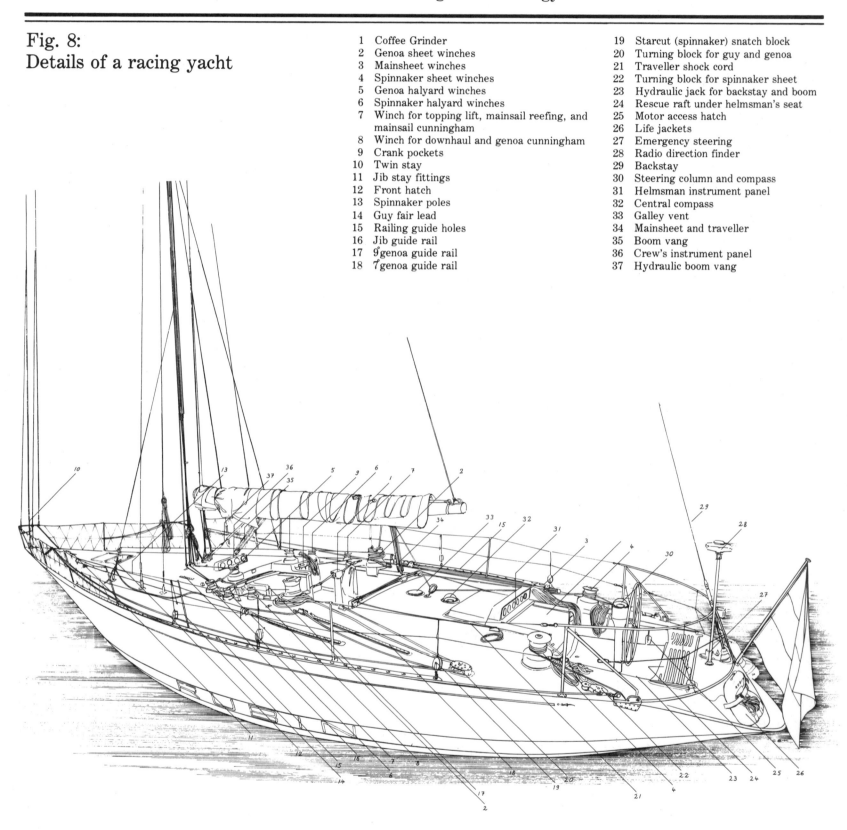

uranium (now prohibited) in their keels. Although the furnishings of an ocean racer are Spartan, bordering on bare necessities, the cruiser may indulge in more comforts.

The multihull boats cover the longest distances. Their characteristics have profited most from space technology but new avenues are being experimented with: a Dane, Paul Elvström, tried a new bulb-shaped bow on a six-meter racer, hoping to reduce pitching motions. A contest for the best cruising sailboat was won by a single hull design with two lateral keels (Fig. 7). An old idea, originated in America, of two centerboards arrayed one behind the other on the long axis of the boat, is being revived; the intent is to obtain better trimming capabilities. The cruise sailor can now appropriate the type of flexible rigs, proven since the Thirties on Stars and dinghies, like the Finns. Masts are bent with boom vangs and boom vang winches with adjustment of the tension of the stays and with the help of hydraulic pumps, with tensioning devices on the sail's leech. As one modern racer noted, today you have to be a mechanic, knowing something about motors, electricity, and electronics, about pumps and plastic.

Wire is rarely spliced anymore; crimps are used instead. The stays on many racers are steel with aerodynamic shapes. The forestays carry aluminum or plastic head foils with grooves that accommodate the foresails. This eliminates aerodynamically troublesome hanks, and precious seconds can be saved when changing sails. Synthetic sails and cordage are not only lighter for the same strength than those made of textile fiber, but they keep their shape better and are impervious to water. Cables and fittings of stainless steel facilitate care and maintenance. The "deck machinery" consists of winches with two or three "gears" that can be linked together; the strongest are called grinders or "coffee grinders," and are hand cranked or pedal driven. Since engine power of any kind is prohibited in races, the goal is to develop manually powered devices that are capable of fast hauling at light levels and high power output under heavy loads. A whole arsenal of rails, turning blocks, clamps, jacks, and fittings serves to give the sails the desired shape and to adjust the leads of the sheets even under load. Sail trim is so complicated that an experienced specialist should be on board in the big races. Aside from electronic navigation instruments such as a speedometer, a depth sounder, radar, and loran (the latter two are not permitted in racing) and good radio direction finders, the yachtsman has at his disposal sensitive wind speed and direction indicators that give readings at every possible point of the boat (Fig. 8). In the table of contents of a modern sailing book, one reads: Construction, Equipment, Accommodations, Mechanics, and Electronics. This can be more concisely stated as: "The Yacht in the Age of Technology."

Hans-Rudolf Rösing

odern offshore yacht racing, with amateur crews competing in boats of between eight and twenty meters, dates only from the Twenties. Before that there were isolated instances of big, professionally crewed yachts being raced across oceans, as often as not with the owner staying ashore to guard the stake money. However, the Great Depression ended this style of sport.

Two American yachting journalists, Thomas Fleming Day, editor of *Rudder* magazine, and a few years later, Herbert L. Stone, editor of *Yachting*, really started the ball rolling. As early as 1904, Day had organized a race of 330 miles, coast to coast, from Brooklyn to Marblehead for small, "everyman's" boats. Six took part, all of them less than ten meters on the water. Two years later, in 1906, Day laid on the first race to Bermuda, a more ambitious project which only attracted three adventurous starters and which, in succeeding years, showed that few yachtsmen were ready for such a test.

Then, in 1922, the Cruising Club of America was born, and a year later Stone was busily promoting the idea of a New Deal race down to Bermuda. This time it seemed that the yachts and crews were ready for the challenge; from 1923 there was no looking back.

That was in 1923. In Britain, in 1925, after much discussion and soul searching, the Ocean Race was started from Ryde in the Isle of Wight. The course led west along the coast and out into the open Atlantic to a small rock, surmounted by a lighthouse off the southwest corner of Ireland; then back to the finish at Plymouth. So the Fastnet Race was born.

The first Bermuda race of the new series was won by the husky schooner yacht *Malabar IV* owned by her designer, John Alden. The first Fastnet race was won by a heavily built converted pilot cutter of French origin called *Jolie Brise* (Fig. 1). When you compare these first handicap winners with the most recent big winners in the sport, you get an insight into the continuous process of intensification and development which has never ceased. In fact, it has in recent years tended to accelerate. The first winners were comfortable, able cruisers, pressed into racing duty. The winners of today are racing machines, hardly suitable for cruising.

From 1923 on, ocean racing spread from one sailing country to another. Today it is one of the most international of all sports, and it could also be said to be the most active side of yacht racing and the one that demands the most talent and enthusiasm.

As with yacht racing in general, the United States went its own way, using its own handicapping rule conceived and developed by the Cruising Club of America. The British and the other Europeans, and later still the Australians and New Zealanders, used the handicapping rule developed by the Royal Ocean Racing Club. This split was unfortunate, for quite soon sharp owners began to build boats especially to the rule, and those with international ambitions had to choose between the two rules. It depended upon whether one wanted to race to Bermuda or around the Fastnet Rock, but many leading Americans wanted to do both.

The first of the new breed of designers of offshore racers was Olin Stephens. Olin and his brother, Rod, dominated the sport almost as soon as they launched their slim and shapely yawl, *Dorade* (Fig. 2). Olin was twenty-one when he designed *Dorade* in 1929. She won the Fastnet races of 1930 and 1931 and the Transatlantic of 1931.

Olin had already designed six-meter-class inshore racers, and he gave *Dorade* much of the slimness and lightness of hull (she was 37.25 feet waterline, 52 feet overall, and 10.25 feet beam) of the meter boats. Just as important, she was raced as intensely as an inshore racer.

Because the two rating rules upon which handicaps were based were originated with the idea of equating yachts that already existed, they soon proved vulnerable to the ingenuity of yacht designers. Consequently, they required constant revision if the discovered loopholes were to be closed and if the continuing competitiveness of older yachts was to be preserved. In basic terms the CCA rule tended to encourage a single type which was close to the existing American coastal cruiser—wide of beam, heavily constructed, with absolute limits on lightness of displacement and highness of ballast ratio. In the years following World War II, led by the Stephens brothers, the

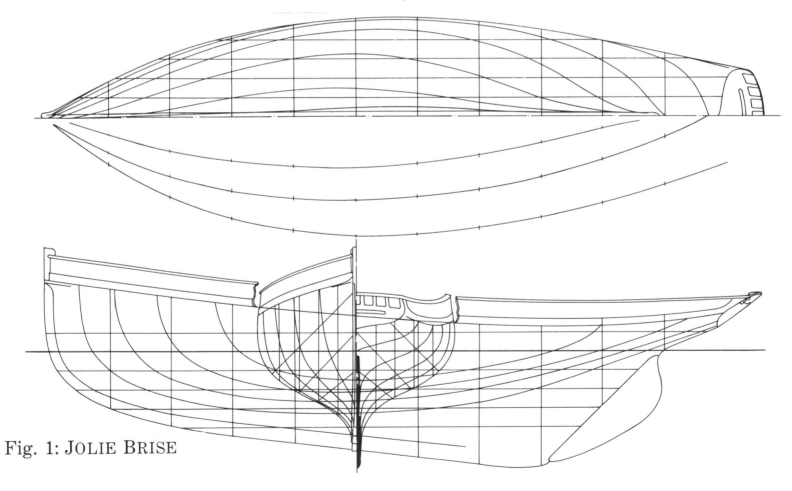

Fig. 1: JOLIE BRISE

rule produced a type of shoal draft center-boarder which was typified by the Stephens-designed *Finisterre*.

The RORC rule tried to be more catholic in its tastes yet unmistakably favored the traditional style of English cutter, or at least designers for a long time thought it encouraged such a type.

British ocean racers tended to be narrower than the American, deeper in the hull, often fuller in the bow, and usually finer in the stern. But then British and American sailing craft had differed in this way for years, since well before 1851 when the schooner *America* came to the Solent and won the Cup that was to take her name. These differences had nothing to do with offshore rating rules.

That the RORC rule, like the CCA rule, was

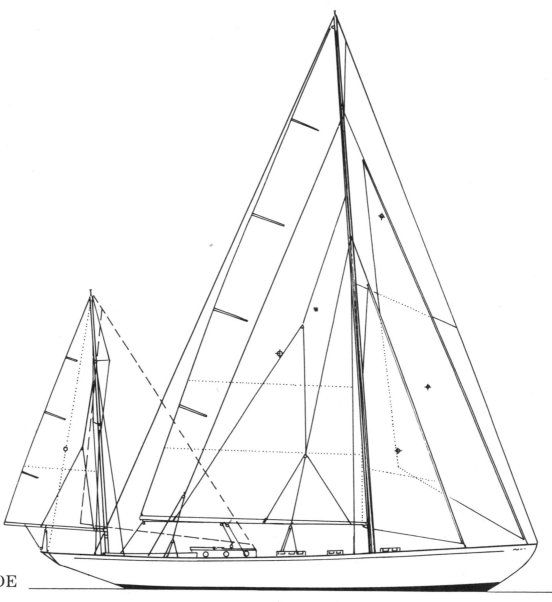

Fig. 2: DORADE

vulnerable to designer ingenuity did not really come to light till 1946 when John Illingworth, an engineer captain in the Royal Navy and leading light in the Royal Ocean Racing Club, commissioned Jack Laurent Giles to design a new ocean racer which would be called *Myth of Malham.* Illingworth had realized that the RORC rule contained a very inaccurate way of measuring displacement — through depth from deck to keel inside the hull (a survival of older British rules which went back to the tonnage or capacity for barrels in the holds of merchant ships). Illingworth's idea was to increase freeboard and reduce actual displacement, for the underbody of the hull was very flat and shallow.

Myth of Malham (33.5 feet waterline, 9.4 feet beam) was virtually unbeatable under the RORC rule; certainly she was unbeatable to windward. She won the Fastnets of 1947 and 1949 and was really only beaten by the rule changes that came as a direct result of her sweeping success and were inevitable if good racing was to continue.

In 1957 came a new event which still further forced the pace of world development—the Admiral's Cup, presented by a group of British yachtsmen to encourage international participation in the Fastnet and Cowes Week. Today as many as nineteen nations send teams of three yachts for this event.

The Admiral's Cup and similar team events are conducted in the old-fashioned way, on handicap. In the early Sixties a diminutive French lawyer named Jean Peytel who had been an Olympic helmsman and hence realized that handicap racing could never be quite as tense and competitive as level racing, had a bright idea which made ocean racing more competitive than ever—a series of races for boats built to rate at exactly the same level under the RORC rule, thus they would rate level and race level without handicaps. For a trophy he took down the old One Ton Cup which had been gathering dust on the shelves of the Cercle de la Voile de Paris.

The new One Ton Cup has done more than anything else to force the pace of ocean racing development. Level racing without handicap speedily showed which boat, which crew, which make of sails, and which designer was better than others. First to get his head and shoulders above the crowd was Dick Carter, another of those self-taught American owner-designers. Sailing his own *Rabbit,* he narrowly failed to win the first new One Ton Cup at Le Havre in 1965. The winner was the Stephens-designed, Danish-owned *Diana III.* The year after, 1966, *Tina* (Fig. 3), another Carter design, won the second One Ton Cup in Copenhagen. Carter's own *Rabbit* and *Tina* were designed like big fat dinghies, with wide beam, low ballast ratios, and abbreviated keels. They were quite heavily built of steel (to benefit from the RORC rule) and would never plane like a true dinghy.

The One Ton Cup in its new guise was so successful it soon led to similar events for other sizes — the Half-Ton, Three-Quarter Ton, Quarter Ton, Two Ton, and finally the Mini Ton.

In 1970, after endless argument and political compromise, the two different rating rules,

CCA and RORC, were finally fused into one of worldwide application called the IOR (International Offshore Rating) rule. Once again Olin Stephens took the lead. Basically the IOR took the American rule for rig and the British rule, with extra safeguards, for the hull. An entirely new system of heeling a yacht to measure her stability was used instead of scantling requirements. It was easy enough to convert the level rating events to the new regulations, though in the case of the One Ton the change to an IOR rating of 27.5 feet led to larger, more expensive yachts.

Carter and Olin Stephens (the latter forced to design ever-lighter boats), never the most daring experimenters (but never), in the Sixties and early Seventies, caught with a slow boat, shared the early One Ton Cup victories. In the first years of the IOR, yachts became steadily larger (and hence more expensive) for the same rating.

Then, from sunny California, along came an unknown hippie in sandals and beard called Doug Peterson. Single-handedly, he reversed the trend to bigger yachts. In no time he designed himself a simple little boat called

Ganbare. Noticeably smaller but with more sail than her leading rivals, *Ganbare* should have won the One Ton Cup of 1973 at Porto Cervo in Sardinia. She was beaten by the larger Italian, Carter-designed *Ydra* only because she rounded a mark in the wrong direction in the final race—an inexplicable error considering the experience and talent of her crew.

Peterson's designs were considerably lighter, as well as smaller, than those from the drawing board of Dick Carter. They tended to be more Vee shaped and narrower in the stern. Keels were deeper and more sharply defined. Sail, in proportion to both displacement and wetted surface of the hull, was larger.

New Zealand had for several years been one of the big centers of really competitive offshore racing. A Kiwi crew had finally won the One Ton Cup in a light displacement Stephens boat named *Rainbow* at Heligoland in 1969. For two years before that, the Cup had been in German custody thanks to the success of the Carter-designed, German-owned and sailed *Optimist* in France in 1967 and in Heligoland in 1968.

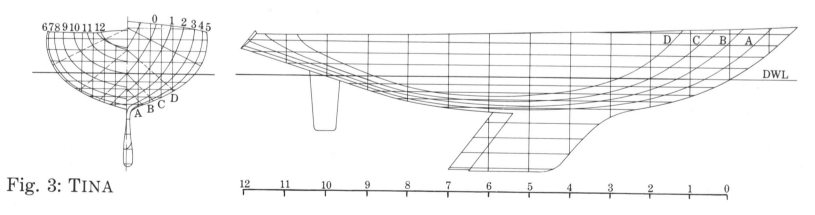

Fig. 3: TINA

Onto the scene came another young designer, New Zealander Bruce Farr, fresh from immense success in the design of racing dinghies and skiffs. Farr was the first leading offshore designer who had already climbed to the top of the other no less demanding game of small boat design. Farr's concept was different. He cut his keels away till they looked like dinghy centerboards. Even though others reckoned the IOR rule did not favor ultra-light displacement, he reduced his to unheard-of levels. He made his boats so flat that he had to cut sail severely to get them to measure for the various level rating levels. Plainly, his boats needed fresh winds.

Farr had to wait till the Quarter Ton Cup of 1975, at Deauville in France, to prove the success of his ideas on the international scene. Here, in a series interrupted by fishermen's strikes, Farr had a runaway win for his little *45 Degrees South*, with a sister ship, *Genie*, not far behind. Many said the success was due to the large amount of crosswind, reaching in the long race across to the British coast and back.

A Farr one-tonner on similar lines and with a similar name, just failed to win the 1976 One Ton regatta at Marseilles. In 1977 the Farr-designed *Joe Louis* did win the Three-Quarter Ton at La Rochelle. Already Farr and others were experimenting with lifting keels and centerboards. A couple of months after *Joe Louis'* excitingly narrow success, the Farr lift keeler *Red Lion* won a tough One Ton Cup and two others made the top five in Farr's home waters around Auckland. A few weeks after this, in Australia now, the Farr-designed *Gunboat Rangiriri* took the 1977 Half Ton, and, to cap it all, in the first few days of 1978 the New Zealand team, all Farr designs, won the Southern Cross Cup. Not since the best days of Olin Stephens had one designer dominated the sport so completely as did Farr at the beginning of 1978.

Meanwhile, there arose a great clamor to have the IOR rule changed. Many thought the Farr type (many other designers such as Paul Whiting, Laurie Davidson, Doug Peterson, and Ron Holland were doing similar boats, but Farr had shown them the way) to be unsafe. They said they were too lightly built, too lightly rigged, and claimed that the lifting keels made them capsize easily. They pointed out that such craft, with their stripped-out interiors and shallow hulls, were completely unsuitable for cruising, and that they were so sensitive that sails had to be changed for every puff of wind and that the crew, to increase their stability, had to sit on the weather rail night and day. They were nothing more or less than ocean racing dinghies and should be banned.

From *Jolie Brise*, as solid as a rock, Fastnet winner of 1925, to *Gunboat Rangiriri*, the delicate, nervous, high-strung Half Ton Cup winner of 1977, is a road fifty years long, full of twists and turns but always pointing in one direction, toward extra speed whatever the cost.

The search for more speed has touched every aspect of the offshore racer. Hulls are being reinforced internally with welded alloy tubing to make them more rigid so that the rig is properly supported, the forestay remains

59

tight, and hence the all-important headsails can set to the shape that their makers intended. Restrictions had to be introduced to limit the number of sails a yacht may carry and these limits have caused strong controversy. The advent of level racing brought inshore sailors of Olympic Medal winning standards into offshore racing, and they, in turn, quickly raised the general standard of sails and rig tune in offshore racing.

Sail handling and changing techniques have undergone a not-so-gradual revolution. Three-speed sheet winches are now common. So, in larger yachts, are paired, interconnected winches with clutches that allow two pairs of winch handles to be directed to turning a single winch drum.

To speed up headsail changing, special headfoils have been developed which allow a replacement headsail to be hoisted alongside the sail it will replace. The luff of each sail engages in grooves in the foil. With this system no speed is lost when headsails are being changed.

In the late Sixties hydraulics were introduced as a more accurate, more powerful method of rig adjustment than the mechanical means that had prevailed till then. These devices are now being limited because of cost and also because of the loads they impose on hulls.

Masts have become so frail that there are demands for minimum sizes. A special rule had to be introduced banning any metal, for ballast and keels, which was more dense than lead. This was because it was discovered that the famous French sailor Eric Tabarly had fitted a keel of spent uranium to his *Pen Duick VI.*

So far, the rule makers have turned away from any attempts to require quarters in offshore yachts, for they realize that such a course would probably cause more problems than it would solve. (There are simple toilet and other requirements for each of the level rating classes.) They also realize that such a requirement could increase costs. Yet there is an increasing demand from average owners — those who race in their own spare time and cruise as well — to bring back the true dual-purpose racer cruiser.

One answer is the Offshore One Design. In the USA, Britain, and Scandinavia, One Design classes are arriving fast and attracting many orders. Another, less certain answer is the creation of new "perfect" rating rules, rules which, by evaluating every speed-making and speed-reducing factor far more accurately than ever before, will restore the chances of older, slower boats and put them back on an equal footing with the latest so-called "throwaway" designs. That would be the ideal solution, and with computers and hull-measuring machines to help, it may just be possible. At least the Americans are trying with a new rule called the Measurement Handicap Rule (MHR). This has been evolved as a spinoff of a very thorough research program into yacht performance conducted by the Massachusetts Institute of Technology.

Yet, when all is said and done, it is difficult in any sport to prevent those willing to go to greater lengths from winning.

Jack Knights

Long before *America* set out on her legendary race against sixteen British yachts, the races off Cowes were already established as a social event among the English nobility and upper middle class. The first races around the Isle of Wight took place in 1824, when the Royal Yacht Club was only nine years old.

During the Victorian era, a large number of sailing clubs were founded, and the races in The Solent became a regular event. The schooner was the favorite racing yacht, especially the American type that had evolved from pilot cutters and from the Gloucester schooners used by Newfoundland fishermen. *Mohawk* (Fig. 13) is an example of this type, which was refined almost beyond rational limits. The ridiculously oversparred *Mohawk* was launched in 1865. She is reported to have measured 120 feet at the waterline and to have had a beam of 9 feet. With her centerboard up, she drew only 6 feet. From her topsail spar to the waterline, she measured 164 feet; and from the end of the boom to the tip of the bowsprit, she measured 234 feet! This schooner sank in 1876 when a strong gust of wind hit her under full sail and capsized her.

The cutter type was used consistently for many decades, as in the regattas off Cowes (Fig. 14). Next to the robust cutters and the oversparred yachts that sailed in The Solent in 1883 (Fig. 15) and in 1905 (Fig. 17), *Valkyrie III* and *Defender* (Fig. 16) racing for the America's Cup in 1895, look like early versions of modern racing yachts.

Toward the end of the nineteenth century, interest in sport sailing was just as great in Germany as it was in England and America. This was due in no small part to the sailing activities of Kaiser Wilhelm II. As commodore of the Royal Yacht Club of Kiel, founded in 1887, he bought *Thistle* in 1901. A number of other yachts, all called *Meteor*, followed. Like *Meteor III* (Fig. 18) they were manned by English crews so that they could stand up to the competition in yachting events dominated by the English and Americans. In 1905, Wilhelm II established a cup for a transatlantic race without handicaps and open to yachts of all types. The German two-masted schooner *Hamburg* (Fig. 20) with an overall length of 150 feet and a total sail area of 18,000 square feet, presented the keenest competition for the American three-masted schooner *Atlantic*. *Atlantic* won the race in the still unbroken record time of 12 days, 4 hours, 1 minute. Her average speed was 10.32 knots.

The Solent continued to be the favorite location for the big regattas. It offered ideal training conditions for the major races: the schooners *Ingomar* and *Elmina* (Fig. 19) are shown racing in The Solent before World War I.

18

19

These schooners (Figs. 21, 26) carried veritable clouds of sail. It was yachts of this type that gave yachting the reputation of being the "sport of kings" after the turn of the century. *Bluenose* (Fig. 23) was the largest and best designed "racing fisherman" ever built in Newfoundland. Her proportions have never been surpassed. She won the International Fisherman Race of Nova Scotia (Fig. 25) in 1921 and has held the cup ever since. Her designer, W. J. Howe, had as great a talent for shipbuilding as Charles E. Nicholson, who built America's Cup yachts *Shamrock IV* and *V* and *Endeavour I* and *II* and who is shown here at the helm of the *Candida* (Fig. 24). This remarkable picture (Fig. 22) from the period between the World Wars shows *Lulworth*, *Shamrock I*, *Westward*, *Britannia*, and *White Heather* competing in a regatta. The Solent has probably never again seen an armada of thoroughbreds to equal this one.

III
AMERICA'S
CUP

Only two yachts sail this race but hundreds of spectator boats accompany them, and the ballyhoo of a spontaneous party reigns on land. The yachts are the most expensive sporting equipment in the world. The smartest designers conceived them. The most expensive materials were used in their construction. Multimillionaires paid for them. They are captained by the best sailors to be found anywhere, who have been training for months. And lofty words are spoken. Some are as pathetic as those about the "Holy Grail of yachting"; others are as somber as this phrase, heard in 1977: "If America loses, Ted Turner's head will roll through the New York Yacht Club."

The duel of the yachts is the oldest and at the same time the most modern spectacle in sailing. It is called the America's Cup.

Ted Turner had made his money as the owner of local TV and radio stations. As well known a sailor as Muhammad Ali is a boxer, and as big-mouthed, he had merely drunk two bottles of aquavit as though they were spring water. Just as he was to explain how he had won the Cup, he slid under the table, and, in the exuberance of triumph, nobody seemed to mind. Because, thanks to Ted Turner at the helm of *Courageous*, America had successfully defended the America's Cup for the twenty-third time.

The story begins in the year 1851. In that year a schooner, described as piratical because of its black hull, raked masts, and sharp bow, appeared off Cowes on the Isle of Wight, the seat of the Royal Yacht Squadron,

Britain's most distinguished sailing club. *America* was its name. John C. Stevens, commodore of the New York Yacht Club, and George Steers, designer of this yacht, which was to become the most famous of all yachts, had dared to go into the den of the British yachting lion in order—as the crew liked to jest over a beer at the pub—to give it a vigorous pinch in the tail. The British turned a deaf ear. Only after Stevens offered huge bets, dollar against shilling, any sum, and the *London Times* asked provokingly, "Where are the strength and courage of our men?" was the challenge finally accepted by the Royal Yacht Squadron.

Seventeen British yachts sailed against the challenger from America in the nearly sixty-mile race around the Isle of Wight. *America* won by eighteen minutes in conditions much more familiar to its competitors than they were to the crew. *Victoria and Albert*, the Queen's steam yacht, was anchored at the finish. *America* breezed by at thirteen knots. "And where, if you please, is the second?" Queen Victoria wanted to know. A courtier looked through the telescope, bowed, and said, "Your Majesty, there is no second."

This anecdote sums up the perplexity created by this defeat. A group of delegates asked in the House of Commons, "What does the government of Her Majesty intend to do to ameliorate this low point of British yacht building?" In addition to countless sums in betting money, Stevens took the Hundred Guineas Cup home with him. This silver jug is 2 feet, 3 inches high, weighs 8 pounds, 13 ounces, and was made by the London jewelry firm of R. & G. Garrard. The jug is not good for anything. It has no bottom, but to its bottomless depth, millions upon millions of dollars and pound sterling have disappeared over the years. It became a fixation with the British: the jug must be won back. The firm wish of the Americans, illustrated by the fact that the jug was bolted to its display case at the New York Yacht Club, was that the jug, now the America's Cup, stays. The fight for this trophy assumed fabulous proportions, unparalleled in yachting and sport in general, in the expenditure of both money and genius. In 1977 alone the old jug swallowed more than $12 million—the cost of equipping nine racing yachts under the American, Australian, French, and Swedish flags. Nothing is too good or too expensive to defend the America's Cup, to win it back, to prove that one possesses the most perfect sailing yacht in the world. Apart from horse racing, the America's Cup brought sport into the world of high performance. Even the physical demands made on the crews of America's Cup yachts compare favorably with land-based

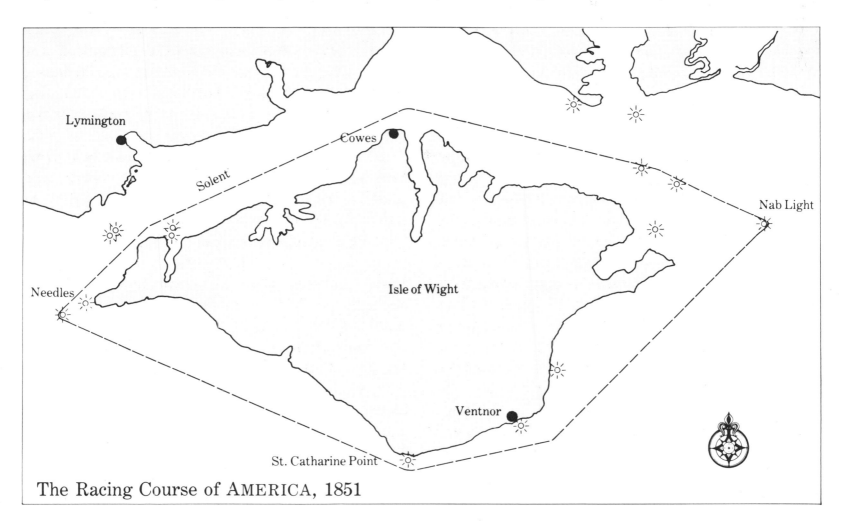

The Racing Course of AMERICA, 1851

athletics. The men are trained as athletes. In recent times, they have worn large numbers on their backs, like football players, so that the videotapes taken from an accompanying motor launch can more easily show if every "number" is in the right place at just the right second, working at the fastest possible pace with the most precise motions on each sail maneuver.

Today a racing crew consists of eleven men. Formerly, there had been as many as twenty or thirty, but they had to handle true clouds of sails. The largest single sail in history was made for the fight for the America's Cup. It was the 17,976-square-foot spinnaker flown by the American *Ranger* from its 164-foot mast in 1937. In a race on a thirty-mile course off Newport, it reached the record average speed of 11.1 knots.

Ranger belonged to the *J* class. The *J* yachts were about 135 feet long. Defenders and challengers had agreed in 1930 so that handicaps and time allowances between the smaller and the larger yachts could be eliminated. Up to then the first boat to reach the finish was not necessarily the winner; a handicap formula decided if the advantage was sufficient or not. In 1930, when *J*-class boats competed for the first time, the complex formula became obsolete. Since then, the first to finish is in fact the winner. The expensive yachts were praised as "racing machines." In any event, they were beautifully perfect yachts. As the duels for the old, bottomless jug were resumed after World War II, *J*-class yachts became unfeasible. No one could afford these yachts anymore. Thus, since

1958 a significantly smaller class, the twelve-meter boats have competed. The "twelve" in the class designation has nothing to do with the yachts' dimensions: twelve-meter yachts are about sixty-five feet long. A *J* yacht cost about $50,000 in the 1930s. Today, $2 million is not unusual for a twelve-meter yacht, as there are immense costs for research and development. This deadly serious form of recreation has only become cheaper in relation to general inflation. "If you have to ask what a racing yacht costs, you can't afford it," J. Pierpont Morgan, the creator of the steel trust, said to his son. As the commodore of the New York Yacht Club, this Croesus of Wall Street was one of the main financiers of the Cup defense. But even at the turn of the century, multimillionaires joined in syndicates when it came to paying the exorbitant fees of such famous designers as Nathaniel Green Herreshoff. Herreshoff designed and built five yachts that, between 1893 and 1920, repulsed all attacks on the America's Cup. The technical competition made the races increasingly expensive. The officials in charge of rules and construction formulas finally had enough: in 1970 someone at the New York Yacht Club thought aloud, "Why not make the keel of gold?"; gold has a higher specific weight than lead. "We will not even discuss it," was the answer from the clubhouse located near Central Park.

The first to want to take the America's Cup from the Americans was James Ashbury, who had the money to do it alone. Ashbury, a British industrialist, was newly rich and was determined, America's Cup in hand, to gain admission to the salons of the London establishment. In 1870 he sponsored *Cambria*, and in 1871, *Livonia*. The first time he had to contend with an armada of twenty-three American yachts, including old *America*, which finished fourth. *Cambria* was tenth. In 1871, only the defender and the challenger raced; initially the Americans allowed themselves the privilege of changing their yachts according to weather conditions. After losing a second time, Ashbury vented his anger in newspaper articles, in which he accused the Americans of "lack of sporting blood," and had the satisfaction of soon being admitted—without the trophy—to British blue-blooded circles. In 1876, when Canada, not Britain, was the challenger, it was agreed that the exchange clause, giving the defender a unilateral advantage, should be dropped.

Since that time the races for the America's Cup have been real match races; disputes over interpretation of the rules, especially when a challenger became really dangerous, had always arisen. It became a real feud when British sailing honor was to be avenged by a man whose name alone called attention to himself: Wyndham Thomas Wyndham-Quin, Earl of Dunraven Viscount Mountearl and Adare, Baron Adara of Adare, of Scottish ancestry, who appears in the result lists as Lord Dunraven. He was elegant, arrogant, and as obstinate as if he had the keel of a yacht for a forehead. After defeats in 1893 and 1895, like Ashbury he continued his feud in newspapers and magazines, but with more vehemence. He accused the Americans of

cheating, dragged two attorneys with him to the inquiry in New York, and was refuted point for point. Because he refused to apologize, as advised by the Prince of Wales, he was summarily ousted from the New York Yacht Club, of which he had been an honorary member. Above all, in these decades permanent racing rules for sailing were formulated from the match races for the America's Cup. The Americans interpret them with extreme strictness; in 1939, for example, they denied a justified protest of the British *Endeavour*, which has come closer to success than any challenger because it had hoisted the protest flag at the finish line (European fashion) and not immediately, as required. After World War II, Australian newspapers howled about alleged unfairness of the Cup defenders, who already had an advantage in their home waters, just as their British forerunners had done. But this expression printed in an American paper remains unassailable: "Britannia rules the waves but America waives the rules."

The dispute for the Cup stoked the feelings of naval supremacy of the Anglo-Saxons, which in turn stimulated the cartoonists. One drew "two nations at play," Uncle Sam and John Bull, kneeling at the edge of a pond and blowing—as grim as they were childish—into the sails of two toy boats. Another pictured the British lion, with *Valkyrie*, the name of Dunraven's yacht, written on its injured tail. As the lion cried a stream of tears into the jug, the American eagle watched mockingly. The importance given to the Cup was best illustrated by an American in 1899: Uncle

81

Sam is reading the year's agenda and topping the list, before the convening of Congress and the Philippine War, is the Race. The jug was also a perennial valve for the remaining historic rivalry between Great Britain and its seceded colony. The Britons gave up trying to reconquer the Cup, lost under such spectacular circumstances, in 1958, after their twelve-meter yacht *Sceptre* was defeated by *Columbia*, captained by Briggs Cunningham, also successful as a racing car driver. Since then the Australians have reached in vain for the "Grail." Their yachts were sponsored by millionaire newspaper owners and real estate brokers. France appeared for the first time in 1970, with *France* of Baron Marcel Bich, the ballpoint pen magnate. In 1977 the Swedes competed. Their *Sverige*, christened by Queen Silvia, was financed by the country's industry. They had seen, rightly, an opportunity to advertise, especially Swedish cars. In the meantime voices in Germany promise a prestigious victory, should a challenge be attempted. In this play of nations, past and present, a vague element of politics and socioeconomics is unmistakable. Four years after the ruckus around Lord Dunraven—a man honored and not mocked as the "greatest loser of the sport"—he saw to the continuation of the yacht match races. His desire for social acceptance had a major part in it, too. Sir Thomas Lipton was head of a grocery empire and the sole ruler of the Ceylon tea trade. He was forty-eight years old when he applied for membership in the Royal Yacht Squadron; however, despite his title, he was not considered good enough. His father had only been an Irish potato farmer. So Sir Thomas flew the ensign of the Royal Ulster Yacht Club on his yachts, all called *Shamrock*, which gave chase to the America's Cup from 1899 to 1930. Although he lost every time, at the age of eighty he was asked to submit his application to the Royal Yacht Squadron; thus he finally achieved his goal.

It is said that Sir Thomas Lipton sailed $10 million away. His other hobby—the steam yacht *Erin*, whose yearly maintenance alone cost a quarter million—proves that he could afford it. Thomas O. M. Sopwith became his yachting heir. He had made millions in aircraft construction, mostly with the Sopwith Camel, a fightercraft famous in World War I. His victorious rival in 1934 and 1937 was Harold S. Vanderbilt, who had also defended the Cup in 1930. He, like Sopwith, stood at the helm as the master of his yacht. Both had their wives with them as "tactical advisors," and because his paid crew had gone on strike in 1934, Sopwith was the first to go to battle with an amateur crew. Before owners had entrusted the helm to their yacht captains. Charlie Barr, an American, was considered the best. Professional sailors were not forgotten, though. Once, as Harold S. Vanderbilt was about to lose, he let Sherman Hoyt, the best-known yacht helmsman between the wars, take over. Even today's amateurs cannot manage without professional help.

Harold S. Vanderbilt and Thomas O. M. Sopwith, like Sir Thomas Lipton, owned 1,600-ton luxury yachts. They were the last of the super-rich to dispute the old jug, first in the waters off New York and, since 1930, off Newport, Rhode Island, which did not become the metropolis of yachting by accident. The gold dollar had found its summer residence in Newport at the turn of the century. One knight of dividends, William Fahnenstock, used to hang golden decorations in the trees of his park, and the new, green riches bore some other strange flowers. The Auchinclosses, Donahues, Drexels, and Woolworths—the people from Gotham—can still be found here in grand stucco palaces or refined, simple cottages. And with Newport as a backdrop we may finally understand the true meaning of the America's Cup: in the final analysis the America's Cup is a status symbol of old, wholesome America.

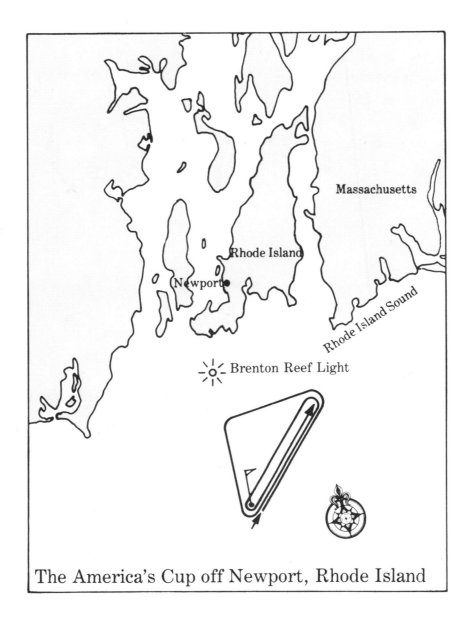

The America's Cup off Newport, Rhode Island

Nostalgia, however, remains farther and farther astern behind the modern technology of yachting. In 1977 the number of challengers was greater than ever. The Australians only made it to the final match race after the French and the Swedes were eliminated in the qualifying races: again, the Americans won. Even if it sounds boring, and even if the once new, green riches are slowly yellowing, the future of the America's Cup is bright—perhaps because in this world of error and bungling the old jug has become a symbol of perfection.

Alexander Rost

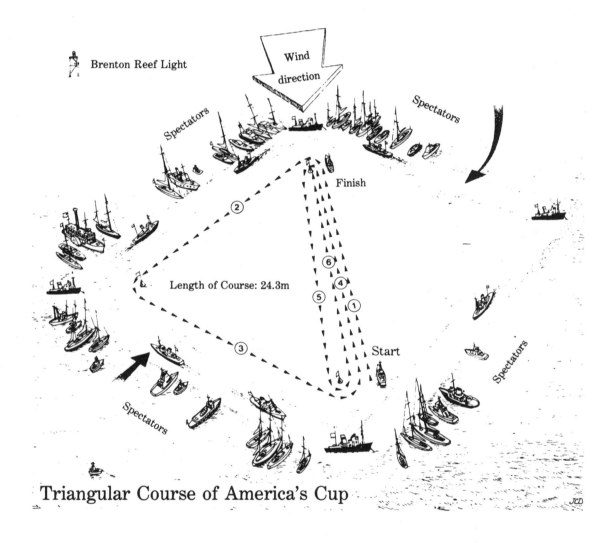

Triangular Course of America's Cup

28

29

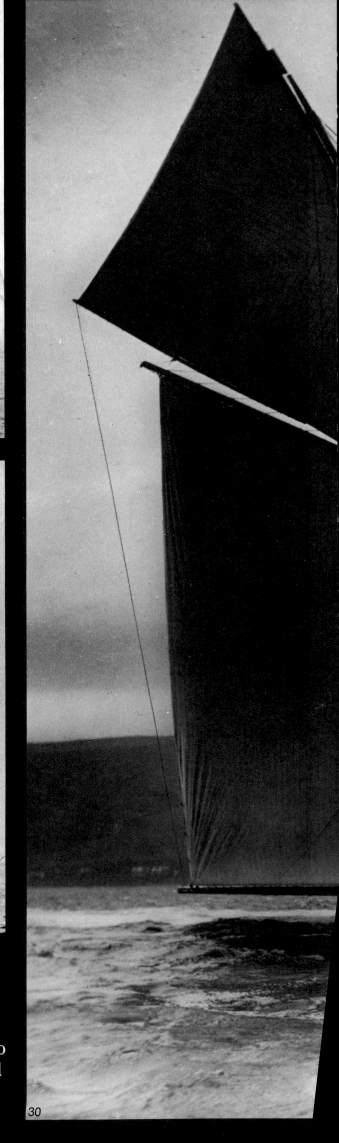

30

It all begin with *America*. George Steers, a famous American yacht designer of the period, and John C. Stevens, the first commodore of the New York Yacht Club, embarked on a project that would make yachting history. In 1851, they built the schooner *America* (Fig. 28). This was the first yacht ever to cross the Atlantic for the sole purpose of participating in a race on the other side. On August 22, 1851, *America*, outnumbered sixteen to one by boats of the British Royal Yacht Squadron, won a spectacular victory in a race around the Isle of Wight,

completing the fifty-eight-mile course eight minutes ahead of the yacht in second place. The prize for this race, the Hundred Guinea Cup, a silver cup weighing eight pounds, thus became a symbol of American superiority in international yachting. Despite all attempts that have been made to take it away, it still stands in a showcase in the New York Yacht Club.

Over the years, the races for the America's Cup have turned into increasingly spectacular duels. Wealthy Americans and British lords invested their prestige and considerable fortunes in hopes of winning the next round. In 1886, the steel-hulled British cutter *Galatea* (Fig. 29) challenged the wooden-rigged *Mayflower*, built by Starling Burgess. But victory in this sixth America's Cup race to be held since 1851 again went to the Americans. *Mayflower* crossed the finish line almost thirty minutes ahead of *Galatea*. The passion both sides invest in this competition was evident in the race of 1895. Lord Dunraven's *Valkyrie III*, launched in 1895 (Fig. 27) and carrying 13,000 square feet of sail on its mainmast alone (Fig. 30), challenged *Defender*, built by the legendary Nathaniel Herreshoff and financed by William Vanderbilt. With skipper Hank Haff at the helm (Fig. 31), *Defender* won easily, but Dunraven protested the outcome, claiming interference on the part of *Defender* and accusing the Americans of cheating. In response, the New York Yacht Club revoked his honorary membership.

Only four years after the scandal with Lord Dunraven, Sir Thomas Lipton, ruler over an empire of colonial enterprises and the Ceylon tea trade, was the next to throw down the gauntlet. With his yachts, which were all named *Shamrock*, he remained the only challenger until 1930. He is said to have invested some $10 million in his boats over the years, but he lost every race.

In 1899 the last race of the series, held on October 20, ended in a clear victory for the Americans. They were represented by *Columbia* (Fig. 32), which was also built by Herreshoff. She was financed by J. Pierpont Morgan. Charles Barr, probably the best professional skipper of his time, sailed *Columbia* across the finish line half a mile and 6 minutes, 34 seconds ahead of *Shamrock I* (Fig. 33). In 1903, *Shamrock III* lost to *Reliance* (Fig. 34), financed by Cornelius Vanderbilt and built by Herreshoff. With the *Shamrock V* (Fig. 35), Sir Thomas Lipton made his fifth and last challenge in 1930. The Americans raced *Enterprise*, which was designed by Starling Burgess, built by Herreshoff, and skippered by Harold S. Vanderbilt and Vincent Astor. *Enterprise* was the first boat of the new J class. It was also the first boat in the history of yachting to have its racing qualities tested beforehand by a model in a towing tank. This technical innovation paid off. *Enterprise*, with its owner Harold Vanderbilt at the helm, won by a large margin, and Sir Thomas Lipton decided to give up yacht racing after this defeat. The Americans gave him a gold cup, dedicated to the "best loser."

The rules for the America's Cup competition were interpreted very strictly. Thomas O. M. Sopwith, who was the next challenger after Sir Thomas Lipton, found this out. With *Endeavour* (Fig. 36), which Sopwith had financed himself, the British came as close as they ever had to defeating the Americans. Sopwith, who was at the helm himself (Fig. 37), entered a justified protest against interference on the part of *Rainbow* (Fig. 38), skippered by Harold Vanderbilt and Sherman Hoyt. The protest was finally declared invalid, however, because Sopwith raised his protest flag while crossing the finish line, as was customary in Europe, rather than raising it immediately, as the Americans did.

39

The last competition between *J*-class boats took place in 1937. Some of the most important yachts in racing history belong to this class. Sopwith's *Endeavour II* challenged *Ranger*, built by the veteran Starling Burgess and Olin J. Stephens, a bright new star in the field of yacht construction. The two boats were much alike in construction, but *Ranger* carried the largest single sail ever made: a spinnaker of 18,000 square feet of fabric.

The sail lockers needed for sails of this kind took up what would today be considered a huge amount of space below deck (Fig. 39). On a course of thirty miles, *Ranger* set a record average speed of 11.1 knots. *Endeavour II* lost (Fig. 40), and the America's Cup remained undisturbed in the New York Yacht Club.

40

41

42

After a break of twenty years, the America's Cup regattas resumed again in 1958 with a challenge from the Royal Yacht Squadron. The war had seen the development of new materials that brought revolutionary changes in yacht construction. Artificial fibers replaced hemp and other materials used for ropes, and sails were no longer made out of cotton but out of nylon and polyester. The rules governing the races also underwent major changes. The minimal length at the waterline was reduced to forty-four feet, and the races were now run with these so-called twelve-meter yachts. The challengers no longer had to cross the Atlantic on their own bottoms; and, finally, both challenger and defender had to be named a week before the first race at the latest.

The new yachts were only half as long as the boats of the old *J* class. Where *Ranger* of 1937 had an overall length of 135 feet, the twelve-meter boats were, like *Weatherly*, for example, only about sixty-eight feet long. *Weatherly*, as defender in 1958, lost to *Columbia*; but in 1962 she won a clear victory over the Australian challenger *Gretel* (Fig. 43).

In 1967, the challenger was again an Australian. This time Sir Frank Packer, a press magnate, entered his *Dame Pattie* against the Americans' *Intrepid* (Figs. 41, 42). In four dramatic races, *Intrepid* won easily every time. This brilliantly designed boat by Olin Stephens represented a new milestone in technological development. *Intrepid* had a mast made of titanium, and her winches were mounted below deck.

44

45

In 1977, the number of challengers was larger than ever. *Australia* (Fig. 46) won the elimination races against *France* and *Sverige* (Fig. 51) and became the challenger against Ted Turner's *Courageous* (Figs. 47, 48, 49). In the American eliminations, Turner and his crew had won clear victories over *Enterprise* (Figs. 44, 45) and *Independence* (Fig. 50).

The tremendous will to win that characterized Ted Turner and his crew was probably a decisive factor because many experts did not consider *Courageous* to be the faster boat. But once the contest with *Australia* was underway, the superiority of the Americans once again became evident. *Courageous* won all four races and an overwhelming victory.

46

47

48

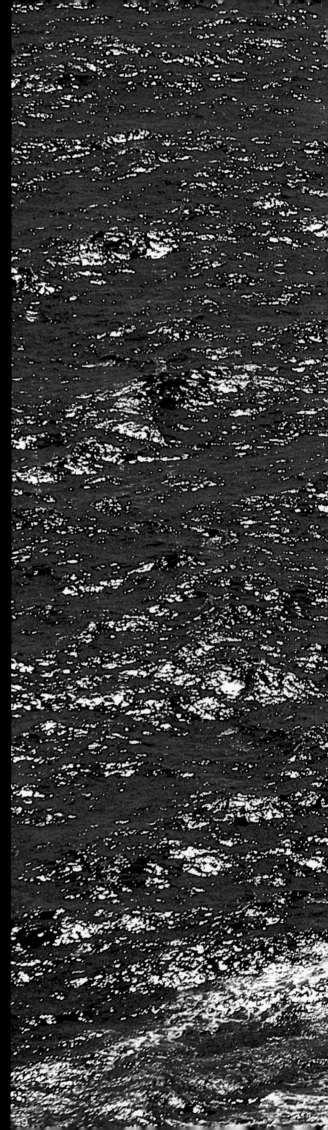

49

Ted Turner, who had become rich as the owner of local radio and television stations, once again secured the status symbol of the wealthy American past by successfully defending the America's Cup against the twenty-third challenger (Figs. 47, 48).

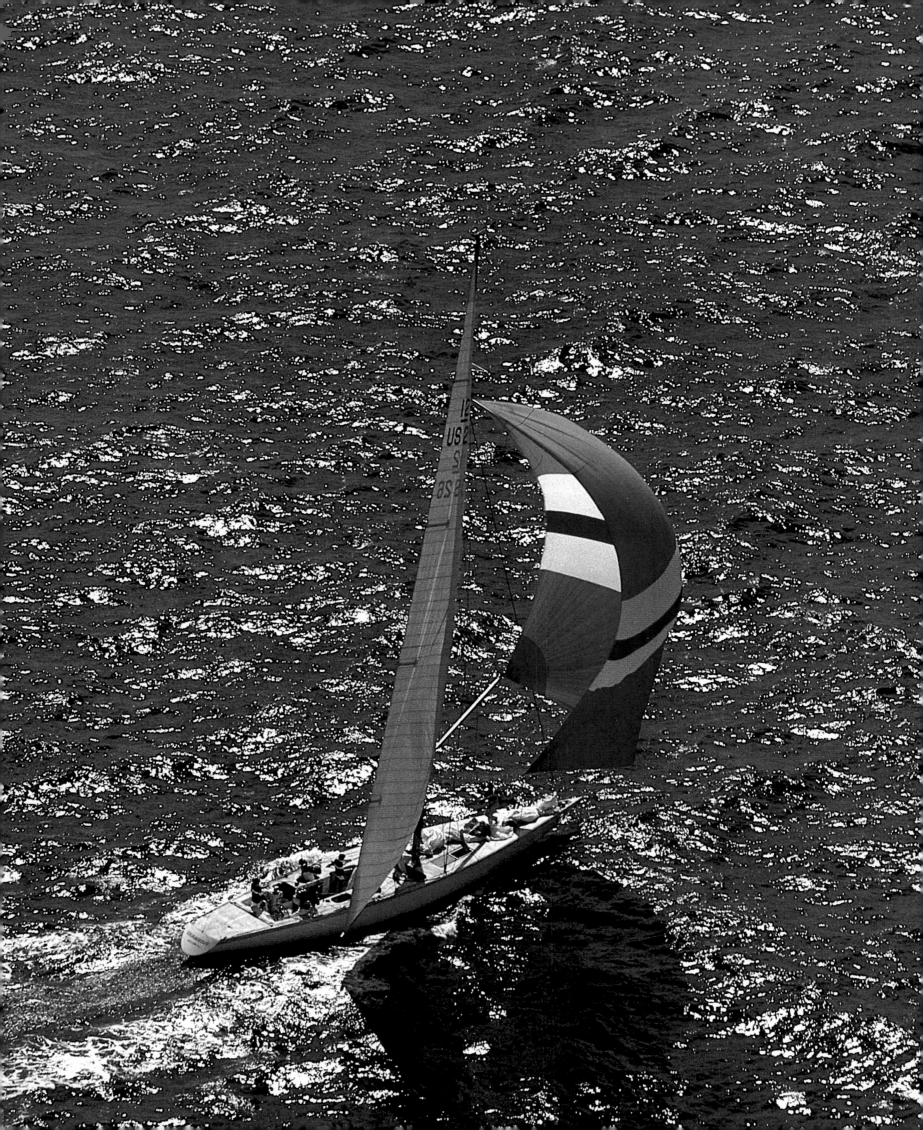

IV
THE
BIG
RACES
ON THE
HIGH
SEAS

Probably no ocean race has ever generated as much excitement as the Tea Race of 1866. The clipper ships that took part in that race started in the Far East and sailed more than 10,000 miles, reaching their destination with only minimal differences in their elapsed times. The clumsy, broad-beamed, unresponsive freighters of earlier days had evolved into beautifully designed clippers, with sleek hulls and almost dangerously large sail areas. Opium smuggling and the profitable trade in tea and Oriental silks created a need for fast sailing ships that would soon become even faster in the race for California gold. Speed was the prime consideration. It is a tribute to the genius of the designers of these ships that speed was not achieved at the cost of seaworthiness.

Although the world's first yacht club, The Water Club of Cork Harbour, Ireland, was founded in 1720, and amateur sailing spread rapidly to many points on the European and North American coasts, not much yachting was done beyond sight of land before the end of the nineteenth century. People then thought that only large yachts measuring close to one hundred feet could safely venture onto the open sea. The first ocean race for yachts took place in 1866 as the result of a bet. Three schooners, *Henrietta*, *Fleetwing*, and *Vesta*, manned by professional crews, set out from New York on December 11, 1866, to sail to the Isle of Wight. The season was unfavorable for crossing the North Atlantic, but by Christmas all three ships had reached their goal. A tragic incident took the

joy out of this triumph. On a stormy night, a high wave swept six crewmen from the deck of *Fleetwing*. Despite a five-hour search, none of the lost men was rescued.

The three-masted schooner *Atlantic* set another milestone in the history of ocean racing. In the 1905 Transatlantic Race, this first modern deepwater yacht sailed from Sandy Hook to Lizard Light—a distance of 2,925 miles—in the still unbroken record time of twelve days, four hours, one minute, for an average speed of ten knots. *Atlantic*'s best twenty-four-hour run, reckoned from noon to noon, was 341 miles; an average speed of 14.2 knots. This race stimulated great interest in blue-water sailing and in racing on the high seas. Deepwater races were established in different parts of the world, and these contests helped encourage the development of yachting and ocean sailing.

The guiding principle in all these races was to lay out an interesting course that would cross stretches of open sea or even entire oceans yet that would be realistic in terms of local geographical and meteorological conditions. Among the many deepwater and transoceanic races held in the world today, some meet these criteria better than others and therefore hold a special attraction for the international sailing set. Participation in these races usually involves a considerable sacrifice in time and money both for owners and crews.

The oldest of all ocean races is the Transatlantic Race. For many years after the first contest in 1866, this race was run with paid crews. In 1928, at the suggestion of King

110

Alfonso XIII of Spain, the first Transatlantic Race for smaller yachts and amateur crews was held. The course was New York to Santander. The 59-foot schooner *Nina*, which was built especially for this race and was small by the standards of that period, defeated all the larger yachts, many on elapsed time. Since that year, transatlantic races have been held at irregular intervals, usually in connection with special occasions like the Admiral's Cup or centennial celebrations of different clubs. The courses have run from the east coast of North America or from Bermuda to the west coast of Europe; i.e., to Norway, Sweden, Denmark, England, Ireland, Germany, or Spain. The distances sailed amount to between 2,600 and 3,600 miles.

As a rule, a transatlantic course skirts the southern edge of the low-pressure zone across which the lows from North America move via Iceland to Northern Europe. Parts of the route follow the Gulf Stream. Much of the race can be run before the wind, and depending on a yacht's speed and on the speed with which the lows travel in a northeasterly direction, a yacht may be driven across the Atlantic by very few or by many different low pressure systems. Sailing the North Atlantic with the lows means, of course, that it can turn very cold even in the summer because winds on the port quarter bring Arctic air with them.

From 1866 to 1978, the Transatlantic Race was held twenty-two times. Sixteen of these races were run after 1945. The longest race, which was held in 1951 and in which only four yachts took part, went from Havana, Cuba, to San Sebastian on the northern coast of Spain. This course covered more than 4,000 miles. The shortest course, sailed in 1969,

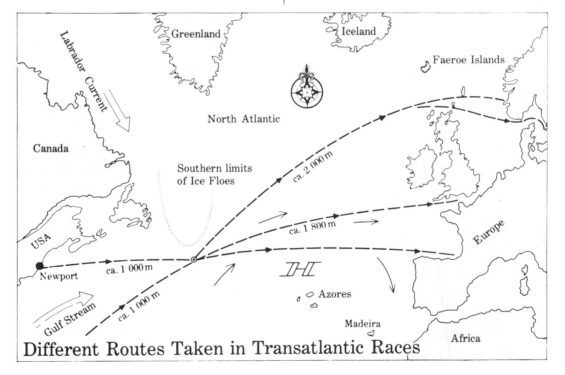

Different Routes Taken in Transatlantic Races

was about 2,670 miles from Newport, Rhode Island, to Cork on the southern coast of Ireland. This race was held in celebration of the 250th anniversary of the founding of the Royal Cork Yacht Club, formerly the Water Club of Cork Harbour.

The American 72-foot ketch *Kialoa II* reached Cork in 12 days, 5 hours, 43 minutes; it averaged 9.08 knots, one knot under the record time of *Atlantic*. The Transatlantic Race of 1966 drew one of the greatest numbers of participants ever when forty-two yachts sailed from Bermuda to Skagen and then on to Copenhagen in celebration of the centennial of the Royal Danish Yacht Club. Sumner A. Long turned in a remarkable performance with his 73-foot ketch *Ondine*. He assured himself of victory when he pulled away in the last third of the race under extremely stormy conditions. When asked how he had done this, he replied, "When the storm got worse and the other boats struck their spinnakers, we hoisted one with wire leech lines." It's that simple! The 1972 race drew the largest fleet, over sixty boats.

Conditions are very different for the Transpacific Race, the longest of all regularly held ocean races. The course runs from Los Angeles, California, to Honolulu, Hawaii, a distance of 2,225 miles. The prevailing winds for this race are the northeast trade winds. Once the yachts are free of coastal influences, they can sail before these usually fresh winds in reliably warm weather and with their spinnakers set for the duration of the race. It is therefore not surprising that this race has gained in popularity ever since it was founded in 1906. In 1969, a record number of seventy-two yachts participated. The best time for this course was set in 1977 when the 67-foot displacement sloop *Merlin* turned in a time of 8 days, 11 hours, 1 minute and an average speed of 10.96 knots.

But even this sunny trade winds race can

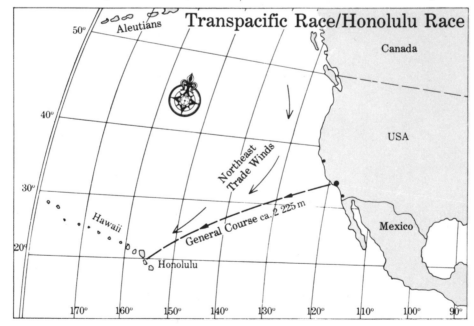

have its stormy moments, and the competition can be fierce. Two top yachts once showed just how fierce it can be when they raced to a dramatic finish. Two 73-foot ketches, *Ticonderoga* and *Stormvogel*, once battled each other for first place, both still carrying spinnakers in a wind of Force 11. The Transpacific Yacht Racing Association sponsors this race every odd-numbered year. The first Transpacific was held in 1906, but the race has been held regularly only since 1947.

The Cape Town-Rio de Janeiro Race has been in existence only since 1971. With a rhumb-line distance of over 3,000 miles, this is the longest ocean race of all. The appeal of this race has been great ever since its inception. Sixty-three participants from fifteen countries entered its first running; and in 1976, when the race was held for the third time, 148 yachts from 22 countries started. The drawing power of this race is unique in the history of ocean racing. Part of its attraction may be that it gives yachtsmen a chance to see something of the exotic continents of Africa and South America as well as to put in at two of the world's most beautiful ports, Cape Town and Rio. The race is also scheduled so that the participants can experience the famous carnival in Rio. Then, too, the course crosses only tropical and subtropical seas where the prevailing winds are astern. At the beginning of the race, the yachts sail before the southeast trade winds. Then at about 15 degrees South, they pick up westerly winds that take them into the northeast trade winds prevailing along the coast of Brazil. These winds drive them on

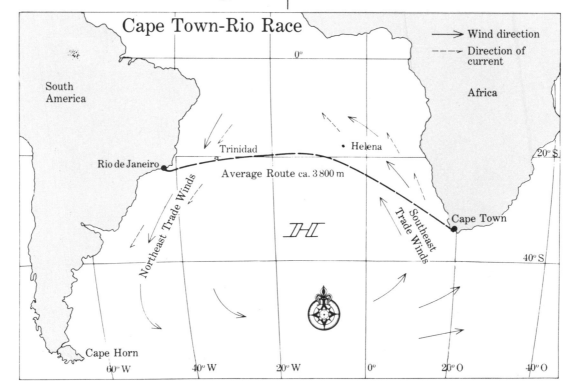

under spinnakers to Sugar Loaf Mountain. Even this summer race is not without its risks. In 1971, the 33-foot sloop *Pioneer* was sunk by a whale at night. Thanks to an incredible bit of luck, the crew of three men and a woman, set adrift in their life raft, was picked up about seventeen hours later by a steamer that had no business being in that area, since no shipping lanes transverse it. The Bermuda Race is the oldest deepwater race still in existence. First run in 1906, it is now held every even-numbered year. Only three yachts participated in the first race. In 1974, 167 yachts set out on the course of 635 miles from Newport, Rhode Island, to St. David's Head, Bermuda. The Bermuda Race is a classic that every blue-water sailor worth his salt feels he has to have sailed. Of course, all the participants want to win and do their best to sail as fast as they can. But victory in this race is not won by speed alone. It also depends on expertise in navigation and on the tactical use of currents. How a skipper deals with the Gulf Stream is decisive in this race. The Gulf Stream, moving with considerable speed, crosses the racer's course about a third of the way along on his voyage to Bermuda. A yacht in the Gulf Stream will

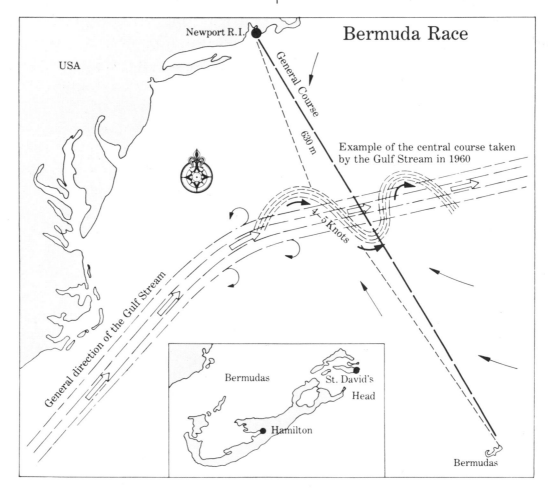

be rapidly carried eastward. Then, because the prevailing winds south of the Gulf Stream are usually out of the southwest, it is usually important to leave the Gulf Stream with Bermuda off the port bow, for a close reach to the finish. Sometimes, however, it pays to come out of the Stream with the island on the starboard bow. Only with the aid of careful navigation involving frequent sextant readings and constant checks of the water temperature can a yacht maneuver into the optimal position. The 79-foot ketch *Ondine* set the record for this race in 1974 with a time of 2 days, 20 hours, 8 minutes and an average speed of 9.32 knots. The well-known blue-water sailor and writer Carleton Mitchell also holds a unique record. He won the Bermuda Race three times in a row with his 39-foot centerboard yawl *Finisterre*, sailing both in fair weather and under storm conditions, in 1956, 1958, and 1960.

Another classic race is the Fastnet Race. First sailed in 1925, it is the oldest race to be held in European waters. This course of 605 miles begins at Cowes and runs westward to the mouth of the English Channel, then to Fastnet Rock, a lighthouse on an isolated shoal off the southern coast of Ireland. Once a yacht has rounded this lighthouse, it heads back for the finish line at Plymouth. Despite the light winds that have prevailed during the last few competitions, the Fastnet Race, usually held every two years in odd-numbered years, has a reputation as one of the world's most difficult races. The strong tides and normally harsh weather in these waters account for unfavorable sailing condi-

tions. The fleet, sailing westward, passes to the south of low pressure systems moving northeast and therefore runs head-on into their peripheral winds. Because such winds are unpredictable both in direction and strength, constant changes in sail are necessary. If the tide and a strong wind are moving in opposite directions, a sailing crew is tested to its limits by rough seas. The return leg of the race is often run under spinnakers, but frequent changes in sail are needed in this part of the race, too.

In one Fastnet Race in the 1950s, an English and an American yacht vied for first place. The Americans won because of their superior sail handling. The skipper of the English boat remarked, "We had to keep changing sail all the time on the return leg. I watched the crew of *Carina* change sail ten times in twenty minutes, but I think I may have missed one sail change when I blinked a few times." Dick Nye, the skipper of *Carina*, and his crew had developed a battle cry to keep up their morale when the going got tough. Skipper Nye spat out his cigar and shouted, "Are you all tigers?" The crew answered, "Grrr . . . Grrr . . . Grrr . . .!" and threw themselves into their work with renewed energy.

Ever since 1945, the Buenos Aires-Rio Race has been held regularly every three years. It soon drew a large number of participants because sailing is such a popular sport in both Argentina and Brazil. Yachts from England, Germany, and the United States also take part in it. This race, too, is scheduled to end at about the same time as the carnival in Rio begins so that the crews, after sailing their race of 1,200 miles, can enjoy this unique spectacle.

The meteorological conditions for this race make their own special demands on skipper and crew. The first leg involves sailing out of the immense La Plata River delta, past Montevideo, and some 300 miles almost due east, all under shifting wind conditions. Once a yacht comes into the northeast trade winds, she can head for the finish, sailing close-hauled, with Rio off its port bow. During the first third of the race, sudden storms called *pamperos* pose a constant threat. They are difficult to recognize, and it is impossible to tell just how much wind they are bringing with them. An Argentine sailing rule prescribes that if a *pampero* is blowing up, a skipper should strike all his sails, then reset them in the storm according to the velocity of the wind. A boat can suddenly be confronted with a wind force of anything from 7 to 12. Sailors who have chosen the shorter course close to land have often found themselves stalled in the calm pocket in the bay of São Paulo. But on the route farther out to sea, a yacht will have 800 to 900 miles of sailing ahead, usually under ideal conditions: fantastically blue water, wind of Force 5, long swells out of the northeast. An angel hovers over every boat, whispering to the crew, "Hurry up! The carnival in Rio is about to begin."

On the other side of the world, also in the Southern Hemisphere, is Australia. There another ocean race is held every year at

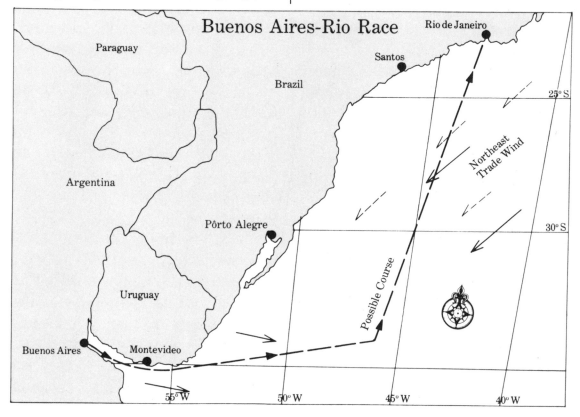

Christmas time. In 1945, a few blue-water sailing enthusiasts founded the Cruising Club of Australia. Talking with the internationally known English deepwater sailor Captain John Illingworth, they said that they wanted to sail to Hobart, Tasmania, over Christmas. Asked if he would like to join them, Illingworth replied, "Yes, but only if you make a race of it." That was the origin of the Sydney-Hobart Race.

In the course of this challenging 630-mile race, the sailor can expect to encounter everything from calms to winds of gale force, and his job is made even more difficult by currents and tides. The course follows a generally south-southwesterly direction along the southeastern coast of Australia with the wind usually astern. Then it crosses the eastern mouth of the Bass Strait, which separates Australia from Tasmania. In this region, which enjoyed a particularly bad reputation in the days of the old sailing vessels, the yachtsman is greeted by often icy and always stormy winds out of the southwest, accompanied by exceptionally heavy seas. These winds can be explained by the fact that they are generated in the "roaring forties," the particularly stormy region of the South Pacific centered on the fortieth parallel. Once the Bass Strait has been passed, the course runs south along the east coast of Tasmania toward Hobart. Here, the winds tend to be weak and shift, as is to be expected on the lee coast of a mountainous island. But despite this slow leg of the voyage, some yachts have occasionally managed to run the course in very good time. The

record of 3 days, 3 hours, 46 minutes, set in 1962 by the 56-foot American yawl *Ondine* was not broken until 1973 when *Helsal*, a 72-foot Australian sloop with a ferro-cement hull, bettered it by 2 hours, 14 minutes. In that race, *Helsal* was sometimes exposed to wind velocities ranging from 40 to 80 knots or, expressed on the Beaufort scale, peak wind speeds of Force 13 or 14. Ninety-two yachts sailed in that race, a record.

Along with the ocean and transoceanic races, we also have to mention the racing series that have become popular in recent years and have changed the character of blue-water sailing considerably. Many sailors found the expense in time and money that ocean racing involves too great for what was often a rather tedious sailing experience. Many called for races that offered more activity and close sailing. As sailing became available to ever-larger segments of the population, more and more small-boat sailors joined the ranks of blue-water sailors, and the demand for nonhandicap races open to ocean-going yachts made itself felt.

Small-boat sailors were accustomed to having their competition constantly in view, to being able to see instantly whether they were gaining or losing ground, and to winning by virtue of being the first to cross the finish line. They were not satisfied with battling the clock and an imaginary opponent for days on end, only to have a competitor who arrived at his goal days later walk off with the trophy. These were the feelings that gave rise to series races. Some of these races are for yachts of different size, some for those of the same size and rating. These latter regattas have come to be called level-rating regattas because all the boats in each series have the same rating.

Series races usually include a mix of day races, medium-length races about 200 miles, and longer races. This variety gives all boats and crews the opportunity to demonstrate their particular strengths. Series of this kind are the Admiral's Cup in Britain, the Southern Cross Cup in Australia, and the Southern Ocean Racing Conference and the Onion Patch series in the United States. Level-rating regattas in the Quarter, Half, Three-Quarter, One, and Two-Ton categories are held in different countries each year.

In the last ten years, a dramatic change has taken place in blue-water sailing. Into the 1950s, yacht owners and crews participated in ocean races purely for the pleasure they found in the sport and in the competition. The boats were designed as cruisers or cruiser racers. In other words, they were intended for pleasure cruises with friends and families

The Courses of the Southern Ocean Racing Conference (S.O.R.C.)

- –··– Anclote Key Race
- —— St. Petersburg – Ft. Lauderdale Race
- –·– Ocean Triangle Race
- ···· Lipton Cup Race
- – – Miami — Nassau Race
- –·– Nassau Cup Race

Anclote Key
St. Petersburg
Florida
Bahamas
Fort Lauderdale
Florida Strait
Miami
Nassau
Andros
Rebecca Shoal
Key West
Havana
Cuba

0   100   200 m

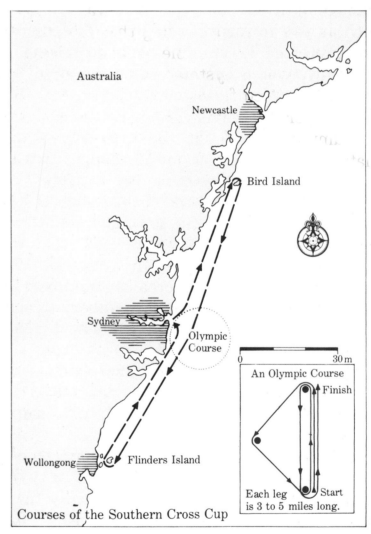

Australia
Newcastle
Bird Island
Sydney
Olympic Course
Havana

An Olympic Course
Finish
Start
Each leg is 3 to 5 miles long.
0   30 m

Wollongong
Flinders Island

Courses of the Southern Cross Cup

as well as for ocean races. Owners wanted these boats to have good resale value. For these reasons, technical progress in the design and construction of hulls, rigging, sails, and equipment was slight.

A key factor in planning ocean-going yachts at that time was the desire to provide those crew members who were not on deck with dry, comfortable bunks and with a galley that was practical in any weather so that meals could be enjoyed in as civilized a manner as possible. Often, the crew ate at a massive mahogany table. The deck, too, was designed with an eye toward keeping the crew as dry and protected as possible. During a race, a strict two-watch system was adhered to. If help was needed for a difficult change of sail, the skipper, the navigator, or the cook would be summoned from below. It was almost a matter of honor that the off-duty watch not be dragged out of their bunks.

The competiveness of the series, such as the Admiral's Cup races, brought about a fundamental change. In a short time, blue-water racing acquired a status and quality that attracted increasing numbers of young sailors of Olympic caliber. Yacht owners began to recruit this talent to help them win races.

For the crew, the whole point of sailing was to win. The new tone that dominated on board was tough, impersonal, and professional. A parallel development was the designing and building of yachts with nothing but victory in mind. The first things to go were dining tables, comfortable bunks, and storage lockers. These days on racing yachts, crews squat among sailbags to gobble down meals served on paper plates. The crew is also expected to place themselves where their weight will do the most good in trimming the yacht. This sometimes obliges them to spend hours perched on the windward side of the boat, facing the weather and being drenched by waves and spray. In earlier days, sailors were reluctant to register formal protests about breaches of sailing rules and tried to settle disputes on a personal level. Now, the hard-nosed professional seizes every opportunity to protest. Long-distance ocean racing is in danger of becoming professionalized, and we can only hope, for the sake of this sport, that such a change can be prevented.

A well-known and successful English blue-water sailor who, as a yacht owner and skipper, has watched this change take place, describes it in these terms.

On both sides of the Atlantic, ocean racing has become a sport in which people with money win fame by hiring good sailors who can make up for the skippers' shortcomings. These people will change boats, crews, builders, and friends to win a place in the sailing yearbook. It may be that I have contributed to this development. If that is so, I regret it deeply because I think it is a change for the worse. I still count myself among the old ocean sailors who know how to sail older boats and have a good time doing it, even if there is no public acclaim to be won in this way.

Rudolf Koppenhagen

It was the summer of 1936 on board the yawl *Hamburg*. We were sailing in the Bermuda to Cuxhaven race on the North Atlantic, and had started on July 4, at 12:30, in the company of six other German yachts—*Arktur*, *Ashanti II*, *Ettsi IV*, *Peter von Danzig*, *Roland von Bremen*, and *Susewind*—and the Dutch yacht *Zeearend*, after a stay at Hamilton.

The next land we expected to see was Bishop Rock on Scilly Island at the entrance of the English Channel. In between lay 3,000 miles—a long way. There must be another 500 miles to Cuxhaven. It was the longest race yachtsmen had ever attempted up to that time. The race started in a light southwesterly and smooth sea. The deep blue dome of the sky, with just a few pyramid-shaped clouds over the receding island, gave us an intoxicating feeling. Then the night obscured this sunny day and enveloped us in its lukewarm wings. Pressed closely together, we six comrades on board *Hamburg* were sitting in the cockpit, dousing our racing fever with pipe, cigar, or cigarette. We now had to master any situation on our own, according to the laws of the sea.

When the sun sent its rays into the sky the next morning, the only sails to be seen were those of the larger *Roland von Bremen*, far to starboard. This fueled the racing fever anew. According to our calculations, that ship had gained a third of a mile an hour on us. That was a 5 percent speed difference, while *Roland's* handicap allowed us only two. We tried in vain to keep the distance the same, but by noon we were by ourselves on the wide sea. Where were our opponents? Who was behind? Where were we in the procession of boats? We had only one point of reference—our daily run! The first day's reckoning measured 139 miles, which meant barely 6 knots. That day it became obvious that covered distances alone would not keep the racing fever at its highest. We had to keep after our opponent even if she was out of sight and we could not constantly keep an eye on her, as in a day race. And so it was only natural to see an opponent in the other watch. Each watch wanted to cover more miles than the other. During the night the barometer fell gradually and the wind stiffened. At seven in the morning the wind was blowing Force 5. We doused the big spinnaker and the mizzen and set our small storm spinnaker, made of the strongest canvas, which remained our workhorse during the whole voyage, even on the worst days. The boat ran well in mounting seas. The wind strengthened even more during the late morning and we sailed 181 miles that day, despite rough conditions.

It got tougher during the morning watch of the third day. The jib replaced the spinnaker. A heavy gale struck around noon. A funnel swirled down from the dark mass of clouds. We were registering Force 9 winds while we furled the mainsail as a precaution. Pity, since wind meant speed and distances covered. Since we could not sight with the sextant, we determined our day's reckoning by the log—185 miles. A proud performance.

The square head of Captain Schlimbach appeared in the companionway. He popped the cork on the bottle and, his face beaming, he announced, "Gentlemen, we have put the first 500 miles behind us. I have mixed an especially good drink for the occasion."

But the next day did not live up to our expectations. The roaring speed of the last few days dropped off. The wind became more irregular, with somewhat decreasing seas. At two in the morning, the wind shifted south, blowing at Force 2 and 3. We unreefed and set the big spinnaker. Around eleven another rainsquall came up from the southeast, with the wind stiffening to Force 7 and veering to the south. Now the spinnaker had to come down and storm sails took its place. In the evening, the wind shifted to the west and north. We did not jibe, since we wanted to stay toward the south. Since the barometer had dropped again, we put a reef into the mainsail. The distance for this day was 140 miles. On July 9 we encountered northwest winds of Force 4 to 6 under a scattering cloud cover. At noon the wind turned back west with heavy gusts. We had now covered far more than 800 miles. In the afternoon, the wind blew Force 6 to 7 under a heavily covered sky and rainsqualls. It got worse at night. After taking another look at the barometer, we decided not to reef deeper. The port watch went below. We were alone. Soon rainsqualls were rustling over us. The bow wave streamed by to the lee, whitish gray. The ocean was alight with phosphorescence! Isolated jellyfish drifted by, hanging in the water like swaying lanterns. Suddenly, silver streaks were blinking—singly, in pairs, and more; dolphins were circling our ship like shining torpedos. It was wonderful to watch this elegant play.

The whistling of the wind increased. The ship labored heavily but not spasmodically. We prepared the reefing pendant, just in case. We would want to reef if the weather worsened, but not before the changing of the watch if possible, so we would not deprive those off duty of their sleep. Midnight drew near slowly. Before the calling out of the new watch, the weather improved a little. At 1:00, both watches could not decide whether or not to reef the mainsail. Our watch finally went below completely drenched. Each surge made the hull groan and the bulkheads and doors creak. When the boat was lifted hard and heeled over by the sea, it made a sound like a moan which, combined with the sound of the waves rushing along the topsides, made a swelling, rustling sound. Then silence fell for the duration of a heartbeat. Even the wind seemed to stop playing in the rigging at such moments, as if wondering; then suddenly it resumed strumming on the steel chords with renewed vigor, and forced the boat along its course. Suddenly there was a crashing blow, as if the boat had run aground somewhere. Slowly she righted herself and got under way again. Muffled commands were given, and the tapping and dragging of our comrades' heavy rubber boots could be heard. What was going on up there? We had stepped into our clothes mechanically and listened for a word from

121

above. We sensed how the watch was trying not to wake us. They doused the jib. But our sleep was over. Were we to take these wet rags off again? Too much trouble. Instead, we smoked for a change and drank a cup of coffee.

The day dawned slowly. We retired below deck for the remainder of the rest period. The wind jumped to the north and carried misty air with it. In an hour we were in the midst of dense fog. The Gulf Stream demonstrated to us again how whimsical it could be. We listened attentively for the ringing of the sirens of oncoming steamers. The rough sea and the rattling sails and blocks made us hear all kinds of strange sounds. We realized for the first time how small our *Hamburg* was in the endless water desert. The ship labored hard in the restless ground swell. Our spirits sank. We did not want to look at each other; we avoided each other or exercised the utmost politeness. It is the famous "cabin fever" in its purest form. I had helm duty from noon to 1 P.M. From yesterday's position, we calculated that we had sailed a total of 990 miles. Today's position was 42° North and 49°5′ West. I finally went to sleep, relieved. But the hoped for, rewarding sleep did not come. The solitude worked like a sedative, despite the pitching and yawing of the boat. While I dreamed of our *Hamburg* sailing for home after a successful run under the big spinnaker, Petersen came silently into the cabin to light one of his long, calming cigars. When he went back on deck the sun had broken through and its rays were dancing over the shiny mahogany planking. The little room became quite festive. The space between the mainmast and the bunk was just big enough so that if you sat on the bench you could lean your head comfortably against the spar. How often had this cranny proved itself ideal for dressing in foul weather. With handholds all over the place, there was hardly a chance to fall over.

A while later, a look at the horizon confirmed the fact that the boat was turning in a circle. All things considered, this was an awkward situation in the heavy and irregular ground swell. We tried to decide if this predicament was worse than the toughest storm could have been. But since we knew that calms do not last on the Atlantic, we did not let our newfound optimism be spoiled. It was as if the ship wanted to direct our attention through its turning, to the magnificent spectacle of the mid-ocean sunset. Each of us might have been thinking different things— the play of the colors, or the symphonic quality of the event, or the fleeting nature of life, or the time when no human eyes would remain to behold it. In a word, we were happy to be allowed to absorb this exquisite moment together without having to say much.

As the disk of the sun sunk behind the clouds, making them fiery red and touching the higher ones with its dying light for a long while, it seemed to us that our ship had wandered through a great bloodred gate into an alien, mysterious world. Only after the descending night had extinguished all daylight did we shake the spell. With the appearance of the first stars, a light breeze rose from the south. We set all sails and the big spinnaker; our boat continued its journey on an east-northeast course. We sighed with relief. Our hope to push *Hamburg* to victory was reborn.

Georg Lauritzen

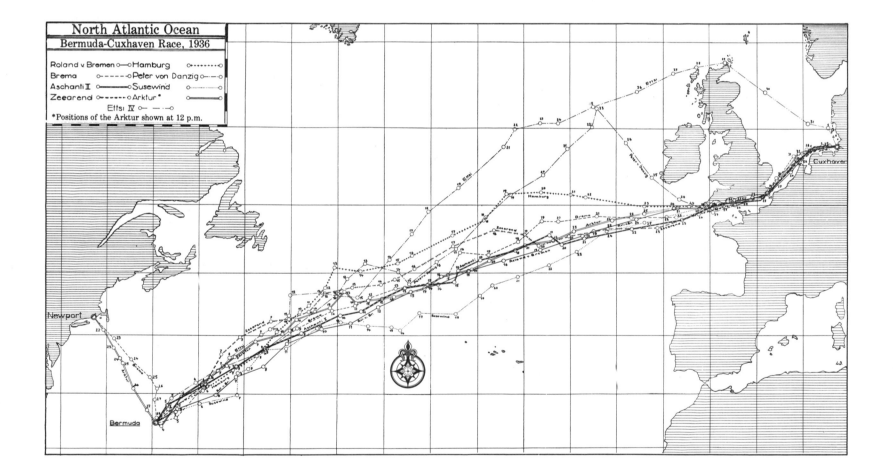

The start of the Sydney-Hobart Race is the most exciting of any race in which I have participated. Traditionally boats cross the line at eleven o'clock on the morning of the day after Christmas. This itself creates an air of festivity which no other ocean race possesses. On such an occasion Sydney harbor is a splendid setting, usually with a bright blue sky and hot sun. All along the shore of this massive harbor house parties are on their balconies ready to toast the adventurous fleet in champagne as it passes. On the water some four thousand boats of every size and description and carrying spectators are ready to move down with the competitors. Sitting on the hills on each side of the entrance to the harbor are half a million people, enjoying their family holiday. In these circumstances it is not surprising that there should be something more than usually electrifying about the start.

There couldn't have been a better morning for the start of the twenty-fifth race on December 26, 1969, in which I sailed the first *Morning Cloud*. This was a Sparkman and Stephens 34, a standard production boat, 24' on the waterline and 33'9" overall. The boat and crew had been sailing in Australia for three weeks as the reserve boat for the British team in the Southern Cross Cup. The series for this trophy is similar to that of the Admiral's Cup in Britain and the Onion Patch in America. A two-hundred-mile offshore race and three thirty-mile races had enabled us to become acclimatized to the heat of the Australian summer and also to get used to the sloppy sea inshore and the long, rolling swell offshore. While we had been preparing for this race we had thought of Capt. John Illingworth, a British naval officer stationed in Sydney who had won the first race in 1945 in his boat *Rani*, just a foot longer overall than *Morning Cloud*. No British skipper since had succeeded in winning the race. The conditions twenty-five years before had been very different. There were only nine entries; the boats had been designed for cruising. When the fleet encountered a southwesterly gale off the New South Wales coast on the second night out, eight of the yachts hove to or ran for shelter. The only one not to do so was Captain Illingworth in *Rani*. After the storm was over the eight other boats were located, but for four days *Rani* was missing. Finally she appeared off Tasman Island to win the race in six days, thirty-eight hours, twenty-two minutes. We knew that Illingworth had followed the tactic of standing right offshore from the beginning of the race, in part to gain advantage from more consistent winds, in part to make use of the "set" or current. This is said to run south at anything up to two knots if one can find the right place; if not, one may very well encounter it coming north at the same speed.

Captain Illingworth's dictum "get out and stay out" had also been pressed on me by Tryg Halvorsen, an Australian of Norwegian extraction, who had himself won the Sydney-Hobart Race four times. The crew and I had spent Christmas Day with him at his home overlooking the Sound and had decided to heed his advice. With a northeasterly wind, once through the Heads, we ought to be able to hoist a spinnaker, get well east of the rhumb line, and run with the current down to the coast of Tasmania. This was the second lesson we had learned from studying the history of the contest. In the majority of cases it is a downwind race, certainly until one hits the westerlies in the Bass Straits or the southerlies from the Antarctic. Two years previously *Rainbow Two*, skippered by Chris Bouzaid, had been successful largely because of her outstanding performance downwind and the ruthless way in which she had been driven with a strong following wind by her crew. I had talked to some of them in Auckland six months earlier and they had emphasized to me the vital importance of being able to sail fast downwind. As a result we had increased the size of our spinnaker and the length of the poles, incurring in the process a small penalty, which we thought worthwhile.

At the time of the twenty-fifth race, the nine boats had increased to seventy-nine, many of them designed specifically for ocean racing. The Australians, who had been to

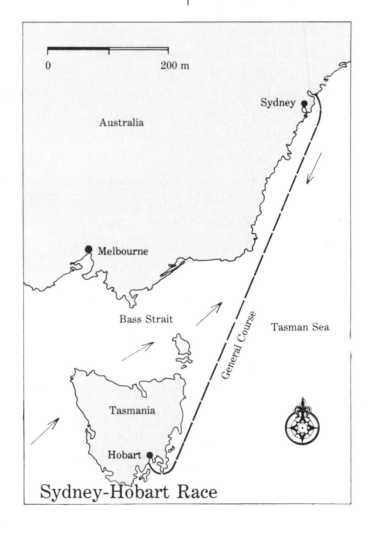

Sydney-Hobart Race

Britain to take part in the Admiral's Cup, had learned a great deal from the international competition there and had transferred their experience of boats and crewing to the Australian scene with considerable success. All the boats, no matter what their class, were on the starting line together, but compared with what we were used to at Cowes there was plenty of room to maneuver. Looking around it was not our rivals who gave cause for apprehension but the enormous spectator fleet. For a newcomer it was impossible to visualize how they could accompany us all the way down the harbor without colliding either with themselves or with us. In any case the chop in the water was bound to be considerable and in the lightest wind could cause us a lot of trouble. On *Morning Cloud* we managed to get a good position on the line, which we crossed just a second after the gun, our wind clear and the biggest boats some distance away from us. That start enabled us, although one of the smallest boats in the fleet, to be one of the first dozen through the Heads and out to sea. In the event the spectator boats caused us no anxieties. Those north kept to leeward, turned away from us whenever we signaled we were about to tack, and gave us a cheerful sendoff, which for the time banished all thoughts of the storms we might meet further south.

As soon as we were out of the harbor we were able to hoist our big spinnaker and get out to sea. We made for the hundred-fathom line where we understood there was the best chance of getting the current running south

at its strongest. This in itself posed a problem because our depth meter didn't go beyond fifty fathoms. The question had to be settled by the usual means of navigation. There were also two other aids. We had been told that when we were in the current the temperature of the seawater would rise to 72° F, and there would be a large number of bluebottles (little jellyfish) around. Unlike some of the Australian boats, we did not have a thermometer built into the hull; we carried one with us on a piece of cord which we dipped regularly into the ocean every half-hour. When we were about seventy miles out from the coast we spotted the bluebottles, but the thermometer never rose above 70° F. That we were then in a fast current running south was never in doubt as my navigator checked his daily reckoning. Indeed, we could never have stayed so far out had I not had a navigator so skilled in the use of the sextant. I was fortunate that two other members of the crew could take his place in case of need.

Once on our course we enjoyed some of the most pleasant sailing we have ever had. A steady twenty-knot breeze from the northeast, a long, rolling swell, which sometimes enabled us to plane down the top of the waves, gave us a good average speed. It was soon apparent from the reports made three times a day to the control ship moving in the center of the fleet that we were the boat farthest out to sea. Occasionally, if the reports were correct, another boat seemed to be moving out toward us but then changed its mind. Only once did another competitor just come into view between us and the shore.

When night fell the wind still held and we continued our speedy progress south. On the other hand, the first reports the following morning revealed that the boats inshore had had a patchy night and made fitful progress. Our decision to get out and stay out seemed to be justified. We continued in this way for three days and three nights, closely watching the battle inshore between the two biggest boats, Sir Max Aitken's *Crusade* and Alan Bond's *Apollo*. In all we kept our spinnaker up continually for sixty-seven and a half hours, a record for all of us on board.

As the third night passed and dawn came the wind gradually got lighter and became less constant. We changed to the floater spinnaker but after another half-hour there was not even enough wind to fill that. What there was seemed to be fickle and moving around all the points of the compass. We tried our lightest headsail; soon we were becalmed. Then we were really worried. If the boats inshore managed to hold the wind our tactics would prove to be disastrous. Or if the wind filled in from the southwest we would be faced with a long tack into the Tasmanian shore which would put us far behind the other boats. If it came in from the southeast we would be well placed. With luck it would drive us not far north of the entrance to the Derwent River on which Hobart stands. The other boats inshore would be at a disadvantage short-tacking right down the Tasmanian coast. As we flapped around it seemed an interminable wait. In fact it was only about an hour and a half. Then the wind filled in. Thank heaven it came from the southeast. It rapidly turned into a gale from the Antarctic. That was when our problems began.

We were soon down to our smallest headsail, and the main was reefed almost down to the numbers on the sail. There were thirty to forty knots on the dial, sometimes gusting to fifty. We were a small boat in heavy seas, yet it was surprising how *Morning Cloud* maintained her balance and kept up her speed. Visibility got less and less with low cloud and driving rain. It became bitterly cold, and the rain turned into hail which hit the helmsman and his crewmen on deck hard in the face. It was then that we found we were taking a lot of water on board, but we could not discover the source. The bilges were full and the floorboards were flooded, but we were heeling so much it was impossible to pump out the water. The only alternative was to bail, and for the rest of that day and all through the night two of us were continuously using buckets. We thought the water might be coming through some keelbolts that had become loose, but there was no way of telling. When later we examined the boat we could just see daylight between the keel and the hull, but that was not the cause of our trouble. It was only when we were back in England that we discovered the fault. The starboard locker in the cockpit was not fitting tightly enough, and the water coming off the side had been able to make its way straight down into the stern. But all through the storm we were encouraged by the fact that at least we were on a good course. We finally came near the Tasmanian coast at the Freycinet Peninsula. This was rather farther north than I had hoped, but I was sure that course had paid off against the other boats. We then had to beat down the coast for some sixty miles until we could turn up the estuary into Storm Bay. The gale gradually subsided and the height of the waves lessened. Ironically, the situation in the Sydney-Hobart Race two years later was exactly the reverse. The second *Morning Cloud* was then set to win the race, but at this point she fell into a hole and floundered, windless, for several hours. Meantime the New Zealand one-tonners came up behind her and, seeing what had happened, sailed out around her. She still won her class but didn't win overall.

To return to the twenty-fifth Sydney-Hobart Race, there was still a lot of wind across Storm Bay. We could see a number of bigger boats behind us, and *Fidelius*, a large New Zealand boat, gradually overtook us. Halfway up the estuary the wind began to die. It was at this point that we first realized that we could actually win the race overall. My navigator picked up the local news bulletin at one o'clock and heard the reports about boats which had already docked or who were in the estuary. He rapidly calculated that if we could cross the finishing line by seven o'clock that evening we would have won. Then once again our anxieties mounted. Was the wind going to die on us completely? We were near and yet perhaps so far. When we came into the final stretch of river leading up to Hobart, we had our spinnaker floater up, which was gently carrying us along. As we got nearer and nearer to the harbor we could see masses of cars parked and crowds watching. Slowly we inched closer to the finishing line across the entrance to the harbor. On the helm I was trying to inch *Morning Cloud* over it but finally there was no choice; we had to jibe the spinnaker. I have never seen the foredeck crew leap so quickly on to the bow. Having jibed we were carried slowly across the finishing line. All the cars sounded their horns and the crowd cheered. We moved slowly into Constitution Dock and tied up. We had been at sea for a few minutes over four and a quarter days. At corrected time the race had taken us three days, four hours, twenty-five minutes, and fifty-seven seconds. This put us fifty-one minutes, twenty-two seconds ahead of the next boat, Arthur Slater's *Prospect of Whitby*. Or just under four and a half seconds a mile in hand over the whole race. It had been a great contest and one that we shall never forget.

Edward Heath

The Fastnet Race, Europe's oldest blue-water race, has been in existence since 1925. The starting point is at Cowes. The racers circle the Fastnet Rock off the southwestern tip of Ireland, then head back to the finish at Portsmouth, a total of over 600 miles. Only seven yachts participated in the first running of this race. To everyone's surprise, the winner was *Jolie Brise*, a rebuilt pilot cutter from Le Havre (Fig. 52). Having won again in 1929 and 1930, *Jolie Brise* is the only boat to have won the Fastnet Race three times.

The Transatlantic Race has a much longer tradition. The first of these races was held in 1866, but seventy years passed before a German port was chosen as the finish. In connection with the Olympic Games of 1936, the North German Regatta Club and the Cruising Club of America organized the Bermuda-Cuxhaven Race. Eight of the nine participating yachts were German. On July 4, this race of 3,400 miles began. Among the German entries was the North German Regatta Club's yawl *Hamburg* (Figs. 53, 54, 55), skippered by Ludwig Schlimbach. The navigator's journal indicates that *Hamburg* did not enjoy exclusively sunny weather on its twenty-four-day voyage:

> July 23: A full-scale southwest storm with winds of Force 8 and 9 is blowing up. High waves develop quickly, and *Hamburg* is

working hard. We are encountering long swells typical of the Atlantic, but *Hamburg* cuts through their breaking crests easily. We're still carrying a double-reefed mainsail, and the boat still responds well to the helm. As conditions get worse, we strike the mainsail and scud for awhile with only the jib set. . . .

Almost twenty years later the Transatlantic Race went from Newport, Rhode Island, to Marstrand, Sweden. The German participant was the yawl *Schlüssel von Bremen* (Fig. 56) from the sailing club, the Bremen Coat of Arms. Skipper Koppenhagen and his crew made the voyage in twenty-one days.

For German deepwater sailors, the North Sea Week off Helgoland, held every year at Whitsuntide, is the first great test. The vicious storms and currents of the North Sea make heavy demands on both boats and crews. The week begins with an opening race that brings the yachts from Cuxhaven and Bremerhaven to Helgoland. Next comes a race around Helgoland, followed by two triangular races and, finally, the return race to Cuxhaven and Bremerhaven.

Another race that is held every two years after the North Sea Week is the Skagen-Kiel Regatta of about 500 miles. The North Sea Week also has the function, every two years, of selecting the German participants for the Admiral's Cup. *Pfeffer und Salz* (Fig. 58) and *Carina III* sail for Helgoland at top speed. Notable features of *Carina III* are the flat working deck, the two working cockpits, and the two steering wheels (Fig. 57). In 1973, along with *Rubin* and *Saudade*, *Carina III* with Dieter Monheim at the helm and Hans Beilken as tactician qualified to race for the Admiral's Cup, which the German yachts then carried off in a sensational victory.

The Kiel Week takes place every year in June and is the most important international racing event. The best racing sailors from all over the world compete against each other on four ideal courses in Kiel Bay. The deepwater yachts sail in a special program of long-distance and triangular races: the Eckernförde Race and the Stollergrund Race, the Rund Fünen Race and the Fehmarn Race.

In the Stollergrund Race of 1977, *Tina-I-Punkt*, designed as a Two-Ton Admiral's Cup yacht, runs before the wind under a reefed mainsail, a radial spinnaker, and a blooper (Fig. 59). Because of her huge sail area, this boat, which was designed in Canada and built in Finland, was considered to be a superb yacht for sailing in light winds. But in the elimination races for the Admiral's Cup of 1975, *Tina-I-Punkt* won the Skagen Race in what proved to be the stormiest running in the history of this notoriously difficult long-distance regatta. This was still not enough, however, to win *Tina-I-Punkt* a place on the German Cup team.

60

Sagittarius, designed by Sparkman and Stephens, is shown in a stiff stern wind during the Middle Sea Race around Sicily. In this race of 630 miles, *Sagittarius* won first place in Class II in 1977 (Fig. 60). The Middle Sea Race, organized by the Royal Malta Yacht Club, is Europe's longest.

Sagittarius shows here what can happen if a yacht carries too much sail before the wind. Running under a spinnaker, mainsail, and genoa, the boat begins rolling uncontrollably. The situation becomes dangerous if the spinnaker begins to dip into the water. The light sail material can tear; the spinnaker pole can break; and, if worst comes to worst, the mast can break and fall.

Rapidly developing gusts are a
constant threat along the
Mediterranean coast. The
International Sailing Week of
Marseille (Fig. 61) offers
especially unpredictable sailing
because the mistral can suddenly
blow up to gale force out of a
blue sky.

At the start of the first race of the International Week at Marseille in April 1977, the wind was already blowing Force 5; but in the course of the day, it unexpectedly developed into a dreaded mistral with gusts of hurricane force. A number of yachts sought shelter in nearby ports like Cassis or Bandol or

broke off the race prematurely. It was not until the next day that the absence of the One-Tonners *Viridiana* and *Airel* was noticed. The crew of *Viridiana* was picked up by a tanker, but the eight men of *Airel* were never found. Despite a search of several weeks, not even a trace of their gear could be found. Only much later was the body of the skipper, Pierre Serinelli, washed up on the east coast of Corsica.

But the race went on with yachts *Emeraude*, *Entera*, and *Gitana VI* (Figs. 62, 63, 64) among the participants. When the mistral still had not subsided by Easter Sunday, many boats again interrupted the race. The mainsail of *Gitana VI* tore twice, and she had to finish the race storm rigged.

June 29, 1972, stands as a remarkable day in the history of blue-water racing. The Whitbread brewery of London announced that it would sponsor a race that would begin on September 8, 1973, and that would be the first round-the-world race for crews of more than one man. The Sailing Association of the British Navy, with its worldwide communications network, was a co-organizer and was responsible for rules governing participation, safety rules, and the enforcement of those rules. Spectacular races had, of course, been generously sponsored in preceding years: the Observer Single-Handed Transatlantic Race, for example, which has been held every four years since 1960, or the Nonstop Single-Handed Round-the-World Race launched by the Sunday *London Times* in 1968. But the Whitbread Race surpassed them all not only in its scope but also in the exemplary care that was taken in the preparation and actual running of the race. All yachts had to have a crew of at least five. Handicaps were established according to IOR rules so that the winner would not necessarily be the biggest boat, even if it did come in first. The race started and finished in Plymouth with Cape Town, Sydney, and Rio de Janeiro as ports of call, a total distance of over 27,000 miles. The course transversed the storm centers of the southern latitudes and rounded both the Cape of Good Hope and Cape Horn (Fig. 65). It was also stipulated that at every port of call all participating boats would start out together on the next leg of the race.

A total of seventeen yachts entered the race, and fourteen successfully completed all the legs of the voyage. Several yachts had been built especially for this race. The oldest boat came from Germany. It was the yawl *Peter von Danzig*, which was built in Danzig in 1936. It belonged to the Academic Sailing Club of Kiel and was skippered by Reinhard Laucht. The most famous skipper in the race was the Frenchman Eric Tabarly with his aluminum ketch *Pen Duick VI* (Figs. 66, 67). He had already won a number of races before: the Single-Handed Transatlantic Race of 1964 with his *Pen Duick II*, the Single-Handed Transpacific Race of 1969, and the Transpacific Race from Los Angeles to Honolulu of 1972, both with his *Pen Duick V*. Tabarly was the clear favorite, but he

disappointment. During the very first leg of the race, his mast broke. He was towed into Rio de Janeiro by the French navy. On the second leg of the race, Tabarly drove his boat and crew hard and was the winner in actual time sailed. But two days after the start of the third leg, Tabarly's mast broke again. Tabarly continued on to Sydney

but quit the race during the fourth leg and sailed directly home to Brest.

The winner of this dramatic race was the Mexican Ramon Carlin with his ketch *Sayula II*, a boat built by Sparkman and Stevens for series racing.

Still another French boat in this race, besides *Kriter*, *33 Export*, and Tabarly's *Pen Duick VI*, was *Grand Louis* under skipper André Viant (Fig. 68). The fifty-three-year-old amateur skipper had had this 60-foot schooner built as a homey family cruiser before the Whitbread Race had been announced. *Grand Louis* was probably the most comfortable boat in the race. It was equipped with a freezer and a desalinator capable of producing ten quarts of fresh water per hour. *Grand Louis* was the only French boat not sponsored either by industry or a government institution. After its launching on June 16, 1973, it raced in France and in the Cowes Week. This training paid off. *Grand Louis* came in fourth on the third leg from Sydney to Rio. Its

remarkable achievement on this lap of 8,400 miles around Cape Horn was due in no small part to Viant's son-in-law, Michel Vanek, shown here at the helm of the yacht (Fig. 69). For the entire race, *Grand Louis* won a spectacular third place, coming in behind *Sayula II* and the English yacht *Adventure*.

On a 27,000-mile race, there is, of course, no jockeying for position between two yachts, and there is no point in comparing the dramatic finish of a race during the Sailing Week at Antigua (Fig. 70) with a race around the world. What they do have in common, however, is that they both push men and material to the limits of their capacities.

73

The Sydney-Hobart Race is part of the Southern Cross Cup Series, which consists of a total of four races and resembles the Admiral's Cup in its scoring and in its arrangement of courses. The 630-mile Sydney-Hobart Race travels down the coasts of New South Wales and Victoria and then crosses the Bass Strait to finish on Tasmania. This regatta attracts many contestants from abroad. It can be a demanding race because violent storms out of the west can develop in the Tasmanian Sea. In 1967, Eric Tabarly's *Pen Duick III* won the Illingworth Trophy with the best sailing time. In 1969, Edward Heath's *Morning*

Cloud was the top contestant, but the most spectacular victory was won by John B. Kilroy of San Francisco in 1975. His ketch *Kialoa III* (Figs. 71, 72) made the Sydney-Hobart run in the record time of 2 days, 14 hours, 37 minutes. In spite of the popularity of this international deepwater sailing event, the Admiral's Cup remains the *non plus ultra* of ocean sailors. Any boat, such as the *Red Lancer* (Fig. 73), that sails in this regatta during the Cowes Week can be counted among the elite of deepwater yachts.

Like many other ocean regattas, the races of the Southern Ocean Racing Conference (SORC) were first thought up in a bar. In the late 1920s, George Gandy and a few wealthy Cubans put their heads together in Havana and planned a race from St. Petersburg, Florida, to Havana. This race was first run in 1930 with eleven yachts participating. In 1934, the Miami-Nassau Race was added to it, and these two races represented the beginnings of the "Southern Circuit." Today, this competition includes a total of six races, the most famous of which are the St. Petersburg-Fort Lauderdale Race and the Miami-Nassau Race. Both present an ultimate challenge for designers, boats, and crews. *Williwaw* (Fig. 74), later called *Pinta*, and *Charisma* (Fig. 75) are shown here on the 176-mile Miami-Nassau course in 1975.

Although the Bermuda Race is not America's oldest, it is still regarded as the classic American race. Beginning at Brenton Reef Light off Newport, Rhode Island, it covers 635 miles to the Bermudas. Repeated attempts were made to break through the "three-day barrier," as here during the 1968 regatta (Fig. 76). Finally, in 1974, the forty-two-year-old record was broken. *Ondine* sailed the course in 2 days, 21 hours, 42 minutes, 14 seconds. Yachts that participate in the Admiral's Cup cannot book such spectacular times. They are smaller and more maneuverable; and, in contrast to the IOR-Maxis, as boats like *Kioloa III* or *Ondine* are called because of their high IOR-rating, they are designed for maximum efficiency within their class (Fig. 77).

V
ADMIRAL'S CUP

Every two years toward the end of July, the town of Cowes on the little Isle of Wight off the southern coast of England is invaded. Like the Vikings of a thousand years ago, the present-day invaders are rugged in build, tanned dark brown by the sun, fearless in the face of storms, and skilled in the handling of fast sailing vessels. When they come ashore, they indulge in strong drink and fighting, pursue the local girls, and make life difficult for law-enforcement officers. These modern Vikings are deepwater sailors, and here, in the waters near Cowes, they compete for the world's championship in their sport. This trophy that sailors from all over the world vie for is the Admiral's Cup. Whoever wins it is the uncrowned ruler of the Seven Seas until the next competition takes place two years later.

The America's Cup and the Admiral's Cup are two of the most important trophies in sailing. Both contests originated in the efforts of two great seafaring nations—Great Britain and the United States—to demonstrate their supremacy on the seas without resorting to armed combat. More than a hundred years ago the British lost a race and a cup, to be called the America's Cup, to the Americans, apparently for all time, but ever since the founding of the Admiral's Cup, the British have been able to win it often enough—against keen competition from all over the world—to prove their dominance in deepwater sailing. The Solent, the channel between the Isle of Wight and the English mainland and the scene of the Admiral's Cup competition, challenges the sailor with myriad sandbars and currents. It remains the focal point and Mecca of ocean sailors today, just as it was 200 years ago. The Admiral's Cup competitions, begun in 1957, are a relatively recent institution, but they have drawn considerable international interest ever since their inception.

The period of great prosperity following the Second World War saw the fleet of ocean-going yachts grow beyond all expectations. The major event in this burgeoning sport was the periodic Transatlantic Race, which offered the ultimate challenge for sailors who, like the clipper captains of the past, enjoyed pitting their skill against each other over long distances. The Americans were the leaders in this field. The next most prestigious event after the Transatlantic Race was the Fastnet Race, a classic ocean race from England to South Ireland and back, and scheduled immediately after the week of racing at Cowes.

The Americans liked to participate in this major European race, and the English enjoyed the opportunity to sail in their own waters against these strong opponents. To establish a reliable standard for testing the sailing skills of the two nations, the Royal Ocean Racing Club, in London, created a prize for which national teams, consisting of three yachts each, competed. The final score for each country was determined by adding together the points the individual yachts in each team had accumulated. Sir Myles Wyatt, the admiral of the Club at the time, donated the gilded cup that has since gone down in the history of sailing as the Admiral's Cup. The competition for this prize is held every two years, in odd-numbered years, off the southern coast of England. Cowes Week, which is held every year in The Solent at the beginning of August, provides the setting for this important sailing event.

Whether consciously or unconsciously, the original organizers of the Admiral's Cup races in 1957 anticipated future trends in ocean sailing when they established the different individually evaluated categories in the series. By the mid 1970s, deepwater sailors were less and less interested in the Atlantic races, in which yachts competed over long distances and against opponents who were usually invisible to them. Shorter coastal regattas, in which ships raced against each other in a closely circumscribed area, became popular. Another type of race that gained in popularity was the ocean race of moderate

length, which called for navigational skills and sailing techniques appropriate to the open sea. The Admiral's Cup series, with its variety of long and short races, offered just the right combination of challenges. By 1977, the series consisted of the following races:

The Channel Race, 220 miles. Points accumulated in the race are doubled in the final tally.

The Inshore Races in The Solent, 35 miles each. Points in these races tallied at face value.

The Fastnet Race, 605 miles. Points won in this race are tripled.

Each of these five races has particular qualities that best suit one type of yacht or another. The Admiral's Cup, which places particularly high value on the long-distance race, used to be the exclusive domain of long-distance sailors. But in recent years, more and more young small-boat sailors have been taking the helm of IOR yachts. For

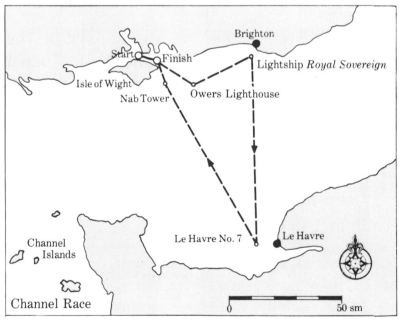

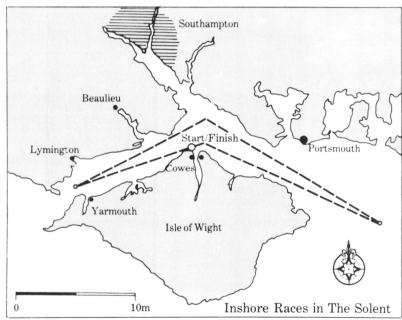

these sailors, a long-distance race like the Fastnet Race is a necessary evil that they must endure, perched on the high side of their heeling vessels and fortifying themselves with chocolate and Coca-Cola.

The Channel Race, because it is only 220 miles long, can be run without sleep. The race begins in Plymouth and follows the English coast past Owers. At the light ship *Royal Sovereign*, it crosses the channel to France, then returns to the finish line at the mouth of The Solent. If the winds are unfavorable for this course, its direction can be reversed. The course forms a nearly equilateral triangle. Experience has shown that the wind rarely allows the fleet to reach around the course. For this reason, the boats that have been most often successful in the Channel Race are ones that are not too large and that can best adapt to shifting inshore wind conditions. The large IOR yachts are rarely able to do well in closed-course races because they are relatively difficult to sail well. The three Inshore

Races, on the other hand, are sheer delight for small-boat crews. Smaller boats have the advantage in coastal regattas held in The Solent, for in these contests, racing tactics and precise control over one's boat are the decisive factors. It is essential to know the currents in The Solent and to know, too, at which phases of the tide it is possible to sail over certain sandbars. The Solent offers some of the most difficult sailing waters to be found anywhere, and crews who take a prize in these inshore races can rightfully count themselves among the world's best sailors. During the Cowes Week regattas, hundreds of bright spinnakers transform the yellowish-green waters of this channel into a veritable orgy of colors. Here, too, the banks of the channel provide natural bleachers, and when huge yachts sail by within a few yards of shore, the spectator can witness a sailing show unduplicated anywhere else.

As a rule, no one can be sure of winning the Admiral's Cup before the concluding Fastnet

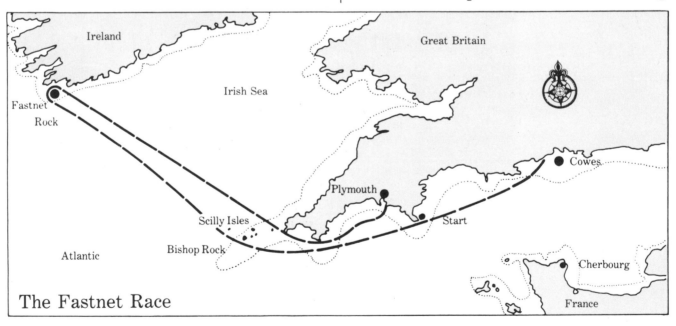

The Fastnet Race

Race has been run, and many a crew that has gone into that race with victory nearly in their grasp have seen their hopes dashed by a calm on the Irish Sea or by a storm their yacht barely managed to survive. The course to Fastnet Rock runs directly against the route that frequent low-pressure systems usually take as they sweep onto the Continent from the Atlantic. The Fastnets of the last few years have been tame affairs, but ordinarily this is one of the toughest blue-water races there is. The fierce storms that plagued it in the 1950s and '60s contributed greatly to its notoriety. In the Fastnet Race, the ratings and sizes of the large IOR yachts give them an advantage over smaller boats, and large boats therefore represent a final trump card for many teams.

The Admiral's Cup was originally conceived to give transatlantic racers an additional incentive to come to Europe, but time has seen the priorities undergo a reversal. Now, the Transatlantic Race has sunk to the status of a mere incidental race that only a dozen or so boats run on their way to Cowes Week. The fact that the Admiral's Cup pits nation against nation makes them of interest to a broad public otherwise not interested in sailing, and in many countries, the press has given them large coverage. Obviously, not just any skipper can enter his boat in the Admiral's Cup. The number of potential participants has grown so large in some countries that preliminary national regattas, modeled on the Cup series, are held to select the best boats to send to Cowes. The competition in these preliminary regattas is often as fierce as it is in the Admiral's Cup series itself.

Nor can just any deepwater yacht compete for the Admiral's Cup. Boats entering the competition must be of a certain size. Originally, a broad range of yachts, from about thirty-eight to sixty-five feet, were permitted. After the adoption of the International Offshore Rule, which is the internationally accepted formula now used for determining the handicap ratings of ocean-going yachts, the organizers of the Admiral's Cup have worked toward ever-greater uniformity among competing vessels. In a few years, the participating yachts will be between about forty-five to fifty feet long. It will then be possible to do away with almost all handicaps and let the boats compete directly against each other, yacht against yacht.

The Admiral's Cup has gained such importance in the sailing world today that boats are specifically designed and built for this regatta. These yachts do not have to set off on endless voyages in the vastness of the open sea, and the large, heavy, solidly built boats designed for Atlantic crossings have now almost entirely disappeared from the Admiral's Cup races. They have been replaced by a smaller, more technically sophisticated, and more maneuverable type of yacht whose greatest strength lies in its ability to sail fast to windward. A large number of technical innovations and a multitude of new sails have been developed to meet the requirements of all possible courses. Structure below deck has been sacrificed more and more for the sake of hull lightness.

161

As a result, almost all the yachts competing for top honors today are nothing but cavernous hollows below deck. Most of that space is taken up by as many as twenty different sails stowed in huge bags. The disadvantage of this kind of construction is obvious. After two or three years, the design becomes obsolete, and the yacht is nearly useless for racing. It is sometimes impossible to sell a regatta yacht that has seen a few years of hard use.

This development, which became apparent in the mid-1970s, has forced the administrators of the IOR to reassess their regulations on boat design. But no sooner are new minimum requirements formulated than yacht designers, who have drawn considerable inspiration from space technology, come up with new designs and materials that leave the new regulations trailing far behind reality. In some ways, the Admiral's Cup Races can be compared to the Formula-1 automobile races. The major difference is that yachts are not usually built and maintained by large corporations but have to be financed by private individuals.

Now for a brief look at the history of the Admiral's Cup competition. As expected, only Great Britain and the United States participated in the races in 1957, the first year the series was held. The British made optimum use of all the advantages they had as host country. They chose the very best yachts available from a large field of first-rate craft; they profited greatly from their precise knowledge of local waters; and, not surprisingly, they won the Cup. In 1959, another major seafaring nation, the Netherlands, entered this Anglo-Saxon dominated contest. But despite the combined efforts of the Dutch and the Americans, the British won again. It was not until 1961, when even more nations competed, that the Americans could finally edge out the British. In 1963, however, the first year German yachts joined the race, the British won the title back and retained it in 1965 as well.

The Australians, like the Americans, are relatives of the British, and regard sailing almost as their national sport. To the dismay of their hosts, they walked away with all the prizes in 1967. The Americans took first place again in 1969, but in 1971 the Admiral's Cup underwent a major change when seventeen nations joined the free-for-all for high honors. The number of competitors obliged the organizers to separate their racers from the swarm of boats participating in the Cowes Week events. Once more the English won the Cup. Not even yachts from such exotic lands as Brazil, South Africa, and New Zealand could deprive the English of their fifth victory. Widespread boredom and despair set in. The Anglo-Saxon countries ruled the sailing world with an iron hand, and nothing seemed able to loosen their hold on it. One or the other of them always walked off with the Admiral's Cup. In 1973, sixteen nations were represented by forty-eight boats, but none of the participants seemed to think the British could be upset this time either. British Team Captain Edward Heath, then prime minister was asked whether the Germans stood any chance of winning the Admiral's Cup, Heath replied, "None at all!" But to the surprise of the sailing world, the German yachts *Saudade, Rubin,* and *Carina III* sailed to an easy victory. The disastrously poor performance of Heath's *Morning Cloud* in the Fastnet Race put the British completely out of the running. The 1973 races showed that a well-prepared outsider who made the best of his opportunities could topple England from her sailing throne.

The wave of euphoria subsided somewhat in 1975 when the Germans ran a strong second but still came in behind the English, who, after their slump in '73, had gone into this regatta as the dark horse. Nineteen nations from all over the world took part in these 1975 Olympics of ocean racing. Two years later, the British reaffirmed their traditional role and won again.

No sailing event, aside from the America's Cup, is talked and written about more than the Admiral's Cup. The English have been accused of everything from shoddy organization and conduct of the races to favoritism on the part of the judges, from arrogance to unfair competition. Indeed, they have been accused of just about everything that a host and habitual winner could be expected to be accused of. The guests have accustomed themselves to all sorts of real and supposed injuries that they will be cheated out of their money in Cowes, that they will be given inconvenient moorings, and that they will be asked to leave the premises of the exclusive Royal Yacht Squadron, or, more likely still, that they will not even be allowed in the first place. But no matter how bitterly they complain, they seem to forget all their injuries after two years' time, and most of them come back for more.

Many improvements have been made over the years. A few start and finish lines have been moved out into open water to give the British less advantage because of local knowledge. Improvement can't alter the fact, however, that Cowes is simply too small to handle the swarm of visitors that descends on it.

It is difficult to say just what it is that constitutes the charm of Cowes. Money and elegance, beautiful women, even more beautiful boats, and the presence of sailors from all over the world all do their part to create a special aura. But there is also a sense that skill, not money, is the decisive factor here, an awareness that the seas on which these races are run make no distinction between the rich and the poor. Not every sailor will think it worthwhile to devote himself to this kind of sailing, but there is no doubt that every sailor can profit from the experience that can be gained in this most demanding of all regattas, for the art of sailing will continue to develop only if there are sailors determined to sail their craft with greater speed, comfort, and safety than have been achieved in the past. The Admiral's Cup, then, is a many-faceted event. Among other things, it is a proving ground for new ideas in sailing and for those sailors who are constantly striving to gain ever-greater control of their vessels. But above all, it is the crown jewel of all blue-water racing events.

Svante Domizlaff

163

A sailboat cutting through the water, driven only by the wind, the most natural of forces, holds an unending fascination for me. Once a boat moves out of harbor and onto the open sea, its crew experiences the natural world in its purest form, its closest proximity, and with the greatest possible force. This is what adds an extra dimension to the sport of deepwater racing, which is otherwise concerned only with sailing as rapidly and skillfully as possible and with proving the quality of one's own seamanship and boat against competitors of comparable rank.

The greatest success that my crew and I have ever had came when my yacht *Rubin* (my fourth boat with this name), together with the two other boats on the German team, *Saudade* and *Carina III*, won the 1973 Admiral's Cup, the world's championship in international ocean racing. My crew and I have been able to win a number of prizes, and the main reason for our success—along with our enthusiasm for the sport of sailing—is that we have been able to put recent technological developments to good use. I have been interested in physics and chemistry from boyhood, and my present work continues to keep me abreast of developments in these fields.

The technological progress we have seen in sailing over the last twenty-five years is astounding. All the materials we use have become increasingly lighter and stronger. There was a time when sheets and halyards would break and sails would tear easily. Nowadays, nothing breaks anymore, unless a sailor deliberately oversteps the limits of his materials. On my boats I have always stayed on the safe side of those limits, for in our sport, seamanship is the decisive element, and genuine seamanship demands that every risk be held to an absolute minimum. However important the role of the natural sciences may be in yachting, we have to remember that *nature* has the final word.

A high jumper or golfer needs intense short-term concentration for each leap or stroke he makes. Sailing calls for long-term concentration. During his entire watch, or sometimes even during two watches, a sailor has to exercise a finely tuned sensibility that can only be acquired through years of experience at the helm. More important than any technical skills he may have is his awareness of his craft as a being with a life of its own. He has to know, for example, that it will begin to slow down if he steers it too sharply into the waves or points it too high into the wind, or that the boat will not balance if the sheets are hauled in too far. In short, a sailor has to feel as one with his boat and respond to every signal it gives him.

Then, too, a sailor's relationship to the weather is just as intense as it is to his vessel. He has to develop a sixth sense for what nature has in store for him: shifts in wind direction, gusts, adverse currents. I have never regarded nature as my enemy. On the contrary, it is—no less than one's boat—the sailor's great ally.

If you ask, then, why I am a deepwater sailor, I would say because no other sport so closely unites competition and a direct confrontation with nature.

Hans-Otto Schümann

The elimination races for the Admiral's Cup in 1973 began in rough weather in the North Sea off Helgoland. Among the top favorites was *Rubin*, a yacht with a laminated wooden hull, owned by Hans-Otto Schümann. Carrying two headsails and a triple-reefed mainsail, *Rubin* headed down into a trough (Fig. 78). *Rubin*, which won these elimination races, later made a major contribution to Germany's victory in the 1973 Admiral's Cup. Two years later, there were many competitors at Helgoland. Germany's success in 1973 had prompted several owners of older yachts to build new ones. Three promising aspirants ran neck and neck before the wind under spinnakers and auxiliary side sails known as big boys or bloopers (Fig. 79). *Jan Pott*, owned by Norbert Lorck-Schierning, is a sister ship of *Rubin*. She was built in 1974. G 33 is *Saudade II*, owned by Albert Büll. Hamburg is her home port. She has an aluminum hull designed by Sparkman and Stephens and was built in Holland. Leading the pack is *Christine* (G 2000), an aluminum hull built in Bremen after a Doug Peterson design.

The most successful racing yacht of 1973 was *Saudade*. Like her British sister ship, *Prospect of Whitby*, she was designed by Sparkman and Stephens and built of aluminum at the Walter Huisman shipyards in Holland. In the Admiral's Cup of 1973, her superior racing qualities were particularly evident in the kind of rough weather that prevailed during the second inshore regatta, which *Saudade* won by several minutes on corrected time. *Saudade* is shown here perfectly trimmed as she runs before a wind with gusts up to Force 8 (Fig. 80).

The aluminum-hulled *Salty Goose* (Fig. 81), designed by the American Bob Derecktor and built at his own shipyard, was the largest yacht in the American Admiral's Cup team in 1973. Boats like this with such high ratings are at a disadvantage on short triangular courses. Although some of the best sailors in the United States were manning *Salty Goose*, it was only in the Fastnet Race that she could show what she could do.

Yankee Girl belonged to the powerful American team that almost edged the British out of first place in 1971. Since she too was a large boat, her crew was hoping to capitalize on the long-distance races (Fig. 82). Her double-head or cutter rig with its two headsails is clearly visible in this photograph. This type of rigging has since gone out of style.

Fastnet Rock off the southern coast of Ireland, the turning mark in the Fastnet Race, has become a kind of symbol among ocean racers. Although hundreds of yachts have sailed around this rock, there are very few photographs of it because the weather is usually so bad that it does not allow any time for taking pictures. All hands are needed for making the turn. The crew of the Swiss yacht *On Dit* has just set a spinnaker and is heading for the finish line with a strong wind at her stern (Fig. 83). The striped flag—flag C in the International Flag Code—flying from the backstay of *On Dit* indicates that the boat has an Admiral's Cup team rating. This photograph was taken in 1975.

Incredible progress has been made in the design and construction of deepwater yachts since the early 1970s. One of the revolutionary innovations is the absolutely flat deck, the so-called flush deck, that carries no superstructures whatsoever. Functionality is the decisive factor for a winning yacht. The living space below deck is of secondary importance.

Scaramouche (Fig. 84), designed by the Argentinian German Frers, was the largest yacht in the 1977 U.S. team. In the inshore races, the twelve-man crew had all it could do to sail one short tack after another with this large boat and maneuver it over the difficult short-distance courses.

Marionette (Fig. 85), designed by Ron Holland, is just the right size for triangular courses near the coast. With *Marionette*, the British team successfully defended the Admiral's Cup in 1977. The German yacht

Champagne (Fig. 86), designed for aluminum construction by Doug Peterson and owned by Peter Westphal-Langlo, is the same size as *Marionette* and has an equally high individual rating. All three of these boats are typical ocean racing yachts of the most recent generation: utterly Spartan below deck, they carry every device conceivable on deck that can make for easier, more efficient sailing.

In 1977, a Japanese team raced in
the Admiral's Cup for the first
time. *Kamatura* (Fig. 87) sails a
closed course in The Solent under
her mainsail, a small genoa, and a
modern triradial spinnaker.

When the wind blows in The Solent, it is powerful and gusty. Italian yacht *Mandrake* (Fig. 88), designed by Ron Holland, rolls violently under her spinnaker. Even though the spinnaker is hauled in tight, *Mandrake* is still heeling sharply to windward. The rolling can be stopped only by striking the spinnaker or setting a smaller storm spinnaker.

The International Offshore Rule (IOR) has produced some rather bizarre hull shapes because every designer tries to exploit the formula as best he can. An unusually long and pointed stern is the characteristic feature of the Italian Admiral's Cup yacht *Vanina* (Fig. 89), designed by the American Gary Mull.

90

Shortly after the start of a race, The Solent is sometimes so thickly populated with boats that it is difficult to see the water. It requires a great deal of care and experience to run a course safely with as large a yacht as *Yachtman* (formerly *Deception*) from Spain (Figs. 90, 91), especially if a skipper runs into a tangle of other boats off his starboard bow and has to yield right of way to them. The narrowness of The Solent, which is aggravated by the presence of commercial shipping and the boats of the spectators, has

brought considerable criticism down on the organizers of the Cowes Week. This is one of the reasons why the Cup yachts now start separately.

Running under a radial spinnaker, spinnaker, genoa, and mainsail, the Argentinian yacht *Recluta* (Fig. 92), designed by German Frers, is perfectly trimmed for this closed course. This bird's-eye view shows the functional and easily surveyable design and construction of cockpits in a modern racing yacht. The cockpit for the midships crew is located directly behind the mast. The smaller cockpit toward the stern is primarily intended for the helmsman, tactician, and navigator.

VI
THE
LONELY
MEN
AND
THE
SEA

England's Francis Chichester, publisher of city maps and in his old age transatlantic sailor, was not the first to sail around the world single-handedly in 1966-67. In the previous fifty or sixty years, some dozen others had done it. But Chichester was the first to circumnavigate in the limelight of world press coverage. Although initially skeptical, the world media had become completely enraptured by the time the voyage was happily concluded. The crowds he attracted—half a million people welcomed him upon his return to Plymouth—frightened this loner so much that after landing he stayed below deck until nightfall. The next day, his queen made him Sir Francis. The abrupt manner in which he answered the questions of ignorant reporters speaks better than words to describe what a miserable time the tough old man had really had.

In Sydney, Australia, where he had stopped en route, he answered a question about the low point of his journey: "When the gin ran out." He radioed a circling plane at Cape Horn: "Jesus, I thought that if there was a place left in the world where no one would bother you, this would be it." The boat which Chichester used to become the first sailor to follow in the wake of the old British wool clippers—from the English Channel to Australia, then around Cape Horn and back to England—was a nightmare to her skipper. On its first run it almost ran foursquare into a breakwater. It was unresponsive; furious, Chichester let it follow the head. Its famous designer, John Illingworth, saved the situation, the ship, and the breakwater by starting the motor at the last moment. There was time only for the most essential improvements to be made on *Gipsy Moth IV*. But he had hardly lain down for his first nap after the start of the voyage, when he got a cold shower from a vent. The first night he had to build a plastic tent over the foot of his bunk because of a deck leak. And the next morning Chichester discovered problems in the self-steering device, which is supposed to keep the boat on course when the skipper is asleep or busy with other tasks.

In the mountainous seas of the "roaring forties," between the continents and the South Pole, Chichester found that the boat did not respond at all to the self-steering mechanism. The device finally gave up the ghost: "First, cold shivers ran down my back. I seemed to be frozen. Then a strange feeling came over me that my personality was split—I watched myself as I furled the sails and cold-bloodedly dismantled the broken steering device. My plan was wrecked."

Chichester, who intended to break the old clippers' record to Sydney, headed for Freemantle, on the west coast of Australia, as an emergency port. He discovered by accident how to keep a reluctant *Gipsy Moth* on course, despite its meager capabilities, by trimming the sails in a special way and linking them to the tiller with an ingenious combination of sheets. Then he lay in a course for Sydney again. "I hate to have to come back. I hate having to give up, and I hate deviating from my course. It is the task of a seaman to overcome such difficulties."

Chichester arrived in Sydney a week later than planned. He almost ran aground in the fog off Australia as he sailed out. He was caught in the fringes of a tornado and capsized, while he lay in his bunk below deck: "This is it, I said to myself, as *Gipsy Moth* keeled over more and more." Then loud creaking and cracking sounds started. "My head was pelted with plates, knives, forks, and bottles. I had the crushing sensation of the boat lying on top of me." But the vessel righted itself again. A sharp serrated knife had landed by his pillow. Chichester: "Just lucky I guess." Chichester came to know fear, became seasick off Cape Horn, and almost ran his boat aground by mistake on the cliffs of Staten Island. He felt wretched, disconsolate, and abandoned—as the British ice patrol ship *Protector*, with the press aboard, turned away after the rounding of the Cape. And after he had put all this behind him and had the solid ground of England under his feet, it was hard for him to feel any joy. A poor fool? No. A man whose late-starting sailing career was marked by cancer but who still believed that there were greater things on earth than his body.

The total neglect of the body—a mark of all great challenges—goes like a red thread through the history of single-handed sailing. It started with an American fisherman, Alfred Johnson, who sailed across the Atlantic in a scantly covered, 15-foot New-foundland fishing boat, and who reached England despite capsizing twice. It wasn't any different for another fisherman, Howard Blackburn, who had lost all his fingers, half of each thumb, and several toes through frostbite on the Grand Banks, and who—a crippled retiree now—crossed the North Atlantic alone twice. He only called off his third crossing when, after capsizing a third time, he became ill.

There was Canadian-born Joshua Slocum who at about the same time sailed around the world in his fishing boat, *Spray*, that he built himself. He was pursued by pirates, Indians, and hallucinations, was almost rammed on the Atlantic, almost drowned off Argentina's coast, and barely avoided running aground in the boiling "Milky Way" northeast of Cape Horn ("God only knows how I got out of there"). Finally, ten years later, when his mind was slipping and when *Spray* was not really seaworthy, he went to sea, never to return.

An Argentinian, Victor Dumas, rounded Cape Horn single-handedly in the dead of the Antarctic winter and braved ice piled on deck as well as a serious head injury. Earlier, he had seriously considered amputating a severely infected arm. A faint saved him: the abcessed arm burst, blood and pus drained out, and the wound healed.

A Swede, Alfons Hansen, cruised around Cape Horn in the snow and ice, and predated Dumas' sailing. Going westward against the prevailing winds, he was later shipwrecked off Chile. Marcel Badiaux managed to round Cape Horn after capsizing twice in Force 11 winds and -14°C temperatures. Edward Allcard, an Englishman, sailed from bay to bay around Cape Horn for six months, living off wild geese and fish, unfurling the frozen sails from the spars every morning. He said, "For me sailing is somewhat of a religion—and a good religion it is." Dentist David Lewis, on the outskirts of the frozen Antarctic, tried in vain for two summers to sail around the sixth continent. He capsized three times, lost the mast and emergency mast overboard, was caught in the pack ice twice, and had his hands badly cut and almost frozen. When he came into Cape Town in his steel yacht, *Ice Bird*, the ship was a wreck—rusted through and through—and he was not in much better shape.

"Stop moaning and groaning!" Scotsman Chay Blyth scribbled into the log of his yacht, *British Steel*, in the midst of the Indian Ocean. "This is what it's all about—not the sun, not the nice days, only this, when survival is the name of the game. . . ." Blyth, a British paratrooper-trained mixture of inferiority complexes, snobbery, and heroism, had undertaken the insane adventure of sailing single-handedly around the capes and the world as no other sailor had done before—against the western storms. His motive: he thought himself a failure and couldn't live with it. There were also a number of sailors who circumnavigated the world single-handedly after Sir Francis Chichester, and made noteworthy headlines.

An English greengrocer, Alec Rose, circumnavigated a year after Chichester; like his predecessor, he was knighted. Robin Graham of California was only sixteen when he started the single-handed journey in his *Dove*, which was only twenty-two feet long. Leonid Telida of Poland was, like Chichester, a sick man when he sailed around the world. He died of cancer shortly after his return. German circumnavigators include Wilfried Erdman, Alfred Kallies, and Rollo Gebhard. One German—Rudolf Konig of Minden—finished his voyage in great pain and died of cancer upon his return. Another—Jorge Meyer, a pharmacist from Unterpfaffenhofen—went under on his second circumnavigation and is still missing somewhere between Australia and Cape Horn.

It is debatable if any of these or the other two or three dozen sailors who sailed around the world after Chichester, started this pitilessly exhausting journey as conscientiously as Britain's Chay Blyth, who sailed around the three capes—of America (Cape Horn), Australia (Cape Leeuwien), and Africa (Good Hope)—in a westerly direction, against the prevailing winds. The voyage around the capes in this direction is a different story altogether from the sun-route of most circumnavigators, which leads around the world through the Panama Canal and the Torres Straits north of Australia. But sailing alone against the Force 8 "roaring forties" of the Indian Ocean—half the length of the equator—and, as Blyth's luck would have it, without his self-steering mechanism for most of the time, is an endless terror: "I realized that I was submitting to a progressive process of exhaustion. Everything on the yacht was wet and uncomfortable. Up to now I have considered wetness to be something unavoidable, but now it seems to permeate my being. I spend half the day in a trancelike state, doing most things mechanically. I limp across the deck like an old man. My backside is forever sore and I constantly have a cold."

A Force 12 storm head on: "As I am furling the jib, I'm seeing concentric circles float toward me—an alarm signal that I am exhausted. I had barely had a bite yesterday, and nothing before that. Enormous seas and they get worse. The boat is heeled over to 50° constantly. My arms and legs hurt. All these symptoms of exhaustion are not really caused by this storm; they are the results of all the exertion since Cape Horn." Two years after his successful return, during the first Whitbread crewed race around the world, Blyth tried to treat a crew of handpicked paratroopers the way he had treated himself. A mutiny ensued and the race was won by a Mexican yacht—proof that achievements bordering both on genius and insanity have their place only with single-handed sailors.

Many have been broken by such a challenge. Englishman Donald Crowhurst, one of the nine participants in the first nonstop around-the-world race in 1968, probably jumped overboard and met death willingly, perhaps as early as the outbound leg in the North Atlantic. More than anything else, Crowhurst was pushed to join this race, for which a prize of $20,000 had been offered, by a mountain of debts. When his boat was found drifting empty in the South Atlantic, England collected $60,000 for his widow and four children. Shortly after, the publisher of the *London Sunday Times*, who had sponsored Crowhurst, admitted on television that the man had been a fraud. An examination of his logs showed that, after making repairs in Argentina, on the outbound leg, he had sailed circles in the Atlantic, abandoning the rounding of the three capes. Obviously, he intended to wait until the other boats were in the Atlantic before rejoining the race and win. Apparently overwhelmed by guilt, he committed suicide.

Others find a completely new life through these challenges. One such man was France's Bernard Moitessier, who had already sailed halfway around the world once, successfully rounding Cape Horn, accompanied by his wife. After rounding the three capes far in the lead, he sailed for Cape Town, threw his diary and exposed film to a passing boat, and sailed on without heading toward the finish, back through the "roaring forties" into the South Seas to Tahiti. This is still the longest nonstop sail, one-and-a-half times around the world. Moitessier, shortly before rounding Cape Horn in Force 9 winds, urinated in his pants from excitement: "An exquisite warmth spread down my leg." He now lives in the port of Papeete with his *Joshua*, and philosophizes, in the company of a few crazy friends, on "the grotesque doom humanity is driven toward by the false gods of the modern world." As Moitessier had recognized at sea, one cannot escape this doom, even with the assistance of $20,000 in cash. His wife is now trying to raise their two children in France. It is rumored that Moitessier has given the proceeds from his book to the Pope so he can improve the world or at least help a few people. Genius or madman?

An Austrian, Wolfgang Hausner, was the picture of rationality when he sailed around the world on his own. His aim was not to win races, find his true self, or lament with his friends about the sorry state of the world. Hausner was—and is—living proof that one can still wander free and unrestrained over the Seven Seas. At the age of twenty-one, this Viennese, just beginning a career as a draftsman, took off for Australia. From there he sailed around the world for seven years on his catamaran, *Taboo*, which he had built himself. One night in the South Pacific, he ran into an uncharted coral reef and only reached the safety of an adjoining island after thirty hours of ceaseless rowing. Seven years is a suspiciously long time for a circumnavigation, but Hausner took his time. He lived on board and, because he cannot imagine living on land anymore, a new boat is already under construction. The little money he needs, he earns by selling shells, for which he skin dives to depths of up to eighty feet. Hausner's single-handed sailing philosophy is: "You come to terms with yourself, smooth out your soul; you gain a new, more tolerant attitude toward the society you left behind, whose good aspects you can still enjoy. I do not think that my inner feelings, my sensations, would have been so satisfying if I had had someone else on board with me."

The voyages of France's Eric Tabarly, who has not yet circumnavigated but who has contributed as much as Chichester to the development of single-handed sailing, are of a different brand altogether. As far as the nonsmoking, nondrinking bachelor from Brittany is concerned, the only true life is life at sea—as long as it's exciting enough. Aboard his various vessels named *Pen Duick*, he proved that without being a veritable single-handed loner he is one of the best sailors Europe has ever produced. With these yachts and some handpicked crews, he has won offshore races all over the world. But for this thick-necked Frenchman, the noblest form of sailing, the form which presents the greatest challenge, is single-handed sailing. The standards set by Tabarly have transformed single-handed sailing from the whim of a few eccentric loners to a sport that, for the last Transatlantic single-handed race, attracted 125 participants. The result of this race was eight hurricanes, two dead, five boats completely destroyed, forty abandonments, and Eric Tabarly the winner. He did it in exactly twenty-four days, three days less than his 1964 Transatlantic victory, for which he was made a knight of the Legion of Honor by Charles de Gaulle. Physical fitness is an important prerequisite for enduring such a transatlantic marathon, according to Eric Tabarly. If one is out of shape, it's easier to fall off the mast or overboard. Tabarly recommends rowing, chopping wood, rope climbing, tennis, and "sports that train you to withstand pain and grind your teeth." Add to this a dose of 400-meter runs, all kinds of swimming and a great deal of sailing, preferably alone, by day or night, in a dead calm or a gale, best of all on the ocean in winter. Says Tabarly, "There are frequent storms, the nights are long, and the weather is cold. . . ."

Tabarly's ideas on boats are just as unconventional. His 45-foot *Pen Duick II*, with which he became the Transatlantic winner in 1964, was an example of his radical method of going to sea. There was no table in the cabin. To eat, he sat on the pivoting saddle of a Harley Davidson motorcycle, in front of a suspended cooking and work surface in the pantry. Compasses mounted over the head of both his bunks showed him the ship's heading the moment he awoke. He could observe the weather and the position of his sails from below decks through the Plexiglas dome of a surplus Sunderland flying boat, built into the cabin roof.

The deplorable losses of life and property obscure the overwhelming fact that in 1976 a total of eighty single-handed sailors, including four women, sailed safely over the North Atlantic against the westerly winds, despite eight hurricanes. This number also included four Germans. The German sailors, not very enthusiastic about solitary sailing, had last distinguished themselves at Cape Horn on the masterfully sailed Flying P liners of the square rigger shipping firm of Laeisz of Hamburg. However, they also tried to formulate a scientific explanation of the solitary sailor phenomenon. Researchers at Hamburg University discovered, with the help of a "quiet room" and several human subjects, that every man has a more or less developed need for stimuli, sensations, and excitement. For some this need could be satisfied by simply rocking or jumping on a trampoline; others were satisfied only by genuinely dangerous situations, or even hallucinations, illusions, and altered states of consciousness, such as those caused by drugs. Or solitary sailing at sea. This is not what you would call sensational news. I greatly prefer the utterly unscientific explanation given by a German single-handed sailor—Friedel Klee. "Why do you sail alone?" he was asked. "Because there is a sea," he answered.

Kai Krüger

It was the 3rd of March when the *Spray* sailed from Port Tamar direct for Cape Pillar, with the wind from the northeast, which I fervently hoped might hold till she cleared the land; but there was no such good luck in store. It soon began to rain and thicken in the northwest, boding no good. The *Spray* neared Cape Pillar rapidly, and, nothing loath, plunged into the Pacific Ocean at once, taking her first bath of it in the gathering storm. There was no turning back even had I wished to do so, for the land was now shut out by the darkness of night. The wind freshened, and I took in a third reef. The sea was confused and treacherous. In such a time as this the old fisherman prayed, "Remember, Lord, my ship is small and thy sea is so wide!" I saw now only the gleaming crests of the waves. They showed white teeth while the sloop balanced over them. "Everything for an offing," I cried, and to this end I carried on all the sail she would bear. She ran all night with a free sheet, but on the morning of March 4 the wind shifted to southwest, then back suddenly to northwest, and blew with terrific force. The *Spray*, stripped of her sails, then bore off under bare poles. No ship in the world could have stood up against so violent a gale. Knowing that this storm might continue for many days, and that it would be impossible to work back to the westward along the coast outside of Tierra del Fuego, there seemed nothing to do but to keep on and go east about, after all. Anyhow, for my present safety the only course lay in keeping her before the wind. And so she drove southeast, as though about

to round the Horn, while the waves rose and fell and bellowed their never-ending story of the sea; but the Hand that held these held also the *Spray*. She was running now with a reefed forestaysail, the sheets flat amidship. I paid out two long ropes to steady her course and to break combing seas astern, and I lashed the helm amidship. In this trim she ran before it, shipping never a sea. Even while the storm raged at its worst, my ship was wholesome and noble. My mind as to her seaworthiness was put at ease for aye.

When all had been done that I could do for the safety of the vessel, I got to the fore-scuttle, between seas, and prepared a pot of coffee over a wood fire, and made a good Irish stew. Then, as before and afterward on the *Spray*, I insisted on warm meals. In the tide-race off Cape Pillar, however, where the sea was marvelously high, uneven, and crooked, my appetite was slim, and for a time I postponed cooking. (Confidentially, I was seasick!)

The first day of the storm gave the *Spray* her actual test in the worst sea that Cape Horn or its wild regions could afford, and in no part of the world could a rougher sea be found than at this particular point, namely, off Cape Pillar, the grim sentinel of the Horn.

Farther offshore, while the sea was majestic, there was less apprehension of danger. There the *Spray* rode, now like a bird on the crest of a wave, and now like a waif deep down in the hollow between seas; and so she drove on. Whole days passed, counted as other days, but with always a thrill—yes, of delight.

On the fourth day of the gale, rapidly nearing

188

the pitch of Cape Horn, I inspected my chart and pricked off the course and distance to Port Stanley, in the Falkland Islands, where I might find my way and refit, when I saw through a rift in the clouds a high mountain, about seven leagues away on the port beam. The fierce edge of the gale by this time had blown off, and I had already bent a squaresail on the boom in place of the mainsail, which was torn to rags. I hauled in the trailing ropes, hoisted this awkward sail reefed, the forestaysail being already set, and under this sail brought her at once on the wind heading for the land, which appeared as an island in the sea. So it turned out to be, though not the one I had supposed.

I was exultant over the prospect of once more entering the Strait of Magellan and beating through again into the Pacific, for it was more than rough on the outside coast of Tierra del Fuego. It was indeed a mountainous sea. When the sloop was in the fiercest squalls, with only the reefed forestaysail set, even that small sail shook her from keelson to truck when it shivered by the leech. Had I harbored the shadow of a doubt for her safety, it would have been that she might spring a leak in the garboard at the heel of the mast; but she never called me once to the pump. Under pressure of the smallest sail I could set she made for the land like a race-horse, and steering her over the crests of the waves so that she might not trip was nice work. I stood at the helm now and made the most of it.

Night closed in before the sloop reached the land, leaving her feeling the way in pitchy darkness. I saw breakers ahead before long. At this I wore ship and stood offshore, but was immediately startled by the tremendous roaring of breakers again ahead and on the lee bow. This puzzled me, for there should have been no broken water where I supposed myself to be. I kept off a good bit, then wore round, but finding broken water also there, threw her head again offshore. In this way, among dangers, I spent the rest of the night. Hail and sleet in the fierce squalls cut my flesh till the blood trickled over my face; but what of that? It was daylight, and the sloop was in the midst of the Milky Way of the sea, which is northwest of Cape Horn, and it was the white breakers of a huge sea over sunken rocks which had threatened to engulf her through the night. It was Fury Island I had sighted and steered for, and what a panorama was before me now and all around! It was not the time to complain of a broken skin. What could I do but fill away among the breakers and find a channel between them, now that it was day? Since she had escaped the rocks through the night, surely she would find her way by daylight. This was the greatest sea adventure of my life. God knows how my vessel escaped.

The sloop at last reached inside of small islands that sheltered her in smooth water. Then I climbed the mast to survey the wild scene astern. The great naturalist Darwin looked over this seascape from the deck of the *Beagle*, and wrote in his journal, "Any landsman seeing the Milky Way would have nightmare for a week." He might have added, "or seaman" as well.

189

The *Spray's* good luck followed fast. I discovered, as she sailed along through a labyrinth of islands, that she was in the Cockburn Channel, which leads into the Strait of Magellan at a point opposite Cape Froward, and that she was already passing Thieves' Bay, suggestively named. And at night, March 8, behold, she was at anchor in a snug cove at the Turn! Every heart-beat on the *Spray* now counted thanks.

Here I pondered on the events of the last few days, and, strangely enough, instead of feeling rested from sitting or lying down, I now began to feel jaded and worn; but a hot meal of venison stew soon put me right, so that I could sleep. As drowsiness came on I sprinkled the deck with tacks, and then I turned in, bearing in mind the advice of my old friend Samblich that I was not to step on them myself. I saw to it that not a few of them stood "business end" up; for when the *Spray* passed Thieves' Bay two canoes had put out and followed in her wake, and there was no disguising the fact any longer that I was alone.

Now, it is well known that one cannot step on a tack without saying something about it. A pretty good Christian will whistle when he steps on the "commercial end" of a carpet-tack; a savage will howl and claw the air, and that was just what happened that night about twelve o'clock, while I was asleep in the cabin, where the savages thought they "had me," sloop and all, but changed their minds when they stepped on deck, for then they thought that I or somebody else had them. I had no need of a dog; they howled like a pack of hounds. I had hardly use for a gun. They jumped pell-mell, some into their canoes and some into the sea, to cool off, I suppose, and there was a deal of free language over it as they went. I fired several guns when I came on deck, to let the rascals know that I was home, and then I turned in again, feeling sure I should not be disturbed any more by people who left in so great a hurry.

The Fuegians, being cruel, are naturally cowards; they regard a rifle with superstitious fear. The only real danger one could see that might come from their quarter would be from allowing them to surround one within bow-shot, or to anchor within range where they might lie in ambush. As for their coming on deck at night, even had I not put tacks about, I could have cleared them off by shots from the cabin and hold. I always kept a quantity of ammunition within reach in the hold and in the cabin and in the forepeak, so that retreating to any of these places I could "hold the fort" simply by shooting up through the deck.

Perhaps the greatest danger to be apprehended was from the use of fire. Every canoe carries fire; nothing is thought of that, for it is their custom to communicate by smoke-signals. The harmless brand that lies smoldering in the bottom of one of their canoes might be ablaze in one's cabin if he were not on the alert. The port captain of Sandy Point warned me particularly of this danger. Only a short time before they had fired a Chilean gunboat by throwing brands in through the stern windows of the cabin. The *Spray* had no openings in the cabin or

190

deck, except two scuttles, and these were guarded by fastenings which could not be undone without waking me if I were asleep.

On the morning of the 9th, after a refreshing rest and a warm breakfast, and after I had swept the decks of tacks, I got out what spare canvas there was on board, and began to sew the pieces together in the shape of a peak for my square-mainsail, the tarpaulin. The day to all appearances promised fine weather and light winds, but appearances in Tierra del Fuego do not always count. While I was wondering why no trees grew on the slope abreast of the anchorage, half minded to lay by the sail-making and land with my gun for some game and to inspect a white boulder on the beach, near the brook, a williwaw came down with such terrific force as to carry the *Spray*, with two anchors down, like a feather out of the cove and away into deep water. No wonder trees did not grow on the side of that hill! Great Boreas! a tree would need to be all roots to hold on against such a furious wind.

From the cove to the nearest land to leeward was a long drift, however, and I had ample time to weigh both anchors before the sloop came near any danger, and so no harm came of it. I saw no more savages that day or the next; they probably had some sign by which they knew of the coming williwaws; at least, they were wise in not being afloat even on the second day, for I had no sooner gotten to work at sail-making again, after the anchor was down, than the wind, as on the day before, picked the sloop up and flung her seaward with a vengeance, anchor and all, as before. This fierce wind, usual to the Magellan country, continued on through the day, and swept the sloop by several miles of steep bluffs and precipices overhanging a bold shore of wild and uninviting appearance. I was not sorry to get away from it, though in doing so it was no Elysian shore to which I shaped my course. I kept on sailing in hope, since I had no choice but to go on, heading across for St. Nicholas Bay, where I had cast anchor February 19. It was now the 10th of

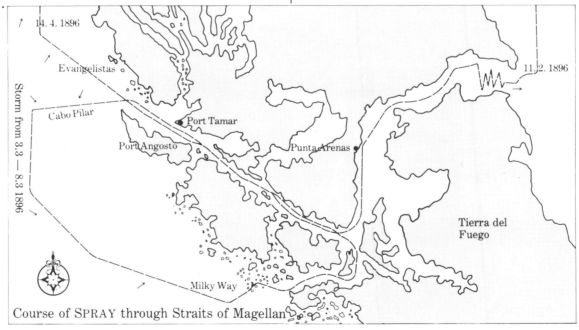

Course of SPRAY through Straits of Magellan

March! Upon reaching the bay the second time I had circumnavigated the wildest part of desolate Tierra del Fuego. But the *Spray* had not yet arrived at St. Nicholas, and by the merest accident her bones were saved from resting there when she did arrive. The parting of a stay-sail-sheet in a williwaw, when the sea was turbulent and she was plunging into the storm, brought me forward to see instantly a dark cliff ahead and breakers so close under the bows that I felt surely lost, and in my thoughts cried, "Is the hand of fate against me, after all, leading me in the end to this dark spot?" I sprang aft again, unheeding the flapping sail, and threw the wheel over, expecting, as the sloop came down into the hollow of a wave, to feel her timbers smash under me on the rocks. But at the touch of her helm she swung clear of the danger, and in the next moment she was in the lee of the land.

It was the small island in the middle of the bay for which the sloop had been steering, and which she made with such unerring aim as nearly to run it down. Farther along in the bay was the anchorage, which I managed to reach, but before I could get the anchor down another squall caught the sloop and whirled her round like a top and carried her away, altogether to leeward of the bay. Still farther to leeward was a great headland, and I bore off for that. This was retracing my course toward Sandy Point, for the gale was from the southwest.

I had the sloop soon under good control, however, and in a short time rounded to under the lee of a mountain, where the sea was as smooth as a mill-pond, and the sails flapped and hung limp while she carried her way close in. Here I thought I would anchor and rest till morning, the depth being eight fathoms very close to the shore. But it was interesting to see, as I let go the anchor, that it did not reach the bottom before another williwaw struck down from this mountain and carried the sloop off faster than I could pay out cable. Therefore, instead of resting, I had to "man the windlass" and heave up the anchor with fifty fathoms of cable hanging up and down in deep water. This was in that part of the strait called Famine Reach. Dismal Famine Reach! On the sloop's crab-windlass I worked the rest of the night, thinking how much easier it was for me when I could say, "Do that thing or the other," than now doing all myself. But I hove away and sang the old chants that I sang when I was a sailor. Within the last few days I had passed through much and was now thankful that my state was no worse.

It was daybreak when the anchor was at the hawse. By this time the wind had gone down, and cat's-paws took the place of williwaws, while the loop drifted slowly toward Sandy Point. She came within sight of ships at anchor in the roads, and I was more than half minded to put in for new sails, but the wind coming out from the northeast, which was fair for the other direction, I turned the prow of the *Spray* westward once more for the Pacific, to traverse a second time the second half of my first course through the strait.

Joshua Slocum

On the afternoon of August 1, 1923, I ran into a storm with very high waves. *Firecrest* dived completely under with the bowsprit, and the wind on the mast was enormous. At this moment I was convinced that a long bowsprit and a gaff rig are only a continuous source of sorrow for the single-handed cruiser. I decided to change my tackle upon arrival in New York and to set a triangular Marconi rig, which would be held steady by a shorter bowsprit. On the same day I gave up repairing another foresail because it would have used up the rest of my yarn.

All during the following night, heavy waves broke across the deck. By the following morning, the equipment was completely soaked. At 4 o'clock I had already noticed that the wind had shifted and that *Firecrest* advanced only with difficulty. The barometer fell still further, and it was clear to me that the worst was still to come. In the early morning the storm intensified and reached its peak around 11 o'clock. In the cabin I discovered true pandemonium. It was hardly possible to fix breakfast. When I tried to cook a little rice, Rasmus came on deck and I spilled the hot water over my knees. When I climbed on deck again, I discovered that high waves had pulled away the hatch of the sail chamber from the quarterdeck.

Since mainsail and foresail were slowly developing holes, I had to take them in. That was the ideal occasion to try out the sea anchor. So, to begin with, I let my boat drift in the storm; I observed that it did not hold much better with the anchor. Many sailors believe that a sea anchor can be very useful when it is impossible to set sail because of a storm—the sea anchor is supposed to keep the bow in the wind so that the boat can ride out the waves. However, my own experience contradicts everything that has ever been written about the behavior of yachts in a storm. I believe that the danger of being capsized varies with the specific type of ship—at least it did not apply to *Firecrest*. It mattered little whether the waves came across the bow, the stern, or the sides, as long as the boat did not drift. The best thing was to sail under as little cloth as possible; that is to say with reefed sails.

Meanwhile, the storm had grown into a true hurricane. The sky was completely hidden behind black clouds, so that day became night. I had to lower the mainsail so far that there was only a little cloth left. The waves rose so high and hit the rigging so hard, that one could believe for a moment that the mast would break. The rain kept getting stronger, even piercing, and it made me almost blind because I could hardly open my eyes. When I did look out I could not look out over the bow. Meanwhile, I had been exposed to rain and salt spray, and the skin on my hands was thoroughly chapped. Only with great effort could I tend to the running rigging. But the storm that had torn my sails to pieces, and the water that was permanently standing in the cabin, and the whipping foam could not decrease my love for the sea. A sailor who single-handedly sails across the ocean has to be willing, from the onset, to get used to such events. My precursors on the square-rigged vessels, which sailed around the Horn, always fought for their existence and they suffered much more from the cold than I. I knew that some day *Firecrest* and I could hit a storm that would be stronger than all the previous ones and that one would send us into the abyss. But this would have been an end which seamen have always reckoned with. Can there be a nicer death for the seaman?

During the night of August 19 it started blowing again. One wave after the other ran over the little cutter, which put its nose deep into the water. I woke up several times because of the strong thumping and the listing. Toward morning I suspected that on this day the peak of all previously experienced storms would be surpassed. *Firecrest* was close to joining the big harbor of lost ships. As far as the eye could see—only foaming, twirling sea and above it ink-black banks of clouds racing along. Around 10 o'clock the storm reached hurricane strength. The waves came short and mean; their crests were broken into white whirlpools and whipping foam. The breakers pounced upon the cutter as if they wanted to crush it. But the boat kept rising up from the inferno, and it fought so courageously against these powers that I wanted to sing a hymn of praise: That was life!

Suddenly, catastrophe hit. It was just noon and *Firecrest* was fighting its way forward abreast of the wind and under a shred of mainsail and a flying jib. On the horizon, a gigantic wave appeared whose white, roaring crest threatened to swallow all other waves. I couldn't believe my eyes, I had mixed feelings because this view was just as beautiful as it was terrifying. With lightning speed I realized that remaining on deck would mean my certain death. With one leap I hastened to the mast. I was hardly halfway up when the wave broke upon *Firecrest* with a fearful roar and before my eyes covered her under tons of foaming water. The ship shook and heeled far over under this blow. I wondered whether she would ever right herself again.

Only slowly did the *Firecrest* emerge from this hell, as the wave broke further leeward. I slid down the mast and contemplated the chaos: large parts of the bowsprit had been broken away. Held by the jib stay, a mass of rigging and sails hung under the lee railing and was hit by each succeeding wave with the force of a sledgehammer against the ship's side. At any moment a leak could develop that would send *Firecrest* and me to the bottom of the sea. The mast had been shaken so strongly and the port shrouds had been so loosened that there was immediate danger of the mast going overboard. The raging of the hurricane was unbelieveable; the deck was covered by waves most of the time.

I had a hard bit of labor to do now. First I had to furl the mainsail. I used a tackle to lower it with the downhaul. It was even more difficult to heave the wreckage back on board. The deck planks were so slippery and the storm howled with such undiminished strength that I had to crawl along so as not to slip overboard. I held onto the shrouds with my hands. The part torn loose from the bowsprit was so heavy that I had to secure it first with the end of a heavy rope, so that I could subsequently lift it back on board bit by bit. I lost my equilibrium several times during this maneuver. Finally, when night came, I had succeeded in pulling the flying jib and bowsprit back on deck and secured both. I felt completely beat.

Nevertheless, I had to try to clear the mainmast again. It wavered dangerously between the single breakers, but I managed to climb it and found the reason for the loosened port shrouds. Twice during this maneuver I lost my strength and was tossed vehemently against the mast. I gave up because I was simply too exhausted and slid down again. In order to release the pressure from the port shrouds, I hoisted the mainsail a little and lay *Firecrest* on the other bow because the starboard shrouds would be able to withstand the storm. The percussions lessened somewhat now and, because it was late at night, I descended into the cabin and closed everything behind me. An attempt to light a fire failed; both burners seemed to have given up their spirit. I went to bed starving, drenched, and almost stiff from the cold. For the first time during this voyage I felt sad and discouraged.

The Bermudas still lay 300 miles to the south, and to get to New York I had at least 1,000 miles to sail via the Gulf Stream. I knew that it would be safer for me to call now at the Bermudas. In a few days this distance could be mastered and the damages could be repaired before continuing to New York. However, I had originally decided in favor of a nonstop Atlantic crossing. Just the thought of giving up almost broke my heart. At this moment I hardly worried whether perhaps one more wave could send *Firecrest* and myself to the bottom of the sea. In vain I tried to sleep, but the vibrations from the mast were so strong that I feared it would snap before daybreak. I remained still for several hours, stretched out in my bunk, and gave myself to despairing thoughts. Despite this lowness of spirits, an *idée fixe* nestled in my brain: although I knew that it would be better to call first at the Bermudas, I couldn't stop thinking that actually I wanted to sail directly for New York.

The decision was made quickly: I had to chance the impossible! I got up and first of all started to fix the burners. For the tasks I faced, I needed a full stomach more than anything else. I found a needle, which I filed so that I could use it to clean the exit valves for the kerosene. At dawn I fixed myself a good breakfast with bacon and plenty of tea. Now I felt good again all around. My plan to call at the Bermudas was forgotten.

Although on the morning of August 21 the hurricane seemed to have ceased raging, there still was a strong storm and the waves were still very high. First of all I had to work on the mast. It was very hard to climb it and then to hold on there. I hung on to it with arms and legs as firmly as I could, and I remained in this position for more than an hour. Only slowly did I succeed in securing the shrouds again, and when I finally could glide down to the deck, I pulled them on tight once again from under—the mast had been saved for now. Now I proceeded to the battered bowsprit. For this job I needed a saw and an ax. With the ax I made a notch in the piece that was broken off, so that I could fit it again into the old spot. I was able to fasten this emergency bowsprit again, although it had come out a little too short.

The hardest work was still before me, however. I had to construct a support to hold the far end of the bowsprit. For this I took a piece of the anchor chain, which I fastened all the way up on the bowsprit so as to then fasten the last link of the chain just above the waterline on the boat. To enable me to work at all on this spot, I flung my legs around the bowsprit and let myself hang down. Because of the continuous pitching of *Firecrest*, I was submerged several times at least a couple of meters each time, but somehow I finally managed to finish this hard chore as well.

When I had finished the repairs, the storm had subsided considerably, as if it had been conquered and could do nothing against my courageous boat and me. I was now also in position to make two observations, and according to those I was at 36° North and 62° West; I was still approximately 800 miles from New York as the crow flies, but the distance to be sailed was 1,000 to 1,200 miles. Even though I was completely exhausted by the repairs, the pleasure of my victory gave me new courage and new force. Now I was also able to repair the bilge pump and discovered that a broken-off piece of a match was stuck in a valve. After two hours of hard work the boat was dry. To convince myself of the reconquered seaworthiness of *Firecrest*, I climbed the mast once again and noticed now that the shrouds had suffered considerably—until I reached New York the mast would require my full attention. With the shortened bowsprit and the reduced sail surface in the bow, *Firecrest* was difficult to maneuver. When she sailed well, I always had to compensate with the tenon; when she sailed close to the wind, the drift was very strong.

Thank God the repairs were now finished. I affixed the tenon and set the sails in such a manner that *Firecrest* could keep on course to New York by herself. Then I threw myself into the bunk, completely exhausted, for a couple hours of well-deserved rest. After having worked as a sail maker, joiner, and mate and having brought my hard sailor's work to a good end, I fell asleep with the comforting thought that my ship was nearing her distant goal, secure on the restless sea.

Alain Gerbault

On June 19, 1937, at four in the afternoon, exactly two weeks behind schedule, I ran out of the harbor at Lisbon with only my jib set. Cheered by a crowd on land, I passed between the harbor walls and among craft of all kinds. No one on shore knew, of course, that the small white bird out there meant to cross the Atlantic alone. Before I rounded the last corner, I set my mainsail. My cruise had begun.

It started with a headwind out of the west. But there was no point in worrying. Farther out to sea, the wind would lie in the north. My diary entries for the first two days were sparse, indicating how many crucial chores I had to do on board. Out at sea the north wind was blowing, and *Störtebeker 3* marched staunchly westward during the first night. Once again I had set out to sail 3,200 miles, but this time alone.

It seems strange in retrospect, but the thought that I was doing something remarkable never occurred to me. The feelings I had at the outset of this voyage were different from those I had experienced at the beginning of any other sailing venture. I had set myself the task of reaching New York single handedly, without any layovers in port, and as quickly as the winds and my sailing skills would allow.

I do not know how many times I heard the admonition: "But a trip like that is dangerous!" And just as many times I explained that it was not, if one had the right boat and the necessary experience and training, had made adequate preparations, and exercised reasonable caution. What were the dangers? You can fall overboard in the Hudson River, too. But since my boat was inclined to make unpredictable leaps, I had run handlines wherever I could, and I also got used to being hooked up to a "monkey line" at all times. Whenever I worked or moved about on deck, particularly forward, I wore a strong rope around my waist. The other end of this rope was equipped with a good solid carabiner hook. The first thing I always did, whenever possible, was to fasten that hook. Then I could set to work with both hands free. This monkey line was not a sign of weakness or cowardice but one of caution. Nonetheless, I have to laugh when I think of myself making my way forward with one end of this line around my waist and the other hooked to the mast. I wore this line even in the fairest weather. I made no exceptions to this rule. Otherwise, I might forget the rope when I needed it most. It reminded me of the watchdog at August Pahl's wharf in Finkenwerder. That dog had a monkey line, too, and much more play in it than I thought. I did not realize that until the dog gave me a sharp nip in the hindquarters.

What about other dangers like injuries, broken bones, sickness, or food poisoning from spoiled provisions? The answer was that I had to be especially careful. Besides, these dangers exist on land, too. Finally, there was the danger of collision. To prevent that, I never left the deck at night without hanging a bright lantern in the shrouds. And as a rule I slept during the day. In foul weather, I carried as little sail as possible.

197

So there I was, alone out there with my boat on the Atlantic. The coast of Portugal disappeared in the evening haze. Several steamer lights moved to the north and south. These, too, disappeared as I headed westward under a stiff northerly breeze with a single reef in my mainsail. The first night left no memorable impressions. One entry in my diary to the effect that the Atlantic was harsh had more to do with what happened above and below deck. When I was sailing at a good speed, the going was far from smooth. I cracked into every available corner with almost every part of my body.

There was so much to do on my first day at sea that I had little time for reflection. By noon on Sunday, June 20, my position was 38 degrees 20 minutes North by 10 degrees 50 minutes West. I had put seventy-six miles behind me. *Störtebeker 3* was sailing on automatic pilot most of the time and doing very well. By Monday, June 21, I had traveled another 120 nautical miles in 24 hours and had reached 38 degrees 10 minutes North by 13 degrees 25 minutes West. That was a promising start. During the night I had seen several steamers, but now I was really alone. You do not meet many ships underway to the Azores. At the helm at night, you have time to think. Many people ask, "Isn't it terribly lonely? What goes through your head at times like that?"

Human beings can tolerate loneliness very well. I would even say that everyone needs to get away from all the superfluous activity of our civilization occasionally, from all the concessions it demands, from all the so-called knowledge it produces. Everyone needs to spend some time in solitude, but you do not necessarily have to cross the Atlantic alone to do that! Of course, a man feels ridiculously small and unimportant in the vastness of the ocean—like a tiny, newborn creature facing its stern creator. That reminds me of a little anecdote that Commander Roosevelt once told me. When a Breton priest blessed his village's fishing fleet before it set out westward for the Newfoundland Banks each

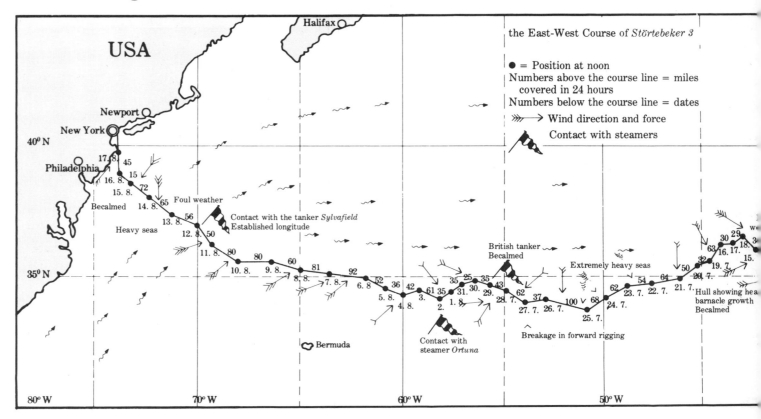

year, he used to say in his concluding prayer: "Dear God, be merciful to them, for your sea is so large and their boats are so small."

I cannot imagine any richer pleasures than those of a satin night sky dotted with glistening stars, of the rushing and whispering of a fresh breeze, of the gurgling of the water at bow and stern, of the pure sea air. From the cabin comes the faint glow of a small kerosene lamp, reminding you of the domestic warmth and comfort that are waiting for you when you go below and leave your boat to take care of itself again. At sea, you forget everything: greed and envy, stock market reports and tax returns. You are freed of everything that might weigh on you. The only other time I have had a similar sense of liberation was years ago on solo ski tours in the majestic silence of the alpine night. There is always so much to observe that tedium is no danger, and sources of amusement are not lacking either. For example, a suitor in the form of a small star once pursued Lady Moon for two or three

nights in a row after she had risen over the horizon. What could he possibly want with her? She wanted nothing to do with him, and one night she deliberately turned her back on him and moved away. That kind of thing happens on land, too.

People also ask me if I might not like to have some kind of animal along for company, a dog or cat or maybe even a canary. No, I am very fond of animals, and I doubt that any such creature could be happy being bounced about on a small sailing vessel. A few dozen flies and a flea boarded ship with me in Lisbon, but even they could stand seafaring for only a short time.

Did I talk to myself on board? I once tried it briefly, but my voice sounded as flat and hollow as if it had come out of an old earthenware jug. I sang for a few nights, everything from folk songs to the "Agnus Dei" and "Ora pro nobis" from old Italian masses that I had sung as a boy alto in Catholic churches in Munich, even though I was Protestant myself. I soon gave that up,

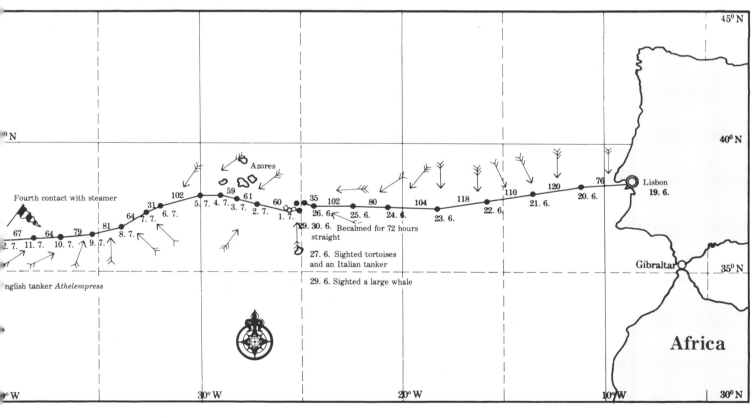

too, but for hours at a time I kept hearing in my head music reminiscent of Strauss.

In all my weeks at sea, I was never bored except for occasional five-minute stretches when I had to wait too long for a breeze. People who do not know me thought I must have suffered from depression. But I did not. Whenever a calm brought on a bad mood, I would curse mightily in three languages. That seemed to act as a safety valve that relieved the pressure. A sign of how little boredom I experienced was that during the whole voyage I never opened any of the books in four languages that I had taken along, with the exception of the nautical yearbook and the table of logarithms when I did navigational calculations.

Tuesday, June 22. Position: 37 degrees 55 minutes North by 15 degrees 45 minutes West. One hundred ten nautical miles covered since yesterday. Wednesday, June 23. *Störtebeker 3* continues to steer itself and make good headway. The wind is tending to swing farther to the east. It this continues, the automatic pilot will not function as well as it has so far. The clouds here, like those carried by the trade winds, run a predictable course overhead. A noon position reading showed that I had covered another 118 miles and that the boat now lay at 37 degrees 30 minutes North. Up to this point I had far exceeded my top goal of eighty miles per day.

At noon the yacht begins to buck and roll and carry on in a totally unreasonable fashion. Like it or not, I sometimes have to take over the helm myself. Ordinarily, my automatic pilot, "Manila Billy," takes care of the steering, but now if I want to prepare a meal or do some writing in this journal, I have to control the helm myself with light lines running out of the cabin. Dr. Wolfgang Frank spent many evenings writing on board when he sailed with me on *Störtebeker 2's* voyage from Newport to Bergen in 1935. He would be surprised to see just how difficult writing on shipboard can be. Toward dusk the seas turned rough, and I had my first misadventure. The bolt at the bottom of the spar used to roll up the jib had worked itself loose even though I had taken particular care to fasten it securely before leaving Lisbon. The bolt had fallen out, and now the almost thirty-foot-long spar, along with its flapping sail, was thrashing about in the air. I secured the helm, tied my monkey line around my waist, and set out to do battle with the dragon. My struggle would have made a marvelous film. It was impossible to work standing up, so I sat down with my legs hanging overboard. Then, perched on the yacht's snout, I bobbed up and down, rising and falling several yards at a time with the speed of an express elevator. Down I plunged, waist deep in the blue Atlantic, then up again into the fresh air. This particular entertainment is unavoidable if you're repairing your jib spar, but you can also partake of it anytime you like for the sheer fun of it.

I finally managed to bring the jib and spar under control and to bolt on a new shackle. After a battle that must have lasted about an hour, I could retire to the stern victorious. There's no doubt about it: All sports, deepwater sailing included, involve struggle.

Ludwig Schlimbach

EARLY on Sunday morning, the 25th of May, I went to Mass; then I fetched my luggage from the hotel. It had been the first time in all my voyage that I had left my 'rabbit-hutch' for a bed. The city was still asleep and the sun was not yet over the mountains when I arrived aboard *Lehg II*.

I was moored astern of the corvette *General Baquedano*, the training ship of the Chilean Navy, where I had often been a guest. With the help of my friends of the Yacht Club, I stowed my stores: wine, spirits, biscuits, quantities of tinned fish; a change from times when I had not been overburdened with such luxuries. I had stores for more than six months and 3,000 miles to sail. It was the shortest leg of the voyage, but also the most tricky. Cook, Bougainville, and all seamen who have navigated in those waters testify to the fact in their books. Hansen, the only lone sailor who had succeeded in rounding Cape Horn from East to West, lay in the depths off the coast of Ancud; only the wreckage of his boat had been found on the rocks. Bernicot and Slocum had chosen to go through the Strait of Magellan.

I knew that a strong current from the West strikes the coast between 37° and 50° S.; it then divides into two branches, one running North, the other South. The danger is the possibility of being surprised by a westerly gale for a couple of days; if the navigator has not had the prudence to steer well clear, he will inevitably be thrown on to the coast. For this reason, my plan was to follow the route of the clippers and eschew the temptation to stop at Valdivia, where the Yacht Club had invited me to call.

Many friends had come to witness my last preparations, most of them convinced that they would never see me again; and I kept stopping work to say goodbye. By 10 o'clock everything was ready; the mizzen, mainsail, staysail and jib were set. . . . The breeze was light. My friend Weddod, accompanied by many assorted persons with whom I had spent pleasant hours, took me in tow. We passed along the line of ships at anchor, including a giant Canadian five-master. She had been lying there for a long time, a sort of black phantom and warning of what might happen to me in the far South. She carried a cargo of wood and had tried to round Cape Horn, but storms had battered her hull to such an extent that leaks had reached danger-point. Her skipper, seeing that she was near sinking, decided to give up and return to Valparaiso with all hands pumping desperately. Was something like that waiting for me? The anxious faces of my friends, whose forced smiles failed to be convincing in spite of their wish to be encouraging, their hints that it might be better to give up the attempt, were certainly not good omens for my departure.

I knew that the problem would be solved for me in the first mile; as soon as I was thrown on my own resources. To escape from outside influences, and firmly to implement my decision, was the only way to defeat 'the impossible.'

We were soon past the breakwater. I looked back at the training corvette, where the signal *'Bon voyage'* must have been flying for me; at that distance it was somewhat difficult to see.

At 16.00 hours I cast off the tow in a very light westerly breeze. I made a board to the N.N.W. to give Point Curaumillas a wide berth. The glass stood at 770, the temperature at 15°C., the humidity 88 per cent. During the evening the wind backed a little to the S.W., the coast and its beautiful colours were bathed in sunshine. One more port was behind me in a sailor's life; but this time I was headed for the imponderables of Cape Horn. What of tomorrow? The day died slowly and the sun sank in a cloudless sky. Astern, above the coastal range stood the peak of Aconcagua.

After sunset I went below; alone in my boat after more than a month—I could not help kissing a panel in a surge of affection for my 'shipmate.'

For the moment I was still a stranger to her; I was so imbued with the memory of happy days in Valparaiso, the land of eternal spring, that it seemed to have been a dream. With its curious and diverse buildings, its narrow streets that wind fantastically as they climb, its romantic old houses of the colonial period, the city has something of all times and a little of every country. Valparaiso is unique.

On Monday the 31st the coast was still visible to the East, but hardly distinguishable between the clouds and the banks of morning mist. The current, stronger than the light breeze, had carried me off towards the North, although my course was set westward. About 5 miles to leeward a schooner from Juan Fernandez was heading for Valparaiso.

Although in my position, 71°30′ West, I should have been well clear of anything, I thought I heard breakers; I was practically becalmed—it would be. . . . No. The noise came from an enormous school of porpoises approaching ahead.

On the 1st of June the sea was flat, without a wrinkle, with little patches of ruffled surface that hardly moved. The wind veered to North-west without freshening much; but by nightfall I was moving well and the boat left a wake of phosphorescence.

On the 2nd of June I caught a better, fresher breeze which allowed me to get some sleep; but the next day it backed to the South, then a little to the South-west. It was intensely humid. I had already travelled 240 miles! Still heading West, and rather wet, I saw ahead Juan Fernandez, 'Robinson Crusoe's' island. I came fairly close, but visibility was very bad and I could not distinguish any details whatever.

I noticed a slight leak aft but was unable to track it down. It was barely a trickle; but if it was running in easy weather, it could be a nuisance when I came to a difficult bit. So I made a painstaking search for the crack; but in vain.

On the 4th of June, my position being 34°58′ S. by 77°15′ W., I began to drift to the S.W. again, which enabled me to get farther from land and reach the high latitudes.

On the 5th the wind was fairly fresh from the S.S.E.; I could not get out of sight of clouds banked up in successive layers off the coast, which they could not surmount because of the height of the continent. They form a barrier that can stretch over 400 miles from the coast.

I was in the zone of variable squalls with low visibility and other obstacles to accurate taking of sights. The number of albatrosses increased as I went down to the South-west.

Up to then I had been at the helm very little; I spent almost all my time resting in the cabin. The boat was behaving very well, both on and off the wind; the prevailing winds made it necessary to sail close-hauled.

The passage of Cape Horn was gradually taking shape. The whistling of the wind was that typical of these latitudes.

The thick mist left me in semi-darkness. None of these things made any difference to my state of mind, for I was always on the lookout for some new developments. Had I begun my voyage around the world by way of Cape Horn, what I found there might have made a deep impression and caused me to worry continually; but, arriving here after such vicissitudes and so much suffering, the only effect was to make me expect the worst. Such weather as this could be compared with my best days in the Indian Ocean. The only difference was the choppiness of the seas, due to the inconsiderable depth.

On the 9th of June the wind seemed to be rising into a storm. As I had rested for several days, I took the helm; the barometer had fallen 10 mm. In the daytime I headed into the waves, but at night, with visibility nil and my cow of a binnacle lamp that still persisted in going out, I could not carry on with this form of sport. The boat having lost way, a wave broke over her and me. The shock was so violent and was such a surprise that I felt I was suffocating. We were well under; it was all I could do to hold my breath; asphyxia was near. For interminable seconds I clung to the mizzen mast, or I should have been washed overboard. Slowly, desperately slowly, *Lehg II* emerged: so did I. I took a deep breath. That accursed binnacle lamp and its tricks! I was so furious that, for the first time, I lowered the mainsail and went below to sleep.

On the 10th I set the mainsail again. As I was sailing very close to the wind, the seas were constantly over the deck and it was impossible to do anything without getting completely soaked. It was only in the cockpit, behind a canvas screen that I had had installed in Chile, that I found some degree of comfort, if I may call it that.

In spite of the wind and the sea, *Lehg II* went on unshaken and that was what mattered. She was going towards her goal, but towards the cold, too. Soon it was 5°C. It was no longer much use to stay at the helm, for my hands could not endure the open air for long. Matters came to the point when, having taken in the mainsail to set the storm trysail, I had to burn matches when I went below to warm my numbed fingers. It was ten seconds before I could feel the heat of the flame.

Very close-hauled, the boat was labouring heavily, shaking, shudddering and creaking under the impact of the heavy seas. My position was 42° S. by 82°45′ W.; the wind, which in the last twenty-four hours had swung to the South, obliged me to get a little closer to the land, whereas I had been more than 400 miles off. On the 14th I was level with the Gulf of Peñas; I had to bail every three hours, for I had been unable to discover the leak.

Hail came rattling down and the clouds were low. The situation was getting worse every moment. That day I reached latitude 47°. I still had another 10° to make to the South in order to round Cape Horn. Waves were crashing down on board. At night I stayed in the cabin, for it was really disagreeable to remain on deck. Not at all like trade wind sailing in the tropics, when a rainstorm is welcome. Here, wet clothes were piling up in the cabin, which was beginning to look like a slop-shop. Hanging them on a wire was useless; they would not dry. Days were short; the sun barely rose above the horizon.

I was disheartened by the recurring squalls and the endless swell; but suddenly I felt that it was vital to go on deck and look around. Why? I don't know. It is one of those odd things that happen to seafaring men. A presentiment inexplicable, as far as our knowledge goes. However that may be, I went on deck . . . and saw an American warship, southward bound and pitching heavily. There were two of us shipping these dirty seas; but we could not make any signals. So we went on our course, each with a different mission.

As the margin of security I had allowed was reduced by the persistence of southerly winds, and I was beginning to get too near the coast, I made a board to the West and, in order not to go too far, took in the storm trysail. On the 16th I was at 48°2′ S. by 82°30′ W. and the wind changing to the South-west, I could resume my course to the South.

The tell-tale which I had installed in the cabin, apart from the very serious deviation caused by the proximity of masses of iron, was useless, as the gimbals had broken and I was not in a position to repair it.

After six days of gales there came a lull and I set the storm trysail once more.

I was 600 miles from Cape Horn. It was time to consider the situations that might arise when I got into the really redoubtable zone. I assessed all the aspects of the problem and drew the most logical conclusion for each of them. This study gave me a more assured plan of navigation.

The cold was so intense that I could not leave the smallest part of my face exposed; on top of the cold, wind and hail lashed down pitilessly. My daily average was 120 miles.

On the night of the 18th of June, Cape Pillar, the entrance to the Strait of Magellan, was 180 miles to the East. This passage tempted me not at all. I had decided to round Cape Horn and neither storms nor risks should shake my determination.

Although not at the helm, I was standing by to surface. Not a detail had escaped me. I had greased two gloves so that the water could not make them useless; I had done the same for my oilskin. I had prepared iron rations on a basis of chocolate, preserves and biscuit for use in the event of being surprised by a spot of weather which might keep me at the helm for several days when close to Diego Ramirez Island, some 30 miles South of the Cape. As it shows no light, constant vigilance is necessary. To keep myself awake, I had benzedrine sulphate ready. Nothing was left to chance, everything had been studied, foreseen and calculated.

I had kept a watchful eye on standing and running rigging in case of wear; they seemed capable of withstanding any unforeseen strain.

As my thigh boots were wet through, I looked about for some means of drying them; and thought of putting a light inside each.

It worked. I was being carried towards the coast, in the zone of icebergs and drift ice. Numerous birds were flying about, hunting for their living. In the cabin, hermetically sealed, the temperature was 5°C.

On the 20th Cape Horn was 400 miles away to the E.S.E. Getting nearer, getting nearer!

Two days later a storm from the North obliged me to take in the storm trysail for the night. I was already sailing due East; the wind was 40 knots; *Lehg II* went on under mizzen, staysail and storm jib. I was not far from the 'mousetrap' and felt that I had to stay at the helm. At 17.00 hours I saw Tierra del Fuego to the North-east and frankly, if the seas were no heavier with the high wind that was now blowing, I could sleep in peace; I had expected worse. Perhaps my imagination had run away with me; if what I had anticipated in the Indian Ocean had been surpassed, I might have exaggerated the difficulties here. I could not deny that the wind was strong, that the waves broke; but

Lehg II was quite equal to it and was never in danger.

What I had had to suffer to get so far! Out of respect for those gallant sailors of old Spain, for all those who have perished in those desolate regions, I had to admit that the danger existed. Still, I had the impression that I should find calm ahead; and that was what happened. I had come here expecting the worst, though convinced that no difficulty would be insurmountable; expecting the 'impossible,' I came to believe that I was seeking death; maybe what was really beyond the limit did not appear so to me and I was being irreverent. The memory of the Indian Ocean must have made me feel *blasé* about all I experienced and it took the sting out of every difficulty.

Towards the end of the afternoon I ran out of the zone of wind into a calmer one, with a clearer sky. To the South I could see, shimmering whitely, the coruscating reflection of the Antarctic ice.

The current was carrying me on my road towards the East. About midday on the 24th the wind veered to the North. Numbers of cormorants came close to inspect the boat; there is nowadays so little navigation in this area that the presence of any ship is a surprise for them. I had still 90 miles to before striking the longitude of Cape Horn.

That night the north wind had already risen to gale force. I only put my nose outside from time to time to see whether there was anything ahead.

How full of meaning and menace is the sound of those two words: Cape Horn! What a vast and terrible cemetery of seamen lies under this eternally boiling sea! Fear adds its chill to that of the atmosphere, the terror that lurks in a name and the sight of these seas.

Here, everything seems to be attracted and drawn towards the depths, as by some monstrous, supernatural magnet. Had I had a larger surface of wood under my feet, I could have calmed my nerves by pacing the deck, but no; I could not walk my thoughts under control.

Fear of the storm? No. Apprehension that sprang, I felt, from legend, from all that I had been told about these regions. Of all storms, that which lurks invisible in an atmosphere of terror is the worst.

As my boat neared the headland I tried to pierce the unknown with the sword of reason, as though this were my last opportunity to think and to live. Perhaps in a few moments all would be over.

Yet that dim light of my compass on this dark Antarctic night made me look with tenderness on these wrought planks, flesh of the beautiful trees of my country, fashioned by human knowledge into a boat. It seemed to me that they were more in their place on land, living under the murmur of warm light breezes; if they had souls, they would reject the present to which I was exposing them. My voyage had been like a stairway which I ascended step by step, until I found myself here. Here, hard by Cape Horn. Had it been announced to me as a child, I should not have believed it.

They were ringing in my ears with a note of doom, as if they came from the depths of the sea or the height of Heaven, those true words that I could not or would not understand, spoken at Valparaiso before I set out for Cape Horn.

'Wouldn't you like to leave your log here? So that your pains may not be wasted?'

The voice that spoke was trying to be persuasive without sounding ominous. What they wanted to insinuate was quite clear to me: they were not at all confident of my success; they felt that I was lost before I started. But I was full of curiosity about Cape Horn. I wanted to see it, live it, touch it, feel it. . . .

Here in my travelling library, close to me, were the records of Cook, of Bougainville, of so many other navigators, books that I had read and re-read. I remembered the enthusiasm I felt on hearing the news that Al Hansen had succeeded in rounding Cape Horn from East to West, a feat nowise diminished by his terrible end. Hansen had been powerless to escape the curse that broods between the 50° of the Atlantic and the 50° of the Pacific. I felt his Calvary in my flesh only to think of it.

Yet I had taken it upon myself to round the Cape as the only way to make port, refusing to admit any other course. All or nothing. As *Lehg II* neared the grim promontory, through hours made infinitely long by impatience and anxiety, I threw my last card on the table of life.

If luck was against me, it would be easy to say:

'It was lunacy to attempt Cape Horn alone, in a 9-tonner — barely that.'

But what if I succeeded?

Imperceptibly, perhaps, the longing of all those who would have liked to make the attempt and were unable to do so, or the hopes of those who had tried without success, crept towards me. Perhaps I had the help of those who perished in this trial; perhaps I was not quite so alone as I thought. Perhaps the seamen of all latitudes were spectators of this struggle against the squalls and the darkness. Perhaps too, this darkness would grow darker yet, that the flickering lantern would cease to glow in front of my eyes, whose lids would close to see nothing any more on earth, now, or ever. This light, of little practical use, was more of an inseparable and invisible companion, standing between me and chaos. Life shone in it, the light of illusion or hope in the possibility —perhaps—of triumph.

It was midnight. According to my speed, Cape Horn should now be abeam. The wind was high and the seas heavy. In the cabin I had to cling to hand holds to avoid being thrown against the panels.

Sitting under the light of my little paraffin lamp, I was trying to repair the tell-tale when a shock threw me forward; my face crashed near the deadlight on the other side. The pain was terrible. I was half stunned, but noticed that I was bleeding violently from the nose. Fumbling, I found some cotton-wool and held it to my face to check the bleeding. Then I let myself fall, sick and dizzy, into a corner. It took me several minutes to pull myself together. I did not know exactly what had happened. I feared that the frontal bone might be fractured; in that case, what should I do? Groggy as I was, I succeeded in grasping the situation; I remembered that the boat was still going on and thought of what could happen. I began to explore my jawbone tenderly, looking for a possible fracture. I stopped for a moment. My fingers were wet with blood. No, the chin was all right. The pain was still acute, but my mind was becoming more lucid. As I touched my nose I felt a sharp stab of pain and noticed that there was an abnormal amount of play. So I had a broken nose. Ouf! that was nothing. I decided to look for the worst, for what I most feared: the eyes. I felt them; no damage. What a relief! I continued along the supra-orbital ridge; my fingers found the lips of a wound on the forehead.

After half an hour, a long half-hour, the bleeding began to ease off.

Cape Horn had made me pay toll. Given the speed at which the boat was travelling, I should now be just past it.

For the rest of the night the wind blew furiously from the North; but in the morning it eased off and backed to S.W.

I could not observe the slightest scrap of land; only a bank of clouds to the North indicated its presence. I took advantage of the relative calm to bail; and I made a trip to the mirror to see what it had to say. My face was a horrid mess, swollen, distorted and bloodstained. But that was nothing. I was back in the Atlantic.

Vito Dumas

ON September 3, 1966, after I had been at sea on my own for 88 days, having left Falmouth on June 14 in my 32 foot ketch *Suhaili*, we crossed the parallel of latitude 40 degrees south. There is no particular significance about this parallel of latitude except that it marks the geographical northern limit of the Roaring Forties and the Southern Ocean. It was not a good feeling entering the roughest ocean in the world with three weeks of winter remaining, but there was, of course, no sudden change in the weather; the effect was purely psychological. My longitude at the time was about 1 degree west, which put me about 1,000 miles south and west of Capetown.

My plan to sail right on round the world at about latitude 40 degrees, going further south only to avoid New Zealand and of course to go round Cape Horn which lies about 55 degrees south. This meant that the next 14,000 miles of the 30,000 mile voyage, nonstop round the world, would be spent in the Southern Ocean. This was the part of the voyage I had been dreading most as I just did not know how *Suhaili* would respond in the enormous seas that can build up in this vast expanse of ocean which no land disturbs in its constant easterly passage around the world. No one had ever tried to sail right through it nonstop before; they had always broken the journey in either Australia or New Zealand for rest and repairs to the boat, and I had no way of telling whether a boat and its equipment would stand up to the fatigue of 140 days constant buffetting in rough weather.

Ordinarily one would not attempt to go into the Southern Ocean at any time other than during the summer, but I had worked out my voyage plan so that I would round Cape Horn at the best possible time, in January, the Southern Hemisphere's mid summer. In order to time my arrival off Cape Horn for mid January, I had no choice but to pass Capetown at the beginning of my passage through the Southern Ocean, and probably an easier rounding of Cape Horn, or an easier passage through the Southern Ocean and the prospect of storms off Cape Horn, and I had decided to take the former choice.

I did not have long to wait for my first taste of bad weather as on September 4 a full gale blew up and lasted for about twelve hours. The wind direction remained north-northwest throughout, so the seas were all from the same direction, and I was able to keep the boat on a steady course with the stern of the boat to the seas. I had reduced sail right down to a 40 square foot storm jib, no mainsail, and a very small bit of mizzen to help keep the boat balanced. This gave her sufficient power to keep moving, but not enough so that she rushed down the front of the waves and threatened to broach. My policy at this stage was very much to put as little strain on the boat as possible and let her ride the waves as comfortably as she could.

Although the wind died a little at nightfall, the barometer continued to fall, and the following afternoon the wind rose again from the northwest. This time, however, a large line of towering dark cumulus came up from the southwest, and as this cloud reached us the wind rose and backed round to the southwest in about ten minutes, and the barometer immediately began to rise. We had experienced the passage of a typical cold front. I reduced sail immediately and put her stern to the northwesterly sea, but as the southwesterly wind continued to blow it slowly built up a cross sea, and we began to have a very unpleasant motion. The northwesterly sea was pitching the boat, and the growing southwesterly sea was throwing her over as the waves hit. For a while I steered trying to keep the stern pointing at each wave as it came along, but after a while the boat seemed to be reasonably comfortable, just rolling heavily, when a cross wave hit, and as I was feeling tired I turned in for a short rest.

My bunk was on the port side and sufficiently narrow to keep me jammed in it when asleep so that I could not be thrown about by the boat's motion. I had been asleep for about two hours when, at 0240, I was awakened to find my whole world on its side. The boat had been smashed over onto her port side by a large southwesterly wave. Quite how far she went over I do not know, my first recollection is of everything stored in the starboard bunks falling straight down on top of me which would indicate an angle of at least 90 degrees. I struggled upright in my bunk, conscious only of the fact that the deckhead was now acting as a bulkhead, and I was being bombarded by biscuits, fruit, jam, nuts, and everything else stored in the starboard bunk which was now the deckhead. I started to clamber up toward the starboard

bunk, getting soaked in the process by water coming in through the skylight when suddenly the boat swung upright, and I was thrown across the boat, landing on my head in the starboard bunk.

I was convinced by the speed with which the boat had swung upright that the masts must have broken, and, freed of the top weight, the boat had swung upright more quickly than usual. So the first thing I did was find a torch, open the hatch, and check the masts and rigging. It was still blowing a good Force 8 on deck, and spray was flying all over the place, but to my surprise the torch's beam showed both masts and all the rigging intact, and the boat was still holding a comfortable course. I closed the hatch and found my oilskins in the chaotic mess below and put them on. The rigging would have to be checked properly, but there was no point in getting soaked doing it, as a cold would only sap my strength. The cabin sole was awash with water, but pumping out would have to wait until I was sure everything was secure on deck.

It was quite impossible to look into the wind, as the spray was coming horizontally off the top of the waves, and when it hit one's eyes it was blinding for nearly a minute. So with my back to the wind I slowly checked round the deck, relashing the sails to the booms where the force of the wave hitting the boat had torn them loose. The only damage appeared to be to my self-steering equipment; one of the wind vane stanchions had been bent over about 30 degrees. The force of the knockdown must have been very strong to

209

achieve this as the stanchion was 1½-inch-stainless-steel tube with ¼-inch-thick walls. Where the ⅝-inch-thick plywood vane had hit the mizzen cap shroud, it had been cut into for about 10 inches, and the shroud was only one inch circumference wire. There was nothing I could do about the self-steering in that wind, so I lashed it to prevent it from putting pressure on the shroud. Then I threw the tail of the mainsheet and the mooring ropes over the stern to check the boat's movement. Provided the boat was hardly moving, she seemed to bob over the waves like a cork. The motion was most uncomfortable on board, but the boat was safer. It was when she ran down a wave front that the trouble developed as the rudder had less bite, and there was a greater chance of broaching.

Having secured everything on deck, I went below and pumped the boat dry and then began to tidy up the mess. A lot of the food had been spoiled and this I collected and threw overboard. It was while clearing away the mess that I became aware of the first serious damage. *Suhaili* has quite a high coach house, and the wave had hit this with the same force that it hit the hull. The hull had taken the blow, but the coach house had been shifted, and every time a wave rolled over the starboard side a lot of water was finding its way below through a ¼-inch gap between the coach house and the deck, sending water cascading down over my chart table and the radio, as well as the starboard bunk. This was not a job I could tackle at night, so I covered the chart table and radio with a piece of canvas to protect them as

much as possible. By 0500 I had things reasonably shipshape and decided to make a cup of coffee. I pumped water up from the water tanks, but what came out was an evil-smelling brown mixture. I supposed this must be bilge water that had somehow got into the supply pipe, but although I pumped for some time the water remained brown and oily. Rather than change tanks, I filled the kettle from one of my emergency containers, had my coffee, and then tried to sleep, fully clothed in oilskins and wrapped in a spare jib for warmth. I slept fitfully until 0800, when I made a big breakfast of porridge with plenty of sugar and condensed milk, and then I took stock of the situation.

The greatest threat to the boat appeared to be the loosened coach house; if it received another blow like the previous one it would probably be carried away immediately, and with an open hole 14 feet by 7½ feet in her deck *Suhaili* would soon be swamped. I got out the hand drill and some brass bolts I had put on board for no particular reason except that they might come in handy and spent the whole day drilling through the internal covering board and tightening the coach house back into place. I managed to get some white lead paste into the gap first to help seal it, but, even so, once I had done the best I could the join remained a source of drips for the rest of the voyage. The wind eventually began to ease in the late afternoon, and I was able to alter course slightly to the north and head up to get clear of this weather pattern until I could effect some half-decent repairs. The constant dripping of water into the boat, apart from keeping everything wet which made life unpleasant, was not good for instruments, and eventually the radio gave up, the salt water having corroded a wire inside. This presented a new problem as it meant that were I to continue the voyage I would have to close land from time to time just to report my position and the fact that I was safe and well.

The self-steering gear I repaired two days later when the wind was down to about Force 3. I carried two spare stanchions, and it did not take long to unbolt the plywood panel from the bent vane and rebolt it in the new one. It was just not the sort of job to tackle in any wind at all, unless one wanted to go hang-gliding in the Southern Ocean holding onto 20 square feet of vane.

Having got the boat as seaworthy as possible, I turned my attention to the fresh-water problem. My tanks held a total of 96 gallons, or roughly ⅓ gallon per day if the voyage took 300 days, as I roughly expected. I had traveled about a quarter of the distance, and for some reason, probably due to a loose filling pipe connection, I had nothing but contaminated water in the tanks. I had about 8 gallons in polyethylene containers and about 100 cans of beer. I reckoned on being able to reach Australia within 50 or so days, so if I allowed myself a pint of water and a can of beer a day I should have no real problem, and at least it would give me time to think of alternative methods of obtaining drinking water. The alternative was to head north for Capetown, now only about 600 miles away, but that meant giving up, and, having got this far, it seemed a little pointless pulling out when I knew that, God willing, I had all the necessities to reach Australia. It might not be the whole way round the world nonstop, but a half was better than a quarter.

My whole objective of sailing nonstop around the world now depended upon obtaining fresh water. The obvious source was rain, and fortunately there was plenty of that about in the Southern Ocean. The next rain squall that came along, I topped up the mizzen boom to bag the sail a little and hung a bucket just underneath the mizzen gooseneck. *Suhaili*'s mizzen boom has a channel cut into it to take the track for the foot of the sail, and as the rain fell onto the sail it ran down into this channel and then down to the gooseneck. I found that if I left the rain for a minute before starting to collect water, all the salt would be washed away, and I was left with beautifully pure water. In an average squall I could usually gather about 5 gallons, which, on an unrationed consumption of 2 pints a day, was enough for 20 days. Later on I tried to clean out the fresh-water tanks, but as they really needed washing out with fresh water, I decided not to bother and filled them with sea water to give the boat more ballast.

In fact, I found it quite possible to gather enough rain water to supply all my needs. The only time I got really short was when rounding Cape Horn, and there was so much salt spray around, the water I collected in the sail was not really drinkable. The only place where I found I could not get rain water at all was in the trade wind belts, but as progress

211

through these was quite fast, a 10-gallon supply was more than adequate to see me through them.

The realization that it was going to be possible to try and complete the voyage, provided the boat held together, gave my morale a tremendous boost which was much needed. By this time I had no dry clothing left, and no way of drying anything out except by wearing clothes when I went to sleep in my sleeping bag. To keep my bunk reasonably dry I had made a counterpane of a piece of canvas so that the constant drips of water from around the coach house fell on that instead of my sleeping bag.

My confidence regained, I stopped heading north and turned east once more. The weather pattern had not changed, and I had six gales of Force 8 or more within a ten-day period, but I was gaining knowledge and confidence with each gale. Four days after the knockdown, the bogey struck again, however, this time at the self-steering gear, and the rudder which was connected to the wind vanes snapped in two. I carried a spare lashed on deck and spent a frustrating morning trying to get the lower end into its socket some 5 feet below the water's surface. I realized that if I could not manage this from on deck I was going to have to dive into the water to do it, and as the sea water temperature was about 1° Celsius, I was not at all enthusiastic. Try as I could, however, I just could not get the rudder in, and so eventually I reluctantly accepted the inevita-ble and stripped off my clothing. Just before going overboard I put a bottle of brandy on deck so that I could get at it quickly once the job was completed. I slowly climbed into the water. It felt absolutely freezing, and the more I immersed myself the harder I found it to breathe. Eventually I was completely in and my breaths were short gasps and getting shorter, and I was going numb with cold. Obviously I would not be able to stand this for long, so I duck-dived down and put the bottom end of the rudder into its socket as quickly as I could. I scrambled back on deck and grabbed the brandy. Looking down at my body I saw it was blue with cold, and I hardly felt the brandy going down my throat. Once it hit my stomach, however, a warm glow began to spread outward, and it was rather interesting watching my skin turn from blue to pink again.

Our first week in the Southern Ocean had been eventful to say the least, but the boat was still seaworthy, I was still fit, and apart from the loss of radio communications we were no worse off than we had been a week before. The remainder of the voyage, some 23,000 miles, was still before us, but having survived our baptism from the Southern Ocean, I felt much more confident of our ability to get round, and, in fact, 224 days later, after a total of 313 days at sea, *Suhaili*, looking battered and worn, sailed back into Falmouth harbor, the first boat to have sailed nonstop around the world.

Robin Knox-Johnston

94

95

96

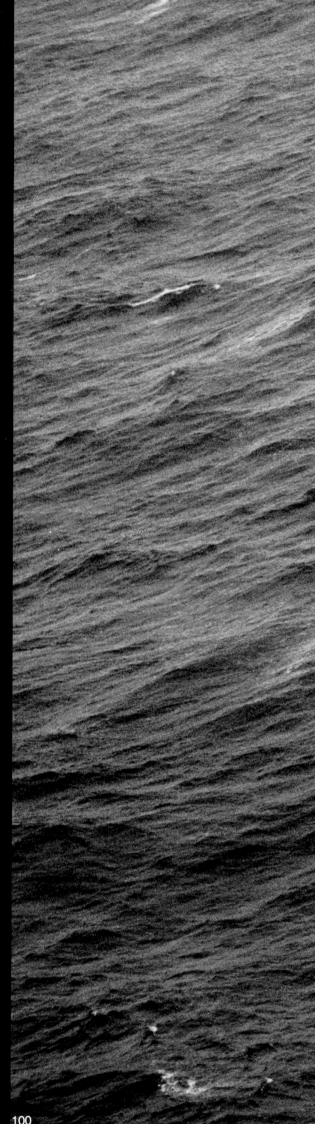

Since the British have a special respect for unusual accomplishments at sea, it is no wonder that Francis Chichester (Figs. 98, 99) was knighted. Not only did he win the first Single-Handed Transatlantic Race, held in 1960, but he also sailed around the world in 225 days at the age of sixty-five. While Chichester and his *Gipsy Moth IV* made one stop in Sydney, Robin Knox-Johnston and his *Suhaili* (Fig. 100) made no stops at all. After 313 days at sea, he reached his starting point in Falmouth in April 1969.

"I stood there and stared at the cliffs. There it was. This was the moment I had dreamed about and prepared for," wrote the sixty-year-old Alec Rose on April 1, 1968, as he rounded Cape Horn. He had to endure two calms in the Atlantic. After a year and twelve days he was back home again (Fig. 101). While Alec Rose, who was later knighted, sailed around the world in his *Lively Lady* "just for fun," Alain Gliksman (Fig. 102) was out for victory. He wanted to be the fastest in the Transatlantic Race of 1968. But, even though his prospects for winning were excellent, he had to give up and put his *Raph* in to port. The steering mechanism had broken. Eric Tabarly (Fig. 105) and his *Pen Duick IV* took part in this race too. He prepared carefully for the lonely voyage at sea. Here Tabarly is shown checking his automatic pilot. Without this device, modern single-handed sailing would be impossible. Chay Blyth crossed the Atlantic, too, but in a rowboat. Then he was drawn to the long swells of the Pacific. Like Knox-Johnston, he too, sailed nonstop around the world. But Blyth traveled from east to west against the winds of the roaring forties." On August 6, 1971, after 302 days at sea, he and his *British Steel* reached their home port of Humble (Fig. 103).

101

102

103

To sail around the world without stopping at any port and without seeing anything but water, the sky, and a boat is a true test of both a man and his craft. Bernard Moitessier, the originator of this idea, set out on such a solo voyage in 1968, as did Robin Knox-Johnston and Nigel Tetley. Tetley's trimaran *Victress* sank just short of her goal. Knox-Johnston was the winner. Moitessier did not complete the loser. He simply kept on sailing, passing the Cape of Good Hope for the second time. He had sailed around the world in 150 days and set a new record. But he did not want to return to Europe. "I'll sail to where I can drop my anchor anywhere I please, where the sun is just as free as the air and the sea."

VII AND THE SEA IS SO FAR

The first human being who set foot on or in the water entered an alien element and learned that life at sea is less comfortable and predictable, as well as far more difficult, spartan, and dangerous than a respectable life on land. Philosophers, poets, scientists, dreamers, and even sailors themselves have tried time and again to answer the question of why men put out to sea. As yet, none of them has come up with a completely satisfactory answer. Why, for as long as we can remember, have men alone or in pairs or in groups or families set sail and voluntarily exposed themselves to hardships and dangers they could have avoided by staying on land? To circumnavigate the world, a sailor has to find his way past dangerous capes, horns, reefs, and cliffs. He has to survive icy storms, searing heat, and oppressive calms. And if he finally manages to reach his home port again, many miles and months later, what does he have for his trouble? Nothing but a wiggly line around a globe, the trail—30,000 miles long—that his wake cut behind him, a distance the equivalent of ten Atlantic crossings or of thirty passages from Cowes to Lisbon or Annapolis to Miami. But for many sailors, a voyage is appealing only if it offers something new, taking them into unknown and distant waters and promising danger and adventure. Driven by the desire to be the first or the fastest, some few sailors bent on breaking records are always putting out to sea to win their places in the annals of sailing history. Joshua Slocum, Vito Dumas, Francis Chichester, Bernard Moitessier, David Lewis, and Jörgen Meyer are all men of this breed, and their names will always be synonymous with good seamanship and a pioneering spirit.

Whoever is the first to accomplish something remains the first. His triumph cannot be taken away from him. But those who hold speed records or who win fame by making a particular passage in a smaller boat than had ever sailed that route before can be dethroned at any time. The American William Albert Robinson, for example, holds two records. He was the first to sail around the world with only a two-man crew, and he made this voyage in the smallest boat that has as yet circled the globe. Starting from New York in the early 1930s, he sailed his 32-foot *Svaap* through the Panama Canal, around the world, and back to New York again. He did not, however, set any records for speed. His Tahitian crewman, Etera, acted as something of an anchor on this voyage. No sooner did Etera set foot on land than he was in trouble with the police or some other authorities. Robinson's departures often had to be delayed until he could beg, buy, or bribe his friend out of waterfront jails.

"The sea calls us to action," Robinson once wrote to a friend in New York. "I am in my element when the breakers come foaming over my bow and my wake is aboil behind me." For him, the open sea was a dangerous and unpredictable opponent, one that no man would ever be able to conquer but one that every man should encounter at some time in his life. Many years later, Robinson won his personal feud against the forces of nature. In a new vessel, 70-foot *Varua*, jointly designed by Herreshoff and Burgess, Robinson went out to meet his enemy face to face in the "roaring forties" of the South Pacific. He engaged his foe and survived.

The sailing clan has always been peopled by rather eccentric individualists. In character, they may be strong or weak, anxious or bold, free or inhibited, but whatever else they are, they are surely descendants of Columbus, Fletcher Christian, Captain Bligh, and Cook, followers in the footsteps of the Luckners, Lindemanns, and Störtebekers. In most sailors, the fierce, untamed, weather-hardened aspect of their character, the one they need to haul in a genoa those last crucial millimeters and the one that sends them on nonstop voyages around the world—that aspect is usually (and fortunately) balanced by a calm, cheerful, contented, and romantic streak that will make a wide detour around anything that even faintly reeks of competition or record-breaking.

The men and women who take to the oceans of the world today and let the wind carry them to sunnier climes expect something very different from a voyage around the world, even if they have difficulty formulating in words exactly what it is they are looking for. "Some people sail to win races," Mac said. He had worked his way up to boatswain on the racing ketch *Sturmvogel*, then turned his back on racing. He has since sailed around the world twice in his own boat. "Others," he went on, "sail just for the sake of sailing or just to get away from one place and go to another. Me? I sail . . . because . . . well . . . why shouldn't I?"

In 1928, Erling and Julie Tambs set out in their 39-foot Colin Archer cutter *Teddy* with the stated intention of sailing around the world. On the first leg of their journey, their son Tony was born.

"Life at sea is good for my boy," the proud father said. "Besides, there's nobody out here to upset him or stuff a bunch of ridiculous pills in his mouth." When the family increased by one more in New Zealand, things got a bit cramped on *Teddy*. Unfortunately, the Tambses were not able to complete their voyage. On May 9, *Teddy* was caught in a powerful current and smashed against the reefs of the Challenger Islands. The Tambses were becalmed at the time and therefore could not sail free of the current. By some miracle, they made their way safely to shore through the dangerous surf, each parent carrying a child.

Professor Roger Strout and his wife Edith were the first married couple to complete a voyage around the world. This couple from Maine made their journey in the years 1934 to 1937 in a replica of Slocum's *Spray* that they built themselves. Although the Strouts had never set foot on a sea-going vessel, they did not let that stop them from building their dream yacht, *Igdrasil*, which was ready for launching in 1934.

"It ought to be a sturdy boat," the proud shipbuilder told his friends before setting out on *Igdrasil*'s maiden voyage. "After all, I've pounded almost 10,000 nails into it." When the Strouts left Jacksonville, Florida, in June, 1934, they had no idea that they had just begun a journey around the world. "It just happened all by itself," the seafaring professor remarked once, and what did in fact happen was a successful 38,000-mile circumnavigation with a long layover in New Zealand. A high point in the Strouts' trip came when Alan Villier's *Joseph Conrad* sped past them under full sail on the Pacific. In recognition of the Strouts' accomplishment, the Cruising Club of America awarded them the club's gold medal for long-distance sailors,

223

the Blue Water Medal.

After careful planning and extensive preparations, William and Phyllis Crowe also made a successful and remarkably storm-free voyage around the world. Both had considerable sailing experience before they set about building their own schooner on the beach at Waikiki in the 1930s. It took them three years to complete their boat, which they christened *Lang Syne*. Then almost another ten years passed before the Crowes could begin their four-year trip around the world. At a Samoan festival in Pago Pago, they kept an engagement to meet their old sailing friends, Irving and Electa Johnson, who were trying out a new *Yankee* at the time. Since then, the Johnsons must have circled the earth seven times in their different *Yankees*. That, too, is a world record.

Whenever there is talk about people who, at one time or another, have exchanged a secure shore existence for a few square yards of swaying deck under their feet and who have then spent part of their lives afloat on the Seven Seas—on such occasions the name of Eric Hiscock, the "pope of long-distance sailors," is bound to be mentioned. Eric and Susan Hiscock, both from Yarmouth, are rarities among voyagers because both of them had been sailors since childhood and had thousands of miles of sailing experience behind them before they made their first cruise around the world. After extensive sailing in the North Sea and a honeymoon voyage to the Azores, the Hiscocks decided, in July, 1952, to take their 30-foot sloop *Wanderer III*, designed by Jack Laurent, on a circumnavigation. For seventeen years, the knife-edged bow of this little sloop sliced through the waters of the world's oceans.

Hiscock, who is well known for his technical books on long-distance sailing as well as for accounts of his sailing experiences, is the very model of the sober, undramatic long-distance sailor.

A successful ocean voyage in a sailing yacht is never a spontaneous adventure that begins whenever it pleases the yachtsman and that leads him anywhere the wind happens to take him. Innumerable journeys have, of course, begun in this casual way, but very few of them have ever come to satisfactory conclusions. Voyages of this kind, like any other enterprise that is worth undertaking at all, require a certain amount of planning. The greater the care that goes into the preparations, the greater the likelihood of a successful voyage.

It is as simple as that.

But even careful planning, a seaworthy boat, good seamanship, and extraordinary courage cannot always guarantee success. Beryl and Miles Smeeton had to learn this bitter lesson the hard way. They were both rank neophytes when they bought their 46-foot ketch *Tzu Hang* in 1950. On their attempt to sail around the world, they were defeated twice by the stormy waters off Cape Horn. They first capsized in the spring of 1956 and barely managed to reach the coast of Chile, sailing with a jury rig. They spent several months repairing their yacht, then took on Cape Horn again almost a year after their first disaster. But once again their fearful opponent struck them down. *Tzu Hang* capsized again. The mast was lost and the cabin smashed. With a combination of luck, ingenuity, and iron discipline, the crew brought the yacht into Valparaíso, both boat and crew very much the worse for wear. When friends asked Miles if he was going to make a third run, he answered brusquely, "Once is enough. Twice is one time too many." He had *Tzu Hang* loaded onto a freighter, and the yacht took a piggyback ride home to England. But Cape Horn was still there. In the third round, *Tzu Hang* and the Smeetons emerged victorious. This time, however, they had Bob Nance, the brother of the famous sailor Bill Nance, on board to help them.

But even if a sailor does not set out to win a victory over the forces of nature, has no personal feud to settle with her, is not intent on putting his boat and himself to any ultimate test, but simply delights in easy sailing, every mile of a world cruise can contain hidden dangers. The tragic voyages of the Baileys and the Robertsons show how a moment of idyllic sailing on a blue ocean can turn into catastrophe within seconds and force a crew into a last-ditch battle for their very lives, even in the absence of Cape Horn or hurricanes. In the early 1970s, the two yachts *Auralyn* and *Lucette* were rammed by whales in the Pacific and sank within minutes. With luck, determination to live, and "a well-developed sense of the ridiculous" (Dougal Robertson), the castaways survived and were picked up after 117 and 37 days, respectively.

"What do you think? Shall we take a trip around the world on this boat? Just imagine drinking milk from coconuts on an island in the Pacific and swimming in crystal clear water while the anchor of our yacht lies on a white sandy bottom and the stern is tied to a palm tree. How would you like that?" With this kind of persuasion, Wilfried Erdmann convinced his bride Astrid to set out on a honeymoon cruise in August, 1969. He spoke with the voice of experience because he had been the first German to sail around the world alone. Astrid's pleasure in this trip was repeatedly dampened by serious bouts of seasickness, which she struggled to combat with the aid of tea, hardtack, and plain boiled rice. Still, toward the end of her trip she wrote, "All I want is a tiny little apartment with a big mirror in it and something to eat and drink."

Where Wilfried Erdmann had to do a lot of convincing to lure his wife on board for a trip around the world, Peter Kammler achieved the same end with very few words. He picked up the telephone and asked Beate, who was studying for an exam, "Wouldn't you like to sail around the world with me?" Another three years passed before the Kammlers had sold their cars, stored their furniture, and saved enough pennies. In 1970, they were ready to "make their escape from soft middle-class living." On their four-year journey, many of their hopes and dreams were fulfilled, but Beate could not overlook the disappointments and hardships either.

I'm very run down. My eyelids itch. In fact, I itch all over. I have aches and bruises everywhere because we're knocked about so much. Every bone and muscle hurts, and we're losing weight. It has become ultimately clear to me that I was made for a lazy and comfortable life.

She added: "You won't get me across the Atlantic in a sailboat again."

Neil Hollander

We have been at sea for two months, out of sight of land, and have not encountered even one ship. The coast of South America lies far astern, and *Fiona*'s bowsprit points insolently and unerringly toward the island world of Polynesia. The sheer, endless expanse of a not-always-peaceful Pacific has sheltered us for 5,000 miles. Two months—sixty sunrises and sixty sunsets—each unique and unforgettable, unspoiled and untouched by smog, haze, television antennas, billboards, skyscrapers.

Only at sea does the sun rise clean, clear, and full of hope and warmth from the bed of nature, and sink softly contented, and utterly fascinating, its work done, with the promise of the next day. Alone in the small world of the boat, forgotten on the wide sea, true value and meaning still prevail, and only here is the sun still regarded with feelings of respect and love. And just as the high points of a play, opera, or story are found in the opening and closing scenes, so the sunrise and sunset become the festive moments of each day. Everything makes sense; again the sun turns around the earth and you, in turn, around the sun.

But now there's land ahead! "Land ho!" rang out this morning just after breakfast. Neil had seen it first, a small irregularity of the horizon, "Land ho!" and the last, carefully hoarded chocolate bar has finally found an owner. Barely visible in the brilliance of the morning sun lies an island, a tropical South Seas atoll, the Tuamotus, Fakakarawa, complete with green palm trees, untouched white beaches, and everything that had built up in our thoughts, dreams, and fantasies. Two months we are at sea, or is it years? In any event, Valparaíso lies 5,000 miles behind us, but I cannot shake the feeling that our last port of call had to lie on the far side of another world and in another life. Have we only proceeded from point *A* to point *B*? Is our voyage only a chain of sixty small pencil marks on some crumpled, sometimes folded, sometimes rolled, and often smoothed second or thirdhand map? What is the true meaning of this undertaking; where is the enticement, the value, the meaning of a voyage under sail across the sea? Maybe in the handling of a manmade object of wood, fiberglass, or aluminum, with two masts, a rudder, and a keel? Maybe in the seamanlike mastery of sextant, log, chart, sheet, and halyard? Or is it in the ability to tie a bowline with one hand in the dark or to heave an eighty-pound shark or marlin aboard? No, surely not! All this is secondary—necessary and important, true—but still a by-product of the true adventure, which is you. You alone, your search for a new contentment, a new identity, and lastly your deep and natural need for spiritual and physical freedom. A return, even a regression, to the nature of your original environment and to yourself—as you were and lived thousands of years ago. Sailing certainly is an adventure, but not one made of and defined by storms, flat calms, masts, and miles. Rather it is coined of the rash and venturesome attempt to make yourself at home in the limitless, all-allowing and all-equalizing sea.

Alone or jointly, trusting only your own abilities, every day and hour at sea becomes an adventuresome experience in nature! What does it matter if the voyage lasts a week, a month, or a year? The danger clings to you—the danger is in you. All too often, hopes, feelings, and dreams have melted away, burst and broken asunder at sea, the pitiful remains of fellowship and friendship spit out by the ocean like so much sun- and salt-bleached driftwood and washed ashore somewhere. They can be found in the waterfront bars of Las Palmas, Papeete, Port Moresby, and Cape Town—lonely, broken, discouraged and powerless, and much poorer because the sea is strong and man is weak; the sea is all powerful and man is man—even at sea.

But should you accept the challenge and step into the ring with yourself, the sea will do its part for your success. It will accept you with open waves, give you sustenance and prospects, the same way it has always welcomed anyone pursuing a dream that could only be fulfilled behind far horizons, where water and air become one in the shimmering light.

I recall as if it were yesterday, the day when, puttering along the all or nothing, I leaned carefree against a sail bag secured to the rail, at peace with myself and my thoughts. My gaze wandered around, and suddenly the whole of the world that was important and relevant to me lay simple, surveyable, and uncomplicated before me. And I was the center of my world! The center point of the "now" looked exactly like the center point of the "yesterday," only discernible by an abstract intersection of longitude and latitude. It suddenly became clear to me that I was not only the center of my world, but that it moved with me and followed me, as long as I stayed at sea, out of sight of land. Much has been said about the overwhelming greatness, stunning beauty, bottomless depth and ever-present lurking danger, about the worth and wideness of the sheer, endless sea. Thousands of attempts have been made to explain and reenact the magic attraction the sea has on man's mind and body—in prose and rhyme, songs and poems, stories and fairy tales. But the final explanation remains open, the final secret veiled. No one will question the deep bond that Joseph Conrad, Herman Melville, Jack London, D. H. Lawrence, and John Masefield have had with the sea—the greatness and power these men have drawn from their love of the ocean, from life and living at sea. Thinkers and philosophers of any time who have never set foot on the swaying deck of a seagoing ship have not been able to avoid the spiritual dispute with the sea:

The sea is the highway of the globe. The sea is the playground of power and enterprise for all. The sea is the cradle of freedom. One who has no part of the sea is shut out from the good things and honors of this world.
Antoine de Saint-Exupéry

But when enticed, attentive, curious, and restless to coast or shore, the last step has to be taken on your own. You have to try to rid yourself of the old habits and ingrained, learned behavior patterns of being, thinking, acting, and feeling, in order to be able to wade into it as the logical consequence of a spiritual growth process—born by the winds of freedom in the cradle rocked by the waves of a different life. "Should even the smallest drop of the open sea touch you, you shall be hers forever."

Much is different at sea; it has its own laws. As soon as the waters have closed in your wake, it has absorbed you without a trace, cut you off from your past. All yesterdays lie astern, and ties and relationships that influenced your action and thought the day before are severed and erased the moment the last mooring is slipped, the anchor lifted, and the sail set. As soon as the breakwater is past and the lighthouse left astern, the eternal urge and the restless dynamics of another element take over, slowly but inexorably permeating your thought, feeling, and action. There is no stopping and no returning at sea, even after you furl the sails and drop anchor. As soon as you entrust yourself to the sea, it carries you farther and farther and farther. The sea helps man become a nomad again at a higher level of being. What lies on the horizon? Where goes the drifting, where are the new pastures of body and soul? What lies ahead? The future, the past? I do not know and it is suddenly clear to me that I do not wish to drink one sip from that cup of knowledge. While I am following my thoughts, recalling days, hours, moments, conversations, and feelings, the coral island has come closer. The unaccustomed but familiar sound of foaming surf carries over, and the eyes, that have found nothing to focus on the horizon for weeks, are drawn magnetically to ragged palm fronds waving in the wind. Somehow they look like great friendly beings, waving us closer with their many green arms. I wake with a start. Oh damn, the anchor! We have completely forgotten about it! Land and anchor are known to be one. The beginning and end of every voyage belong to the anchor—at least according to Joseph Conrad—but our "forged symbol of hope" is still stowed nice and clean in the forepeak. I hasten to the forepeak, bang my head on the same beam for the hundredth time, pull the trysail away, heave a sack of potatoes aside.

"Hello anchor, wake up, there's work to do!" I know only too well that land means danger, and that approaching an atoll and sailing into a lagoon always require the utmost concentration. The sea does not forgive mistakes. Too many ships were lost when the men, a successful crossing almost behind them—"We have done it"—became negligent and superficial, and endangered the success of the voyage unnecessarily and carelessly.

We do not have to worry whether or not the motor will start because the slim hull of our seventy-year-young, gaff-rigged boat was never shaken by the vibration of a piston, nor have exhaust fumes ever fouled the air of the cockpit. We have to be doubly careful. We approach the channel. The two natural breakwaters open like a gate. A wide gate? A narrow one? At the moment it is trivial; we

228

have to make it through. We could use a little more wind, since we need momentum to pass through the entrance. The narrow openings of such lagoons occasionally spew forth veritable floods and masses of water that can easily put powerful ships in difficulty and danger. If the wind and the tides have driven and pumped too much water into the lagoon, and if they then decide to change at the same time, any attempt to sail into the lagoon will mean extreme danger for boat and crew.

We are lucky—*Fiona* moves slowly toward the entrance. A self-made leadline in hand—the weight is a heavy shackle given to us by a Spanish fisherman years ago—I stand leaning far out of the bow pulpit, looking for the best and least dangerous passage. I turn briefly toward Neil, trying to read his expression, to guess his thoughts. What is going on inside him? As if I did not know! All too often we have talked about this moment, discussed it, lived it over and over in our thoughts, read about it, dreamed about it: entering the lagoon of a tropical coral island! Robert Louis Stevenson, Jack London, Bernard Moitessier, and all the others were here to fulfill their dreams. Now it's our turn.

But we are not there yet. "Careful, over to starboard," I signal aft, when a dark head of coral appears in the middle of the passage. In the current, *Fiona* does not respond to the helm in the usual manner. We have to bear off to keep her moving, drifting toward the bare point of the breakwater. I hold my breath—a grinding sound from the keel? Is this far enough? It has to be! And then we are through. The water under the keel becomes noticeably shallower and changes color from moment to moment. Then it turns into glass; corals bloom in a variety that is hard to describe. Fish, in never-before-seen splendor and colors—striped, spotted, dotted—swim curiously around the boat like birds, as if they are welcoming us to their paradise. We make the shore in three short tacks. The anchor chain rattles and jumps all over the deck and capstan. The anchor drops with a releasing splash; the chain reels out. The anchor slides over coral, falls on the side, turns, then one of its arms buries itself deeply into the soft sand as if to say, "Hold it, that's it, this is good enough."

Harald Mertes

Whenever I leave a harbor, all the small worries that plague me fade away, and the clock that dominates our lives on land ceases to exist. A time of dreaming begins, a time when hours pass by as we dangle our feet over the bow of *Trismus*. The waves, like the flames in a fire, are always in motion. They hold a fascination similar to flames, catching our attention for hours at a time. Watching them, we leave our everyday world behind and enter a state in which our fascination borders on hypnotic trance and in which our thoughts run free.

And whenever I return from what I call my expeditions into the world of dream, I feel enriched, as though I had understood something that had been hidden from me on the day before. This feeling is particularly strong during a calm when the body, too, is at rest, when there is nothing to do, and when *Trismus* lies on the ocean with slack sails. We pass these hours watching the rise and fall of the slow, gentle swells that call up images of a sleeping giant's breathing. Off Mar del Plata, the *pampero* that had brought us from Rio left us becalmed among a flock of sea birds. Albatross, petrels, cormorants, and gulls were all there on the water, waiting, as were we, for a wind.

This was the day we made the acquaintance of the albatross. This bird has a powerful body covered with a fine, dense down that is usually white. It has a proud head with a long, yellow, hooked beak. Its wing span is immense, sometimes reaching as much as twelve feet. Its flight is every bit as intriguing as the motion of the sea. It usually travels alone and will follow a boat for hours or days on end, hardly ever moving its wings. It glides along majestically, following the contours of the waves with great precision. I never saw it dive for food. It never paid the slightest attention to the bread or the delicious leftovers we threw onto the water for it. It glided along on its course, oblivious to us. I think it must be a mythological creature that is nourished by the wind.

By comparison, it seems unimportant to know that at eleven in the morning on Wednesday, May 10, 1972, the wind died down to Force 2 on the Beaufort scale, the barometer read 1029 millibars, and that we had to keep the engine running until 7:40 that evening. Is it of the slightest interest to know that the wind shifted to the east and was blowing Force 3 and that on the next day we had to take a reef in the sail, only to shake it out three hours later and take it in once again soon after? Who really cares that we crossed the fortieth parallel with our engine turning over at a sedate 1,200 revolutions per minute, that we sighted our first penguins off the bow of *Trismus*, and that our position reckoning after ten days at sea showed us to be 960 miles from Rio? That makes an average speed of something under four knots. Nothing to write home about. Banal stuff.

I began to understand better and better why Captain Pedro Margalot was not the least bit astonished during a conversation in the Nautico when I told him about our plans. "Around the Horn from east to west? Why not? It's the best time of year." He said this without a trace of irony and as if it were the most natural thing in the world. A man in his mid-forties with graying hair and a physique that makes him look capable of hauling in a genoa of a thousand square feet with one hand, Capitan de Navio Pedro Margalot is justifiably regarded as one of the world's greatest specialists in sailing the high southern latitudes. Before he assumed the directorship of the Argentinian maritime office, he was captain of the schooner *El Austral* and plied the waters between the Falklands and Tierra del Fuego for years. To these by no means insignificant achievements, we should add that he skippered *El Gaucho* on the most difficult legs of her voyage around the world and sailed in *Ondine* when she won the Buenos Aires-Rio Race. The opinion of a man with these credentials has to be respected.

I would not have been surprised if he had reacted to my plans by shrugging his shoulders and saying, "You're crazy . . . ." But he did not. Instead, he said,

> That can be done. I'm not saying it's easy, but it can be done. Rounding the Horn from east to west . . . people make too much of a fuss about that. If you're going to do it, the winter is certainly the best time. When I say "the best time," all I mean is that the storms out of the west occur less frequently than in the summer, and, even if the ones out of the north and east are pretty rough, they can also help push you through. It will be cold, of course. What kind of heat do you have on board?"

I mentioned a good solid firebrick. Captain Margalot seemed a little surprised but not overly so. Captain Margalot has the capacity—rarely found in Latin Americans—to keep his feelings to himself. "Well, with a firebrick . . . The cold isn't really as bad as everyone says, you know. The worst it ever gets is around zero degrees Fahrenheit, but as a rule it ranges somewhere between 15 and 25 degrees. What's probably harder to take are the short days and the very likely absence of the sun. If you see it at all, it will barely bring the temperature up to 50. If you make it, *Trismus* would be, I think, the first yacht to round the Horn from east to west in the winter." I mentally strike the "if" and the subjunctive in his last sentence. The chances of success are not overwhelmingly in our favor, but, viewed from an optimistic perspective, they are reasonably good.

Better than Francis Chichester would lead us to believe when he writes: "More dramas have taken place in the waters off Cape Horn than in all the oceans of the world . . . ." Fine. We know that. I slap Chichester's book shut. There is no point in worrying my head over that, no point in giving the book to my cousin, who is absorbed in the cartoon adventures of Asterix. The nights are long and silent. Every day the sun describes a somewhat smaller arc on the horizon. Every day the temperature on *Trismus* sinks a little lower, and yesterday the flight of the albatross was accompanied by our first snowflakes.. I automatically cast a glance at the thermometer. It is 45 degrees at 6 a.m. A little heat from our brick before breakfast? Outside everything is still, too still. In less than twenty-four hours we will be in the strait of Le Maire. I have gotten more and more keyed up in the last two days, and I have even developed a tic: ten minutes cannot go by without my looking at the barometer: 1027, 1027, 1025, 1024, 1025 again. It creeps down very slowly as though it were hanging onto each millibar for all it

231

was worth. "Well, cousin, when do we get that homemade lobster bisque?" The pointer has just dropped down to 1022 . . . .

It started undramatically, a northeast wind of Force 2 that gradually picked up steam, jumped to 4, passed 6, and reached 7, accompanied by rough seas. The night before, I took two sextant readings that placed me one hundred miles short of the Strait of Le Maire. The day had been short and without sun. Now the darkness descended on us again. That's just as well. We can make out the lighthouse at San Diego better in the thickening blackness of the night. I keep expecting to see its beam between the starboard shrouds. I'll see it blinking soon. It will have to start blinking soon.

I don't think I have ever smoked as much as I did during the night of May 21. No sooner had I thrown one cigarette away than I had lit another. Then I would forget it until it began to burn my lips. Nerves! Nerves that had me mechanically chewing on the starboard side of my moustache or scorching the port side of it off because I kept holding the flame of my lighter to a still-burning butt without taking my eyes off the horizon.

The barometer keeps on falling until it hits 1016. Then I hear what sounds like a stroke on a bass drum. The first breaker runs off the deck. We're carrying only a staysail, but *Trismus* still shoots ahead, driven by a north-northeast wind of Force 8. Force 8? By midnight it may have reached 9 as we approach the Strait of Le Maire. I can't really judge this wind force. It is difficult to estimate the speed of a wind over thirty-five knots. There are too many factors that can distort your judgment. The roughness of the sea and your own emotional state are not the least of these factors. The anemometer? *Trismus* doesn't have one. I'm guessing that the gusts are peaking at Force 8. That estimate is good for my morale. It has a quieting influence. I'd like to pull it down to 7, but that would be cheating, and I wouldn't believe it anymore. I'm keeping Captain Margalot's pointers in mind. "Wait for the tide to turn before you go into the strait . . . ." Okay, I'll wait. When the wind strikes head on into the current coming out of the strait, it churns up immense, chaotic waves. The breakers intersect with each other, clash, and rise up in towers of foam that are swept away immediately. Sometimes, just after *Trismus* has climbed up a mountain of water and just before she plunges into the trough again, I can see the lighthouse on Cape San Diego marking the entrance to the strait. It is cold.

The waiting is nearly unbearable. But a lesson I learned on the thirty-third parallel is bearing its fruit now, and I'm glad to have had that experience. I suspect that *Trismus* would broach again if I forced my way into the strait too soon. My cousin is asleep. I envy him. Finally, at three in the morning, we make our approach to the strait. The sea is still rough, but the turn of the tide has calmed it considerably. The north-northeast wind continues to whistle unabated through the shrouds, and it drives us through the strait in three hours. At 6:45 a.m. the blinking of a lighthouse pierces the darkness briefly, then disappears again. The lighthouse of Buen Successo. *Buen Successo*! Good Luck! That is the message this lighthouse sends to sailors who reach the safe waters off Tierra del Fuego. Once we have left the

232

lighthouse at Buen Successo behind, there is nothing, not a flicker of light. Nothing but blackness. Cape Horn lies before us.

The morning of May 22 dawns pale. Snow is falling and it is cold. After holding steady at 1009, the barometer drops to 1002, 999 . . . . It is incredible, but the sea has grown rougher despite the protection that the coast of Tierra del Fuego should be giving us to the north. Swells out of the south-southwest rise up into steep, nearly vertical waves. Sometimes a genuine abyss opens up beneath our bow, a gorge whose pale, foam-streaked bottom lies some fifteen feet below us. Fifteen feet? How do I know how deep it really is? The albatross is no longer with us. For the seafarer in southern latitudes, the albatross is as useful a measuring instrument as the carpenter's folding rule is for him. The sailor knows that the albatross's wingspan is between nine and twelve feet, and when the bird glides close to the surface of the sea, a sailor can judge the height of the waves by the bird's wingspan. But the albatross left us long before we reached Le Maire. We don't see them anymore, those friendly companions that in the higher latitudes take the place of the merry dolphins that accompany the seafarer in tropical waters. We miss the albatross.

The barometer drops further to 994, to 992. The cold is biting, but in the cabin it is around 45 degrees and almost comfortable. When we heat up our firebrick on the Primus stove the temperature rises as high as 55. Downright toasty! But I can't tear myself away from the cockpit. I am fascinated by the spectacle of the sun rising from a crater of clouds whose sharply defined edges seem cut out by a scalpel. A stripe of light imparts a reddish glow to the snow-laden mountaintops of Tierra del Fuego and paints icy colors on the sea where the breakers leave patches of glistening jade in the dark, foam-streaked water. Petrels fly around our boat and dive now and then after some invisible prey.

The barometer reads 990. The Horn is less than a hundred miles ahead. The wind will surely shift into the west without abating. Not very promising conditions. The barometer is at 986 now and continues in its determined descent. We have no choice but to accept the evidence it presents. We are in a low. Sailing around Cape Horn under these conditions. Temptation creeps up on me; I force it away only to feel it sneak back again: a slight change in course and *Trismus* could be heading for the shelter of the Beagle Canal. A few hours later we could put in at Ushuaia. Then there would be a warm meal, sleep, solid ground under foot, quiet, warmth.

The freezing cold, the salt stinging your eyes, the exhaustion in every bone in your body, the battles with flapping sails, the struggle to wrestle them into sacks, the sheer effort of staying awake—all that was nothing. What was really hard, what we could hardly endure, was that temptation to change course and head for shelter. And of course, things got much worse. By 4:30 in the afternoon it was pitch dark. A little snow fell. At 6:15 the barometer read 983. The pointer has almost made a full backward turn around the dial. And then, as if my cousin and I didn't have enough problems, another turns up. We are only thirty-five miles from Cape Horn, and if we continue to sail at this same speed, we'll

233

round it in the middle of the night. It seems ridiculous to have sailed *Trismus* from Belgium and then not see Cape Horn when we round it. Would anyone travel to Rome to see the Sistine Chapel, arrive at night, make a tour through the Vatican, and then fly away again before dawn? No! We have to pass the Horn in daylight and close on, too, at arm's length if possible. So we put on the brakes; that is to say, we heave to. Only then, at that moment, do we become fully aware of the force of this storm. The legendary winds out of the "roaring forties" are no legend. They actually roar in the shrouds as *Trismus* heels over sharply. Before we close the hatch, I notice the height of the seas. Thirty feet at least, with or without an albatross as yardstick. The wind? Ten, maybe 12 on the Beaufort Scale.

The barometer has settled down at 983. It hasn't dropped any further for three hours. The low is stable now. We shouldn't always believe what the meteorologists tell us. We shouldn't make an oracle out of technology with all its instruments, electronic gadgets, omniscient computers, and barometers that supposedly can predict catastrophes. For there it was before us: the Horn, lying there peacefully in a gentle southwest wind, Force 3, that was hardly able to ripple the smooth surface of the water.

The storm has abated suddenly and unpredictably at about four in the morning. An alarming stillness sets in and we start up in panic. What's wrong? But nothing happens, nothing at all. We hear nothing but the whispering of a gentle breeze, Force 1, if that. It's a mere zephyr, like those you sometimes experience during races on the Mediterranean when you're hunkered down in the cockpit with just your nose sticking up above the rail, waiting for any faint stirrings of the air.

At this snail's pace we'll never reach the Horn before the best light for taking pictures is gone, and since we don't want to disappoint my photographer cousin, we start up the engine. This is the only way we can keep to our schedule and still catch the light we need for our historic photographs. At 11:30, an hour later than planned, we finally approach the Horn. It gradually becomes visible between the southern points of Decett Island. The east side of the Horn is green and wooded. It looks almost inviting. But at the foot of the cliffs, we see the ruins of a lighthouse. Scattered rocks and fragments of concrete are all that is left of this building that was swept away barely a month ago, in the last westerly storm. But now the weather is beautiful. We have the sunshine a tourist might wish for on a gray day in Saint Tropez. Not a cloud in the sky except for a few fluffy cumulus domes in the east. A formation of *pato libets* or cormorants—large, black, diving birds with white heads—fly around *Trismus*. Prompted by curiosity, they come in close and watch us spread our gear and clothing out on the deck to dry. We look like a floating laundry line. In the cockpit, a bottle has been cooling in a bucket for over an hour. The cork pops. Let the champagne flow!

So that is Cape Horn, this peaceful promontory touched by a springlike breeze. This is the place that sailors have nicknamed the "Himalayas of sailing." Himalayas? Today we could go up to it and touch it, as if it were a sleeping animal. Why not admit it? Along with my feelings of pleasure, to which the champagne is contributing, I also have a sense of disappointment. It's as if a beautiful, apparently unapproachable girl fell into your arms after your first compliment.

But I have even more to confess. I would have liked to present a dramatic picture of the Horn, one that the Dutch masters of the eighteenth century could have painted, one with deep, tragic shadows, towering waves, and howling winds that make your hair stand on end. In short, I would have preferred to tell a wild tale that would leave the reader grateful for his cozy hearth and slippers. I can't do it. My chance for a grand literary gesture is gone. Too bad. By the time you read this, I'll be busy building a thirty-five foot centerboard boat. I want it to be a reliable boat that I can take on long voyages and even venture to Antarctica with. I want this hull to be able to broach, roll over, take a triple somersault, and stand up straight again, undamaged and ready to receive its well-deserved applause from the crowd. But I'm beginning to think I may arrive at Terre Adélie under a spinnaker and in weather so warm that there are parrots nesting on the roofs. With my kind of luck, I wouldn't be surprised.

Toward evening *Trismus* came around onto the west flank of the Horn. It looked the way Cape Horn was supposed to look. It was a bare, craggy cliff against which high swells out of the west crashed in a haze of spray. There, at least, the decor lived up to the legend. But night was falling.

Trismus sails into the Bay of Nassau under a full moon. The glaciers over the bow glow in the silvery light. For the first time in three days, I can wash the dishes in the cockpit.

I am enjoying this domestic chore to an unusual degree, and I mention this to my cousin, who ascribes my euphoria to the champagne. Possible. But there can be other reasons for my intoxication besides the wine. The beauty of nature, for example, or the seals that are frolicking in our wake or, in some deep, hidden recess of the soul, the satisfaction of having realized a dream. Everything seems a bit unreal to me, and I slow down in all my movements in an effort to savor these remarkable moments that are passing too quickly. Now it is over. All that will remain of this day, May 23, are some memories that will quickly fade, some photographs, some slides taken on a bright blue-water voyage, a log book in which dampness has already begun to blur the entries made with a magic marker.

"Why Cape Horn? Why from east to west? Why in the winter?" Behind those questions there is still another that goes unasked. "What was the point of it?" Why did you do it?" My only reply is: "Why does anyone train five hours a day for four years to swim a 400-meter freestyle race in the Olympics? Why did Hillary climb the Himalayas? Why do people collect stamps, butterflies, or beer coasters? What's the point of those things? Only the wind knows."

Patrick van God

235

Spitsbergen—at 78° North, the northernmost of the inhabited lands—has always bewitched man. First, the whale and seal hunters came to its shores, often kept free of ice by the Gulf Stream. After the Atlantic whales had been decimated by abuse, and whaling was no longer profitable, explorers and scientists followed; at the end of the last century men like Nansen, Andrée, Amundsen, and Nobile used Spitsbergen as a point of departure for their expeditions. What could move ten German sailors to pick this unreal, foggy region, with subfreezing temperatures, for their vacation, while other sailors were spending the summer of 1976 in warmer climates? Of course a measure of adventure was involved. We wanted to sail where no yacht had ever gone before. We were challenged by the proximity of the ice; our wish was to sail between the ice pack and the icebergs. It might sound crazy, but we wanted to experience all that we had read in voyage and expedition journals about Spitsbergen and the Arctic. Like so many before us we were captivated by the charm of the Arctic. The English call it "Arctic bitten"—a very fitting description. Thus we decided in early 1975 to attempt to sail the 53-foot yacht *Wappen von Bremen*, flagship of the sailing fellowship with the same name, around Spitsbergen. Our group included myself, Rainer Persch, Otto Jeschonek, Klaus Tänzer, and Wolfgang Behrens, among others, who had undertaken several voyages with me to Greenland and Iceland. All four were experienced sailors. The group also included Christian Hetzer, Ulf Vagt, Tom Hamman, and Michael Rapp, whom I knew were good seamen and sailors, despite their youth. Finally, also among the crew was Hans-Georg Will, whose fifty years included a full measure of sailing experience.

Naturally, a voyage like the one we intended had to be planned and prepared carefully. My goal as a skipper was above all else to bring ship and crew back safe and sound on schedule. The ship itself was in excellent condition. In addition to the already existing charcoal stove we installed a kerosene oven. Even if it became very cold outside, we wanted to have a minimum of comfort inside the boat. The crew bought special polar underwear lined with artificial fur. We had some extra-large foul weather gear made so we could wear heavy overcoats under it.

Otto Jeschonek offered to sail ahead with the majority of the crew to Trømso in northern Norway. The others would follow by plane. On July 10, 1976, I took off from Hamburg with Rainer, Hans-Georg, and Wolfgang. It was one of the hottest days of the year, the temperature measuring 95°F (35°C). Trømso welcomed us with a temperature of only 50°F (10°C), a little taste of what was to come. Otto and the crew had prepared everything so that all we had to do was slip our moorings after making a little toast—an alcoholic tribute to Neptune, the ruler of the seas.

We left the Trømso Fjord under engine power. Despite the midnight hour, the sun was bathing the slopes of the mountains in a light yellow. The mountaintops disappeared in the fog that at times sank to water level. It

236

was to accompany us all the way to Spitsbergen. At times it lay as mist on the water; at other times it came at us in banks so dense we could hardly see the foredeck. After four days, Bear Island suddenly loomed out of the fog. The temperature had sunk to 39°F (4°C). The *Wappen von Bremen* anchored in the lee of this treeless island, which is inhabited only by a meteorological team. The only things visible were the ruins of a mining ghost town, abandoned since 1925. When financial conditions forced an end to mining, everything was left as it was. The cold of the Arctic has kept the wooden houses and the tools in good shape. Before we continued to Spitsbergen, the crew paid the ghost town a short visit. We sailed before the wind in a nice breeze, making decent headway, but were reduced to blundering around in the fog. Approaching Isfjord with a visibility as low as 150 feet was no mean feat, but with the help of the depth sounder and a conscientiously manned navigation board, we managed to make Longyearbyen, the capital of Spitsbergen. *Wappen* hove to at a wooden pier, right next to the coal-loading facilities. When the shifts changed, a few miners came to take a look at the rare guest. Longyearbyen exists only because of the coal, which has been mined here since the beginning of the century. The whole place consists of a few barracks and the loading docks. Long conveyor belts converge on the docks from the shafts, located outside of town. All buildings are covered with coal dust—four inches thick in places.

The next day visibility had improved and we left this unfriendly place called Longyearbyen for Ny Ålesund. A light drizzle fell from the low and shredded clouds; there was no wind anywhere. We tried to reach a point on the northern side of Isfjord under engine power. Soon *Wappen* was sailing out of the fjord under a light breeze, but in the meantime the thick fog had returned. We were feeling our way around Prins Karls Forland, situated in front and to the west of Spitsbergen, when, at its northern tip, the fog was ripped away and Spitsbergen lay in front of us in the brilliant sunlight. Snow-covered 3,000-footers reared up, with tremendous glaciers arching in between, reaching down all the way to the water. Ice chunks calved from the glaciers and crashed loudly into the water. As Rainer was admiring this awesome panorama through his binoculars, he called out in surprise:

"Look here, aren't there two red points moving on the north tip of Prins Karls Forland?" We went in closer immediately since people could be in danger. It proved to be Norwegian cameramen, whose boat was not seaworthy and who were stuck on the island. They had been waiting for rescue for fourteen days. We took one of them with us to Ny Ålesund.

The Kongsfjord, on which the settlement of Ny Ålesund lies, was still full of icebergs. We gingerly sailed around the ice chunks, under a bright blue sky, and dropped off our Norwegian on the old wooden pier. He was eager to organize the rescue of his colleagues and their bulky gear from here.

Ny Ålesund, the northernmost settlement in

the world, was inhabited by only fifteen scientists, who were studying the effects of the aurora borealis on radio communications. Curiously enough, because of the high northern latitude, the aurora appears there to the south. After a short side trip to Bloomstrand and Magdalenefjord, where we met the passenger ship *Europa*, *Wappen von Bremen* rounded the northern tip of Spitsbergen. The remains of the camp of a Russian expedition were still visible in Smeerenburgenfjord, close by the water on a mound of gravel. Those were the last markers of human civilization. Now the crew of *Wappen* was completely on its own. A flat, gray plain, called Reindeer Plain on the map, stretched to starboard. The wind fell progressively and we had to abandon our intention of visiting Woodenfjord. *Wappen*, rocking gently in a light ground swell on an otherwise smooth sea, headed northeast toward the island of Moffen. The edge of the Arctic ice shield would soon appear on the horizon. The compass started acting wild because of magnetic disturbances. The dial kept turning from side to side up to 60 degrees, without any apparent cause. The leaden silence was broken only by the puffing of a pair of walruses, which were swimming around inquiringly. The large-tusked and bearded male got as close as a few feet to *Wappen*.

We had already crossed 80° North a short while before, but we intended to penetrate as far north as possible. The wind had picked up; it now came from the north directly from the Pole and drove large snowflakes ahead of it.

The temperature sank below freezing. The helmsman stood on watch all bundled up, his hood strapped tight. Our hourly water temperature readings showed only 31°F (−0.5°C). We could not be far from the ice. Below decks, the two stoves were spreading a pleasant warmth.

Wappen still headed for the seven islands to the northeast of Spitsbergen. The captain of the watch on duty woke me before dinner. "Ice blink ahead!" A narrow white stripe on the clouds, caused by the reflection of the ice, was clearly visible above the horizon. An hour and a half later, the edge of the ice could be seen clearly. It ran generally northwest to southeast, and from the vantage point of the mast we could see that it touched land in the southeast. The ice was now thick enough to make passage impossible in that direction. We had to tack right by the edge of the ice and sail parallel to it to the northeast. But a new ice blink appeared ahead of us. The ice edge causing it was not as sharply defined as the first. *Wappen* penetrated into the world of the eternal ice. We had to run a slalom between the ice floes. Slowly the ice became denser again. Another tack. From the mast we could see some loose ice to the northeast. The wind blew ice cold from the north, but because of the tightly packed ice floes, no wave motion arose. At the change of the watch in the morning, we routinely measured the air and water temperatures. The water and the air were both 30°F (−1°C). The ice floes were getting closer and closer. Driving snow obscured everything. Around 8:00 it became impossible to continue sailing. At

81° 1′ 20″ North, we turned around. To our knowledge this was the northernmost position ever reached by a yacht. The North Pole is less than 539 miles away. *Wappen* threaded her way among the ice floes toward the Hinlopen Strait. Our goal: to go around Spitsbergen! After thirty miles of good running before the wind, we saw only isolated floes, but the driving snow was getting worse all the time. Waiting for improved visibility, we anchored in a bay at the entrance of Hinlopen Strait, right by the remains of an 1898 Swedish geodetic expedition. On the opposite side of the bay was the place where the German Spitsbergen expedition, led by Scroder-Stranz, froze to death.

A day later the blizzard stopped and *Wappen* entered the Hinlopen Strait on a wide port reach in a wind well over Force 6. Despite our expectations, only a few icebergs were drifting in the water. The countryside on both sides of the Strait was covered with thin, white, almost blue-looking snow. Huge glaciers were there, among them the Walhalla Glacier, with a twenty-mile leading edge stretched far into Hinlopen Strait. The sun shone a blinding light on ice and waves and it reflected, iridescent, off billions of ice crystals. Despite the cold, the whole crew assembled in the cockpit to admire this spectacle of nature. We all realized how alone we were in the midst of nature, and that in case of an emergency no help would be able to reach us from the outside. Here on the east side of Spitsbergen the landscape was completely different from the west; the steep mountains that gave Spitsbergen its name

were missing. In the east, the gigantic glaciers have polished and rounded the mountains. The effects of the temperature decrease in the polar regions were clearly visible on the glacier faces, which are receding every year. Then the glaciers became slighter and the ice floes more numerous. The second slalom run among sixty-foot high icebergs and ice floes that are sometimes over 300 feet long was about to begin. Klaus stood in the bow pulpit and guided *Wappen* through the ice with hand signals. The wind stiffened further and *Wappen* made headway fast at seven or eight knots. From the crow's nest I could see only solid white ice in the direction of Olga Strait. Any passage in that direction was impossible. But I seemed to make out some thinner ice along the shore of Edgeøya Island. So we stood close inshore and sailed for Freeman Sound—our last hope for a successful circumnavigation of Spitsbergen. The ice conditions did not seem too bad here under the shore of Edgeøya. Should we not have made it through Storfjord, we would have to retrace our steps in order to reach Norway again. Over a thousand miles back! And what would we do if the ice had closed behind our backs in the meantime? We did not wish to think about that! We would make it.

After rounding the southeast corner of Edgeøya, Freeman Sound was before us. Disappointment! A thick, impenetrable ice pack lay across the Sound. The ice towered many feet high. I secretly decided to turn back. Descending winds of up to Force 8 came down from the mountains and congealed everything. Heavily bundled up with a pair of binoculars around my neck, I let them hoist me to the top of the mast in a bo'sun's chair. From a height of seventy-two feet I could see blue, ice-free water only a few miles away behind the ice barrier. Would we fail only a few miles from our goal? We had to make it through this barrier. The question was: how? Maybe the ice was somewhat thinner at the edge of the glacier to the north. But, according to the map and the handbook, the water was too shallow for us there. Carefully, under engine power, we made our way toward the glacier, watching our depth sounder constantly. Contrary to the chart, the water here was just deep enough. The tides had caused some movement in the barrier. Cracks and channels had developed, into which I immediately steered *Wappen*. The crew kept pieces of ice away from the boat with boat hooks. *Wappen von Bremen* snaked its way very slowly through the ice, going backward and foward under engine power. The blue water drew ever nearer. After a few miles, we made it. Ice-free water—Spitsbergen had been circumnavigated.

With this, *Wappen von Bremen* became the first German yacht to sail around Spitsbergen. At least one other yacht, from which accurate logs are available, had sailed this dangerous route before us: Carl Emil Petersen sailed with his companions, Cato Strøm and Johan Jerndahl, around the Svalbard archipelago in his Colin Archer type, gaff-rigged ketch *Rundø*, flying the colors of the Royal Norwegian Yacht Club. The archipelago basically consists of Spitsbergen, Nordaustland, Barantsøya, and Edgeøya.

After another three days of fast sailing in good winds, *Wappen* anchored off Hopen, a small island between Spitsbergen and Novaja Zemlja, where we visited the two men from the weather station. The radio operators were very happy to see us, since they are relieved only once a year.

On the way back from Hopen to Norway, it was stormier than we had expected. Considering these temperatures, it is not exactly a pleasure to stand on the foreship in the smooth water and change the foresail. But *Wappen* slowly entered the influence area of the Gulf Stream and the temperatures rose. Four weeks after our departure, we reached our starting port of Tromsø, safe and sound and without damage to our ship.

Jochen Orgelmann

Man, his boat, and the sea all take part in an eternal game. When the sun sinks into the sea, sailing imparts a feeling of profound satisfaction and great happiness (Fig. 106). "I don't know anything in the physical and intellectual realm that can equal it," Ernst Alexander Römer once said. "Human nature needs change, and nowhere else is change experienced as often and as profoundly as it is on a sailing voyage." A day in the Pacific comes to an end (Fig. 107). A gentle trade wind cools the air. The colors of sea and sky blend together. A beautiful night at sea is about to begin. Illuminated by the golden glow of the rising sun, *Fiona* sails toward Tahiti with the wind at her stern. Position: 9° 20′ South, 143° 04′ West. This gaff-rigged pilot cutter was built in England in 1911 and still plies the seas today, like the windjammers of old, driven by the wind in her linen sails (Fig. 108).

The whale hunters and seal hunters were the first to come, then the scientists and explorers. Men like Nansen, Amundsen, and Nobile used Spitsbergen as a base for their expeditions.

Adventurers of our time have followed in their tracks, men who love their yachts and the sea above all else and who, in their search for untouched and unspoiled landscapes (Fig. 109), leave the traditional sailing waters and press on to the edge of the polar ice.

After *Walross* of the Academic Sailing Club of Berlin made a sensational voyage around Spitsbergen in the summer of 1972, *Wappen von Bremen* attempted this same journey four years later. Led by skipper Jochen Orgelmann, the nine-man crew even bettered the performance of *Walross*. The unusually small amount of free floating ice allowed them to approach within 540 miles of the North Pole. Position: 81° 01′ North. No other yacht has ever reached this latitude.

With the water temperature at 37 degrees and the air at 40 degrees, the *Wappen von Bremen* passed NyÅlesund, the most northerly settlement in the world, then anchored in the Magdalene Fjord (Fig. 110). "Then we used our engine to pick our way through the icebergs and come in closer to the crumbling wall of the Waggonway Glacier (Fig. 111). Ice blocks weighing several tons each kept calving off the wall and falling into the sea."

Then the voyage continued
northward. *Wappen von Bremen*
sailed through an unfriendly and
inhospitable world that gave the
impression of a cold, abstract
backdrop in a theater. "We all
sensed how alone we were with
nature (Figs. 112, 113, 114). The
coast was harsh and unreal, and
when the landscape was not
hidden by clouds of mist coming
down from the mountains, it lay
bathed in a glaring light."

113

114

Time and again it was a chance encounter, an evening's chat, or a mere impulse that determined the itinerary of the world traveller Patrick van God. At twenty-seven, he built *Trismus*, and at twenty-nine he gave up his profession as a dentist. He spent the next three years in a series of adventures that ended with the sinking of *Trismus* on the coral reef of Rangiroa in the Pacific. Van God's response was to build a new boat and make new plans. The Antarctic was his next goal, and his voyage to the polar ocean (Fig. 115) was anything but conventional. He was the first man to circumnavigate Antarctica. Then, as he and his wife were returning to Europe, he lost his second boat in a hurricane off the coast of South America. In a rubber life raft equipped with a sail, they drifted for six days and over 250 miles before they were picked up.

In the fall of 1977, van God put out to sea alone again. He has not been heard from since.

The desire and the curiosity to
see nature where it still exists in
its original grandeur are the
motives that send Carl Emil
Petersen out to sea. In 1957 he
set out on a three-year voyage
around the world in his *Rundø*, a
34-foot boat with a pointed stern,
built in 1925 after a Colin Archer
design. Now the two-inch-thick
oak planking was carrying him
into Arctic waters (Fig. 116).
Spitsbergen was his goal. His
was the first and still remains the
only yacht to have sailed not only
around Spitsbergen but also
around North East Land.

117

On July 11, 1977, *Rundø* left the little harbor of Akureyi on the northern coast of Iceland. This time her goal was Greenland. Skipper Petersen, his crew, and his boat were all ideally prepared. The stem of *Rundø* had been reinforced. The hull carried copper plating to protect it from the ice, and the ship carried an emergency trans‒ mitter, a life raft, and even fifty pounds of dynamite in case she had to blast her way through the ice.

With patience and good luck, *Rundø* picked her way into Musk Ox Fjord (Fig. 117), but the journey had taken a lot of time. By September 3, the situation had become critical. Winds of Force 10 began to press the ice floes together. The stern of *Rundø* was squeezed up into the air and the hull crushed. The crew's attempts to rescue the ship failed (Figs. 118, 119). With much creaking and groaning, her ribs bent and broke. *Rundø* was lost (Fig. 120). Petersen sent out "Mayday" on his transmitter, and the entire crew was rescued.

VIII
SAILING
TO
HELL
AND
BACK

I was shocked with the scene that full daylight revealed; scared, then gradually fascinated; though still terrified on looking out through the dome. It seemed as if the yacht's stern could never lift to each wave that reared up behind us. But rise it did; each time with a sensation like being whisked up in a lift. The yacht was being steered by the wind vane, assisted from inside the cabin by occasional tugs at the tiller lines. "She's bloody near airborne," I wrote, and added that she was running incredibly smoothly. But was this in spite of, or because of, my tactics? Were they the right ones?

This last is a perennial query in storms. Vito Dumas, the heroic Argentine farmer who in 1944 circumnavigated alone through the roaring forties in a yacht the same size as *Ice Bird*, never took in his jib. He did the same as I was doing now. Bernard Moitessier, after his memorable non-stop voyage from Tahiti to Spain, had also suggested the tactics I was adopting — running before gales at an angle under headsail, the sail being necessary for control and maneuverability.

Dumas and Moitessier had been two of the successful ones, but so many had come to grief in the Southern Ocean. . . . Yet here I was, traversing even stormier waters than they. No wonder I was scared. The gale seemed to be bearing out what I had somewhat wryly termed Lewis's law—for every point the wind increases your boat shrinks and becomes one foot shorter. This great truth has been my own discovery. I was brought back from my musings about other voyagers by bilge water surging up over the 'permafrost' that coated the inside of the hull these days, as an exploding crest threw the yacht over on her beam ends. She righted herself, water streaming off her decks. . . . These repeated gales were at last seriously beginning to get me down. Gradually my morale was being sapped and increasing physical exhaustion was taking its toll. My whole body was battered and bruised and I was suffering from lack of sleep. Increasingly I dwelt on my in many ways disastrous personal life; what a mess I had made of things. I could hardly remember when my storm clothes had last been removed; standing in squelching boots had become habitual but was hardly comfortable. To make matters worse, my left hip, damaged in a skiing accident the previous winter, ached intolerably. I no longer day-dreamed about the voyage and its outcome—I had already dreamed and was now living it.

Instead, present reality became illusory. In my exhausted state the wild irregular seas that were tossing us around like a cork were only half apprehended. I jotted down in the log that everything was an effort; there were constant mistakes of every kind in my sight workings; I could no longer grasp simple concepts. Twice, I recorded with scientific detachment that I heard ill-defined imaginary shouts. I drifted out of reality altogether . . . such was my mental condition on the eve of disaster.

On the 28th the bottom fell out of the glass. . . . Nothing I or any other man might do could control the barometer. The pointer moved right off the scale and continued downwards to about twenty-eight inches or 95

258

omb during the night. This time it was for real. Long before the barometer had reached this point it was apparent that something altogether new had burst upon us—a storm of hurricane intensity. This was the home of the unthinkable 105-foot waves the Russians had recorded, I recalled with dread. A breaker half as tall, falling upon *Ice Bird*, would pound her flat and burst her asunder.

The waves increased in height with unbelievable rapidity. Nothing in my previous experience had prepared me for this. Yet I had known the full fury of North Atlantic autumn gales when homeward bound in 25-foot *Cardinal Vertue* from Newfoundland to the Shetlands in 1960 (coincidentally, the Shetlands straddle the 60th *north* parallel).

Barry and I had weathered Coral Sea cyclone Becky in *Isbjorn*, only partially sheltered by an inadequate island. Severe gales off Iceland, Magellan Strait and the Cape of Good Hope had been ridden out by *Rehu Moana*—the most seaworthy catamaran built so far—in the course of her Iceland voyage and her circumnavigation.

But this storm was something altogether new. By evening the estimated wind speed was over sixty knots; the seas were conservatively forty feet high and growing taller—great hollow rollers, whose wind-torn crests thundered over and broke with awful violence. The air was thick with driving spray.

Ice Bird was running down wind on the starboard gybe (the wind on the starboard quarter), with storm jib sheeted flat as before. Once again I adjusted the wind-vane to hold the yacht steering at a small angle to a dead run, and laid out the tiller lines where they could be grasped instantaneously to assist the vane. This strategy had served me well in the gale just past, as it had Dumas and Moitessier. But would it be effective against this fearful storm? Had any other precautions been neglected? The Beaufort inflatable life raft's retaining strops had been reinforced by a criss-cross of extra lashings across the cockpit. Everything movable, I thought, was securely battened down; the washboards were snugly in place in the companionway; the hatches were all secured. No, I could not think of anything else that could usefully be done.

Came a roar, as of an approaching express train. Higher yet tilted the stern; *Ice Bird* picked up speed and hurtled forward surfing on her nose, then slewed violently to starboard, totally unresponsive to my hauling at the tiller lines with all my strength. A moment later the tottering breaker exploded right over us, smashing the yacht down on to her port side. The galley shelves tore loose from their fastenings and crashed down in a cascade of jars, mugs, frying pan and splintered wood. I have no recollection of where I myself was flung—presumably backwards on to the port bunk. I only recall clawing my way up the companionway and staring aft through the dome.

The invaluable self-steering vane had disappeared and I found, when I scrambled out on deck, that its vital gearing was shattered beyond repair—stainless steel shafts twisted and cog wheels and worm gear gone altogether. The stout canvas dodger round the cockpit was hanging in tatters. The jib was torn, though I am not sure whether it had split right across from luff to clew then or later. My recollections are too confused and most of that day's log entries were subsequently destroyed.

I do know that I lowered the sail, slackening the halyard, hauling down the jib and securing it, repeatedly unseated from the jerking foredeck, half blinded by stinging spray and sleet, having to turn away my head to gulp for the air being sucked past me by the screaming wind. Then lying on my stomach and grasping handholds like a rock climber, I inched my way back to the companionway and thankfully pulled the hatch to after me.

I crouched forward on the edge of the starboard bunk doing my best to persuade *Ice Bird* to run off before the wind under bare poles. She answered the helm, at best erratically, possibly because she was virtually becalmed in the deep canyons between the waves; so that more often than not the little yacht wallowed broadside on, port beam to the sea, while I struggled with the tiller lines, trying vainly to achieve steerage way and control.

And still the wind kept on increasing. It rose until, for the first time in all my years of seagoing, I heard the awful high scream of force thirteen hurricane winds rising beyond 70 knots.

The remains of the already-shredded canvas dodger streamed out horizontally, flogging with so intense a vibration that the outlines blurred. Then the two stainless steel wires supporting the dodger parted and in a flash it was gone. The whole sea was white now. Sheets of foam, acres in extent, were continually being churned anew by fresh cataracts. These are not seas, I thought: they are the Snowy Mountains of Australia—and they are rolling right over me. I was very much afraid.

Some time later—I had no idea how long—my terror receded into some remote corner of my mind. I must have shrunk from a reality I could no longer face into a world of happier memories, for I began living in the past again, just as I had in my exhaustion in the gale two days earlier. It is hard to explain the sensation. I did not move over from a present world into an illusory one but temporarily inhabited both at once and was fully aware of doing so, without feeling this to be in any way strange or alarming. My handling of the tiller was quite automatic.

Mounts Kosciusko, Townsend, the broken crest of Jagungal; sculptured summits, sweeping snow slopes streaked with naked rock; all this mighty snow panorama rolled past like a cinema film. It was moving because those snow mountains were simultaneously the too-fearful-to-contemplate watery mountains of paralysing reality. . . .

But why are those snow mountains rolling onward? Where are they going? I have drifted away even further from the present and my tired brain baulks at the effort of solving the conundrum. . . .

The intolerable present became too intrusive to be ignored; the past faded into the background. Veritable cascades of white water were now thundering past on either side, more like breakers monstrously enlarged to perhaps forty-five feet, crashing down on a surf beach. Sooner or later one must burst fairly over us. What then?

I wedged myself more securely on the lee bunk, clutching the tiller lines, my stomach hollow with fear. The short sub-Antarctic night was over; it was now about 2 a.m.

My heart stopped. My whole world reared up, plucked by an irresistible force, to spin through giddy darkness, then to smash down into daylight again. Daylight, I saw with horror, as I pushed aside the cabin table that had come down on my head (the ceiling insulation was scored deeply where it had struck the deck head) . . . daylight was streaming through the now gaping opening where the forehatch had been! Water slopped about my knees. The remains of the Tilley lamp hung askew above my head. The stove remained upside down, wedged in its twisted gymballs.

Ice Bird had been rolled completely over to starboard through a full 360° and had righted herself thanks to her heavy lead keel—all in about a second. In that one second the snug cabin had become a shambles. What of the really vital structures? Above all, what of the mast?

I splashed forward, the first thought in my mind to close that yawning fore hatchway. My second—oh, God—the mast. I stumbled over rolling cans, felt the parallel rules crunch underfoot and pushed aside the flotsam of clothes, mattresses, sleeping bag, splintered wood fragments and charts (British charts floated better than Chilean, I noted—one up to the Admiralty). Sure enough the lower seven feet of the mast, broken free of the mast step, leaned drunkenly over the starboard bow and the top twenty-nine feet tilted steeply across the ruptured guard wires and far down into the water, pounding and screeching as the hulk wallowed.

The forehatch had been wrenched open by a shroud as the mast fell. Its hinges had sprung, though they were not broken off and its wooden securing batten had snapped. I forced it as nearly closed as I could with the bent hinges and bowed it down with the block and tackle from the bosun's chair.

Then I stumbled back aft to observe, incredulously, for the first time that eight feet of the starboard side of the raised cabin trunk had been dented in, longitudinally, as if by a steam hammer. A six-inch vertical split between the windows spurted water at every roll (it was noteworthy, and in keeping with the experience of others, that it had been the lee or down-wind side, the side underneath as the boat capsized, that had sustained damage, not the weather side where the wave had struck).

What unimaginable force could have done that to eighth-inch steel? The answer was plain. Water. The breaking crest, which had picked up the seven-ton yacht like a matchbox, would have been hurtling forward at something like fifty miles an hour. When it slammed her over, the impact would have been equivalent to dumping her on to concrete. The underside had given way. . . .

The proud yacht of a moment before had become a wreck: high adventure had given place to an apparently foredoomed struggle to survive.

David Lewis

Until now the sea had shown itself benign—a long regular swelling, gently waving hills of water that helped us forward without presenting any difficulties for us. Slowly, however, high backs appeared. Thus dawned the morning of May 17.

Around noon the wind reached a strength of seventeen or eighteen knots. Often, strong gusts forced us to turn the bow of the boat two or three degrees off course. Meanwhile, our day's run showed 199 miles. But the sky started to look nasty and threatening, and it soon became clear that we were in for bad weather. At 3:00 in the afternoon we brought the boat into the wind, furled the mizzen, and tied double reefs into the mainsail. When we attempted to set the storm jib, the sheet broke and the sail, which was whipping around with its two heavy blocks, tore a hole in the foresail; thus our two heavy weather headsails became useless.

Since there was less damage to the storm jib, I decided to repair this sail first.

I left the foresail and took the drenched storm jib down to the cabin to make the necessary repairs. It was long, tiring work, during which I kept an eye on the barometer, which had started to fall quite rapidly. Once in a while I looked out on the deck. Whipped up by the howling wind, the waves all around us grew into true mountains of water. Nevertheless, I didn't worry about the safety of the boat. At 7:00 that night we had to put two men at the helm. Kaare Tveter and Thorleif Taraldsen. There was no time for supper that day. The storm jib had to be fixed soon; then I wanted to heave to.

At 7:30 the jib was repaired and could be put to use again. We were just about to bring it on deck when Kaare Tveter shouted as loud as he could down the hatchway. "Skipper! Come on deck! We can't hack it any more."

We left the jib below and ran on to the deck. The wind was gusting hard all around. This was no longer a storm but a full-grown hurricane. The boat was thrown thundering through the roaring waters, while spray and gulfweed hit our faces mercilessly and the sweeping rain pricked like needles. A quick glance at the compass showed me that the wind had turned to the southwest. I yelled at the helmsmen: "Watch that we don't capsize, but be careful that we don't get beam-to the seas."

During the previous half-hour the sea had completely changed. Certainly, before it had been mountains of water but those were more gentle giants that would have hurt us only if we hadn't been careful. Now the sea was in a wild uproar, as if those giants had gone completely mad. They carried on in a nasty, drunken way, and suddenly they all banded together to stretch up powerful towers toward heaven, forming terrifying breakers where they were least expected. Never have I seen the sea like that.

Yes, it wasn't blowing just a little! The forward hatch, a small but very heavy part, was opened by the storm, pulled out of its steady joints, and sent flying through the air. Three of us—Peter Archer, Einar Tveten, and I—slackened the foresail and tried to douse it, but the sail ties broke. While Einar

262

Tveten clung to the front of the sail next to me, I sent Peter Archer amidships to get a piece of heavy rope that was under the lifeboat, where we had all sorts of equipment stowed away. At this very moment the ship stuck her bow deep into a wave, and I jumped up and grabbed the staysail as the water reached my hips. Not even now did I believe that danger was imminent. Einar was hanging on to the rail close to me, while Peter—on hands and knees—was crawling on deck. None of us noticed the huge wave that was coming across the bow. However, Thorleif Taraldsen, who was steering, saw it and swears it was as high as the top of our mast.

None of us knew what happened when the boat suddenly went under all at once. Suddenly my surroundings vanished. How I lost my grip on the staysail, I do not know. It seemed to have melted between my hands. The boat was gone, the sky was gone, my mates were gone. I was floating quite alone in a twirling nothing of boiling foam, a helpless toy of the powerful, wildly bubbling mass of water. Then I found myself being pulled down by a wildly whirling stream; that had to be the suction from the sinking ship. I could find no other explanation than that the planking had been torn loose from the stem and that *Sandefjord* was going down with every soul on board. I did not feel any fear, just a hopeless resignation. That, then, was the end. Would death be very painful? I sank deeper and deeper through the white foaming waters and did not fight. Why fight for a few short minutes of life when death seemed to be inevitable? What kind of hope could a swimmer have in such a sea? I was consciously breathing in water. The quick sequence of horrible events seemed to have dulled my senses; I felt no pain. Something hit against my breast; I hardly noticed it. I knew that I was deep, deep under the agitated surface of the sea.

Perhaps it is not so easy to end one's life rationally. Whether nature resists to the very end or whether I suddenly realized that my children would lose their father, the will to live reawakened and I swam with all my might to the surface, almost suffocating, aghast at the possibility that I might lose consciousness before reaching the surface. I managed to breathe only once, then I was torn down again; now I gave up. Why prolong the torture with useless attempts? Until now I had seen nothing but foam all around me. The ship was gone and with her the possibility of life for all of us. The mates were having their own struggle with death now; they could not help me. Yes, those poor, brave mates!

Meanwhile, I shot to the surface again. This time I saw the boat! It was afloat about twenty-five yards away, sailing by slowly on a starboard tack, driven by a tiny remnant of mainsail. Despite everything, salvation was possible; life was beckoning. Fear hit my heart—the fear of not being able to reach the ship before she sailed by. I didn't see a soul on board, but as I got nearer I heard voices and asked for a life buoy. It was thrown to me, but I couldn't find it and instead swam toward the boat, which luckily I managed to reach. Somehow it

263

seemed as if the wave that had submerged us had flattened out the surface of the water around us.

Thorleif Taraldsen was the only one who was still on board. He had been jammed in the seat by the mizzen tackle. The mast had been broken about two feet above the deck. Thorleif pulled me up; I was too exhausted to climb the side without help. At the same time, Einar Tveten and Peter Archer came back on board—Einar was washed up at the poop and got hold of the mizzen horse; Peter climbed over the mizzen boom, which, still hanging from one of the shrouds, was dragging behind starboard. We cut the boom loose so it would not hit the planks. Peter Archer had gone through roughly the same experience in the water that I had; however, he had surfaced on the opposite side of the ship, approximately twenty yards away.

But Kaare Tveter was missing! It hit me like a bomb. I had lost a man. The thought was too terrible; I didn't want to admit it. Had nobody seen him? I called his name. We all called, we screamed, we begged him to come back, but we received no answer other than the thundering of the waves and the shrieking of the storm. We peered out for a sign over the broken water but the waves kept their secret. The sea had taken him and we never saw him again.

But we would be with him soon. When I recognized the condition of our boat I was almost sorry not to have drowned at the first submersion. *Sandefjord* was a wreck and it didn't look as if she would stay afloat much longer. One hour perhaps, then she would be finished. One hour of useless fighting against the rising water, then we would sink. We still had an hour to prepare—an hour of despair, of self-pity—an hour of unspeakable fear of death, far worse than death itself. And meanwhile we would be slaving away like desperadoes, like lunatics—resembling men who have been condemned to death, who are rattling at the prison bars while they are awaiting a grisly execution. Lucky is he whose thread of life is being cut suddenly and compassionately, so that he is spared the dreadful fear of death of consciousness.

I alone was responsible. Yes, even on a small ship the skipper sometimes is a rather lonely person. I had been proud of my strength and dexterity; I had relied on my skills. Now I had seen how totally insufficient they were. Well, I had seen this before, but something like that is always easily forgotten.

However, *Sandefjord* remained afloat! Our desperate struggles with buckets and pump indeed lowered the water level, despite the waves that every now and then thundered in over the open hatchway. Now we started to work in a more organized way. If we wanted to save our boat and our lives we could not merely think of remaining afloat. We were in a part of the ocean where we might not encounter another ship for months. Our provisions and drinking water could run out, if indeed we still had any drinking water left. We had to try to get away from here into regions where there was ship traffic; we had to sail.

A preliminary examination of the ship was

not encouraging. The deck had been swept bare; lifeboats, cabin and compass, and several sails, and a great part of the mooring gear had been washed away. The starboard lantern plank had disappeared. The rail had taken such a beating that there was little left but the bare supports. The port anchor was missing, as was a part of the gunwale. I suddenly remembered that something had hit hard against my breast while I was floating deep under in the churned-up waters. I was convinced that it had been that anchor. It had broken one or two of my ribs.

The worst of all was, of course, the condition of the rigging. The mizzen had been lost and the heavy mainmast, which had broken off a bit above the deck, was swinging wildly between the loose stays and threatened to go overboard any minute. The starboard shrouds had been partially broken, the chain plates were all bent, and the forestay—the only stay that supported the rig forward—had been so badly damaged and had given so much that I had serious doubts whether our efforts to save whatever was left of the rig made any sense.

Meanwhile, we found a few heavy pieces of rope and used them to tighten the shrouds and secure the mast. When we were done, the upper deadeyes were hardly one meter above the deck. It was not much of a success but, as an emergency measure, the best we could do.

Next, we took down the gaff, which was whirling around halfway up the mast and was hitting the shaky rig in a terrible manner. Because the throat had been torn loose, there was nothing to stop the wild swaying back and forth but the aft bolt-rope of the shredded mainsail. At first it looked like an impossible job. The upper part was an entangled ball of frayed ends and ensnared wires, entangled with cloth strips and shreds of hawser. Even in the daylight and in good weather it would have been a difficult task to untangle the mess. However, the rig was banging about constantly in mighty pendulum swings and heavy thrusts; it suddenly came to a standstill with an unexpected jolt. Holding our lives in one hand, we feverishly worked with the other and tried to clear up the mess. The whirling gaff was threatening to hit us, and the wires of both backstays, each with a huge block at the end, were constantly spinning around in the air, slung around the mast with unbelievable speed and then turned free again. They were a threat to our lives until we managed to get hold of them and secure them. Again and again we had to grapple to free ends and clear the blocks. We even had to climb to the peak of the gaff which was swaying back and forth—a tricky job that Peter undertook—because it was necessary to clear the peak halyard blocks there before we could lower the gaff. And during that whole time the boat rolled around in a sea that was acting wild, while breakers were constantly sweeping over the unprotected deck, where not even a handline could protect us from slipping overboard.

We finally made it, but it had been a terrible fight and we were all exhausted when the gaff lay on board, securely lashed up. But we still had no rest. Below everything seemed spoiled: bunk furnishing, clothes, provisions, maps, and personal belongings floated in two feet of rust-colored water over the floors, which were covered with fragments of glass and dishes. We were enveloped in pitch-black night—the lamps had disappeared, all our matches were wet. In the wild mess downstairs we couldn't even find shoes with which to protect our bare feet from the countless shards of glass in which we were wading around. Suddenly I remembered a matchbox that I had put in a tin can and had tucked away in a safe place, an old habit I had already practiced on *Teddy*. That came in handy now. I found the matches; they were dry. We found candles and soon thereafter we had light.

Just then Einar collapsed; he was too exhausted and had lost too much blood. In the darkness none of us had seen that he had blood streaming down his body from a deep slash on his scalp, and he had said nothing. Well, perhaps we would not have been able to do much for him anyway, and even now we couldn't help him very much. The medicine chest was wet through and through; the bandages had been spoiled by dirty water. We poured some iodine in the wound and put him in the least flooded bunk. Then we started to scoop out the water to get at the water tap; we were hoping with all our might that our fresh water had not been spoiled. Progress was slow. Now that the worst exertion was over, we realized that none of us was worth very much. Badly injured, we were all limping and bleeding; none of us had an unscratched arm. But we toiled on until

the pump showed that the boat was free, and we thanked God when we found that our fresh water had not suffered.

When Einar regained consciousness, he climbed out of his bunk and asked, a little subdued, what had actually happened. We told him and advised him to lie down again. "And you?" he asked, "I should have helped you." I answered that we would all go to sleep as soon as we had cleaned up the floor a little and had bandaged his head. "Won't a cork do?" he smiled weakly, "At least it would prevent the sawdust from coming out." Einar tried even now to cheer us up. A valiant guy, our Einar, even though he wasn't the greatest cook.

The mates lay down on the wet floors in the cabin, which was the most comfortable spot on board. Then, quiet settled on the unhappy ship, while I stood a worried watch in a restless night.

Although I didn't know then what had happened, later it was easy enough to reconstruct the event, partially on the basis of the actual observations of each member of the crew, but mostly on the basis of the traces heavy objects had left on the bulkheads and the underside of the deck below. In a series of rough sketches I want to try to explain what happened to the boat and how it happened.

Figure 1 shows how the boat, speeding along, is lifted up by a wave from aft and then stomps heavily into the sea. Since she is abruptly braked but is still pushing ahead, she digs into the water with the bow. The wave coming from the stern—a powerful

266

breaker—pushes her stern simply over her bow as Figure 2 shows, so that she winds up keel upwards, as illustrated by Figures 3 and 4. The latter also shows the angle under which the anchor-chain fell out of its deep-lying locker and hit the deck—in this case underneath—and left deep indentations in the woodwork. When the ship turned right side up again, because of the weight of its iron keel and internal ballast (a total of fifteen tons), the chains fell in a starboard bunk, as seen in Figure 5. The capsize took place at 26 degrees North and 63 degrees West.

Erling Tambs

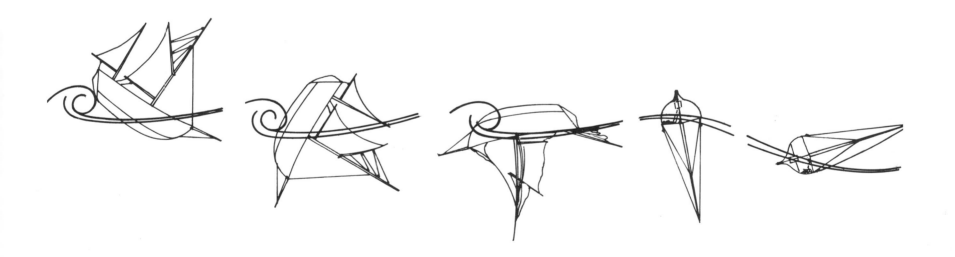

It is cold, damn cold. The North Sea is rough, especially here in this corner where it narrows down like a funnel into the English Channel. We were underway from the Zuider Zee to the small island of Helgoland, heading out of the funnel, and Helgoland lies in the direction where the wind is coming from with a solid wind of Force 7. A northeast wind blows and the crew of the *Rubin* told us later on Helgoland that they had chipped ice off their deck that morning.

We had not slept the night before when we had crossed the Zuider Zee. It was midnight before we had finished stowing our sails and provisions and were finally able to get underway. Then, shortly before dawn, we had to navigate the lock to the open sea. We waited until broad daylight before we began our slalom course between the wooden poles, called "perches," that mark the channel through the Wadden Zee. Small buoys and the perches trembling in the strong ebb tide showed us our zigzag path through the treacherous waters.

Apart from being cold and tired, we had found our trip a pleasant one so far. We went ashore on Terschelling to catch a nap until noon. No one felt like cooking so we had some bread and cheese before setting out again. We had hardly turned the corner of the island before we were up against it. The wind had come up strong. We changed the jib for a smaller one and reefed the mainsail even more. Then we hunkered down in the cockpit and on deck and let our tub have her head, tacking far out into the North Sea, coming about, heading in toward the coast again, then heading out on a new tack, zigzagging back and forth against the wind until we reached Helgoland. We would be there tomorrow afternoon.

I sat and waited—waited, that is, to get seasick. I was not alone. Reimar was the first. He had a sore throat and felt miserable to begin with. All of a sudden he was hanging over the lee rail where the deck of the sharply heeling yacht sometimes dipped under water. He unloaded his bread and cheese. He cursed, then disappeared muttering below deck. There was nothing much left to do anyhow. Albert, the boat's owner and skipper, was at the helm, and two men were enough to handle the sails when we came about. I was next, or was it Frank? I don't remember anymore. God damn this seasickness!

Our scow was heeled over so far it kept scraping one ear on the bottom. Water we had shipped sloshed up the cabin sides into the bunks, the mattresses, and the sleeping bags. We pumped and puked, and our boat ran up and down like an elevator. You sit below deck on the slanted table and brace your feet against the wall. You pump and heave your insides out. Oh, the joys of sailing! We nearly piled up on the reefs in the middle of the night and might well have drowned like rats because the light buoy we were to round suddenly was no buoy at all but a small lighthouse on a well-scoured reef! Two days and two nights this torture lasted—why did we put up with it?

And then there was that trip home in the

268

Baltic from Karlshamn, Sweden, when we ran head on into a southwest wind between Bornholm and the mainland. Or that time in the Gulf of Finland when everybody ran for the stern because a ridiculous wind force of 6 was making the foredeck fly up and down like a roller coaster. Why do we endure this madness?

And here we are spending Easter on the North Sea again, for God's sake. The decision to go below makes things even worse. You squat on deck; the cold creeps up your legs; your breakfast creeps up your throat; you have no choice but to struggle against your fate until it gets the better of you. You rush to the lee rail. Relief. I know very well I'll feel even worse below. The trick is to get undressed and prone without vomiting.

Once you're lying down, things are better. Your feet are ice cold halfway up to the knees. Have I slept? My feet are warm now. I must have slept. In the meantime, Albert has settled into his bunk for the second time. He had just stuck his head out of the companionway a few minutes ago. His stomach must not have been quite empty.

I doze off. My mind begins to work; so does my stomach. I leap up, run out the passageway in my underwear and sweater, hang head and shoulders over the lee rail. If a wave sweeps over the deck now, I'll be drenched to the skin. It is still daylight; the sky is gray; the sea is gray; everyone's face is gray and stiff with cold. No one speaks; hardly anyone moves. We're still heeling to port, heading farther out to sea. I doze off. Then it hits you. No, it's not your stomach this time. This time it's your bladder. If you get up and put on some clothes to go out to the railing you'll be sick again. You can't roll over in bed. The boat is sailing close-hauled and is heeling sharply. Your mattress has an angle of thirty degrees. You can lean your back against the side wall, but not your stomach. That doesn't work. Just hang on and a solution will present itself. You doze. No solution presents itself. You finally brace yourself for the struggle, decide to do without more clothes, climb up on deck. Still dressed only in underwear and sweater, you stagger astern, grabbing for one handhold after another. The railing and the after stay provide you halfway solid support.

With one hand you hang onto the boat. With your other, you grope for your masculine member. That member has shrunk to its smallest state. Despite your scant clothing, you can hardly find it. The sea rises up; the stern of the boat rises with it. With your bare feet and legs planted firmly on the deck you press yourself against the railing. Cramps threaten to seize up your muscles when the last thing you need is a cramp. The stern begins to buck again, as it always does just as everything is about to flow freely. Your muscles tighten involuntarily.

Relax! It's all a matter of concentration. You look down at the water shooting out under the stern below you and try not to think about the possibility of an unwanted bath, a bath that can quickly become an eternal one. After twenty minutes in water at this temperature, the body is under attack by lethal hypothermia. The wind is cold, icy. The

269

supply of warmth you brought with you from your bunk has long since been used up. But you're beyond caring now.

Back to your bunk. Your chums in the cockpit grin. Just wait, you think. Your turn will come. Sleep is impossible on this tub. The wind howls in the rigging. The water pours over the deck. The heaving of the yacht sets something knocking repeatedly against something else. Every footstep on the deck echoes through the cabin because the deck is made of aluminum with nothing but a layer of cork on top and a thin ceiling inside. Every word the helmsman utters can be heard through the open passageway, and Harald, blast his soul, talks all the time. He and Matthias are the only ones left on deck. I haven't heard any more gagging and heaving for some time.

Michael was the last to turn in. "Call me if you need me." He and the other two are stretched out in the main cabin, maybe in their bunks, maybe among the heavy sailbags that are piled up there. The ship is trimmed for racing, and to keep the balance we want, we store the sails we're not using amidships in the main cabin, not forward where they really belong.

Sometimes the boat plows into a wave that you think will knock the mast down. In the darkness, you can't avoid the big waves. The helmsman may sense that one is coming, but he can't see it. If anyone has managed to fall asleep in spite of everything, a blow from a wave like that will have him wide awake again. The comment from above is usually, "Shit!" A full shower—only a few degrees above freezing—is always included. "God damn! Is that cold!" That was Matthias. He doesn't say much as a rule, but what he does say is usually to the point. Harald's flood of words finally subsides, and he says, "We ought to take half-hour shifts at the helm. It's easier to stay awake that way." Night on the North Sea with wind of Force 7 or 8 head on out of the northeast. I can think of better ways to spend my time.

Daybreak. It's a clear morning. The wind has swept the sky clean. The ship is quiet, if you can call this quiet. I pry myself out of my bunk, dig out my socks, pants, sweater, insulated suit, and rain gear. Dry socks are essential. There's nothing worse than cold, wet socks early in the morning when you've just tumbled out of a warm bunk and you still don't have any breakfast in your belly. Boots on, then out of the cabin.

The two men in the cockpit look like plaster statues. "Morning." "Morning. How's it going?" It's hard for them to talk. Their faces are so stiff with cold that they can only mumble. Salt, white and fine as powdered sugar, clings to their rain gear and skin. Harald is the first to stagger below deck. Matthias follows. He takes over my bunk. It's simpler that way. All the others are occupied, some of them with sails. The cold, fresh wind out here feels good. So does the slowly rising sun. It isn't warming, but it is enlivening. The sky is a pale blue, hazy along the horizon. The sea is still rough and choppy, a cold blue-back with whitecaps that seem stationary in the distance but move faster as they draw near. Horizon and sea are as empty as the sky. The sun and our boat are the only things to be

270

seen in this expanse. The wind seems to have let up a little even though the anemometer is still spinning furiously. It reads twelve knots, but we must have more than twice that. The wind still whistles in the shrouds, and from the crest of every wave a shower of drops sprays against deck and sail.

The helmsman is never seasick. Everyone knows that. I have to accustom myself to the helm again, but then the yacht skims along through the waves like a little dinghy. As we climb a wave, I ease off on the helm a bit. The bow drifts slightly to one side, then dives down into the next trough. If you want to step on the gas in a yacht like this, you do it with the sheets and blocks and tension levers and zippers for trimming the sails, with the hydraulic system for putting tension on the stays and bending the mast, with travellers and leechlines and boom vangs. You also do it with a light touch on the helm, with the gray matter in your head, and with muscle power on the winches that tame or—if you're not on the alert—unleash massive forces.

This yacht is a good forty-five feet long and weighs thirteen tons. Close-hauled, she plows through the seas like a thoroughbred. "Thoroughbred" is no poetic term. It's the word English sailors have always used for beautifully designed boats. The forces that lay the mass of this ship over on its ear, that drive it up hill and down dale on the sea, the forces of wind and water have been so carefully calculated that a man can control them with two fingers on the helm. I'm alone on deck, alone on the sea this morning. It's not every day that a man can be alone on the broad sea with forty-five feet of concentrated technical perfection at his command. At a moment like this, he forgets seasickness and his two sleepless nights.

A lot of praying gets done on these boats, too, praying with wide open mouths from which no sound comes. Wide open eyes stare fascinated from the stern of the yacht at frothing waves and deep troughs into which the boat plunges, drawn on by a huge spinnaker billowing out before the mast. The speedometer needle can't go any further up on the dial, and boltcutters are at the ready in case the whole kit and caboodle comes tumbling down and all the wires and lines have to be cut loose to keep the shattered mast from damaging the boat.

Fascination holds the crew speechless when a wind of Force 8 or more is coming across the stern and they raise a spinnaker, booming it out on an aluminum pole tested for eight tons pressure yet only loosely guyed by two lines or wires. Or when the wind presses the bow down and everyone runs for the stern railing to keep the boat from plowing under the water. Or when it takes two men to handle the helm and when tons of aluminum hull and lead ballast slice the water with a speed it would take an engine of some 500 horsepower to equal.

It is difficult to conceive of the forces that storm conditions exert on a yacht's hull, on the rigging of the mast, on the winches and fittings. Difficult to imagine, too, how this spinnaker, this bulging, mast-high nylon balloon hanging loose in front of the boat and nearly bursting with wind, can ever come

271

down again without smashing everything to ribbons as it is taken in.

A yacht like this costs a quarter of a million dollars. So what? Somebody on board had that much, and that's why he sleeps aft in a double bunk on the starboard side. For the crew, his money is like the water they sail on: something they take for granted and don't waste any words over. It doesn't matter on board what a man has. All that matters is what he can do. The steady crew of this boat is made up of three businessmen, three recent university graduates, a machinist, two ship dealers, and a man doing alternative service. None of the crew members is over thirty, none has money. Two will come into an inheritance someday; one will inherit banks, the other, shipyards. And so who cares?

The most expensive part of a racing yacht is not the hull. What drives the total up so high is the sophisticated technology that is necessary to control the force of the wind and convert it into speed. Every last item of a yacht's highly technical equipment has to be light yet still function reliably under extreme stress. Damage can involve more than just a loss of time. Damage at sea always brings danger for both yacht and crew. As often as not, breakage is the result of the wrong move at the wrong time. Anyone who is not familiar with racing boats had best keep his hands off if he doesn't want to get hurt. But those who do understand them will find what many men seek in vain: one of the last forms of adventure left in the modern world.

And this is why men sail, even when sailing is torture. Our skipper Albert says, "A man needs freedom for his hobby. If he doesn't have it, then the trouble begins. First he starts playing poker; then comes the booze, then the women." That's the way it is. Albert's great hobby costs him more than money. It also costs him immense amounts of time. His secretary knows that he is always available for his sailing comrades. He always has a telephone line free for shipbuilders, equippers, designers, and sailmakers. She knows the dates of the boating shows and the races by heart. And all Albert's money isn't of any use to him on board if he makes a mistake and everyone curses him out in elegant tones. On board, he is one of the gang. No one is handled with kid gloves. His only privilege is to worry about competition—not business competition; he has everything under control there—but competition at sea. Who is building a new yacht? What is he building? Do we have to build something new?

The latest thing in yachts will be obsolete in no time. The designing and building of yachts is an arms race with no time out. The Admiral's Cup, the unofficial world championship in deepwater sailing, takes place every two years. The races that are held in between are only test runs for new ideas, new people, new boats. Money is not the decisive factor. All you can do with money is pay for everything. It's you alone who has to set the boat in motion, or, more exactly, it's you alone who has to control it. Sometimes with two fingers, sometimes with two fists.

Kai Krüger

272

122

123

"Anyone who wants to know the age of the earth need only look at a stormy sea. The gray of this immense surface, the lines the wind cuts in the face of the waves, the huge masses of churning foam tossed about like the white hair of an old man all make the sea in a storm appear ancient, drab, lusterless, and bleak, as if it had been created before the first light ever dawned." *Joseph Conrad*

Rough-weather scenes: In the America's Cup of 1962, *Weatherly* (Fig. 121) competes against *Gretel* (Fig. 122) in winds of Force 6. These pictures give an idea of how physically demanding modern yachting can be. The crews are in top shape, and, as here on *Gretel* (Figs. 123, 124), they have to perform to the outer limits of their strength. But despite their efforts, *Gretel*, like all challengers in the America's Cup, lost to the American yacht.

Wind Force 10. High waves with slowly breaking crests form. Patches of foam blend together in dense white ribbons that follow the direction of the wind until the whole surface of the sea seems white. The water rolls heavily and erratically, seeming to play with the yacht as though it were a ball. But man intent on technical perfection is out to dominate nature and stand up to her. He does not want to be at her mercy but to determine his own fate.

The Skagen Race is one of sailing's greatest challenges. It covers 500 miles from Helgoland to Kiel by way of Horns Reef and the Skagen Lightship, passing through the Kattegat and the Belt. The 1975 regatta began in a northwest storm that soon reached hurricane force. Sailing close to the wind, the thirty-six yachts fought their way through the seething North Sea. Ground swells up to fifteen feet high sent yachts crashing into the troughs in free fall. For seconds at a time, seventeen tons hung in the air (Fig. 126). When the 53-foot *Inschallah* dove into a deep trough for the second time, she was forced to withdraw from the race with a broken shroud.

The skipper of *Saudade II*, which reached Kiel with her aluminum hull dented all over, described the beating his ship had taken: "It sounded as though someone had thrown a bathtub out of an eleventh-floor window" (Fig. 125).

127

Christine (Fig. 128) also took part in this race. She is shown here, sailing close to the wind with reefed sails, on her way to the Skagen Lightship.

But the North Sea is not the only place that offers rough sailing. Here we see the crews of American twelve-meter yachts straining to the limit (Figs. 127, 129). Anyone who has ever been on a racing yacht and changed a foresail at winds of Force 8 or more knows how much sheer physical strength the maneuver demands despite modern technology.

131

132

133

The mysterious quality of the wind lies in its invisibility. It blows wherever and whenever it wants to. Every kind of wind has its own unique features. Hurricane, typhoon, and *pampero* are the colorful names of exotic winds. There are many kinds of storms at sea, but in the end it is, as Joseph Conrad says, only the human voice that puts the print of human consciousness on the character of a storm.

Every part of the world has its special kind of wind. In the western Mediterranean, it is the *mistral*, a cold wind that blows up quickly, rushing from the Alps to the sea along the Rhone valley. In the 1978 Sailing Week at Marseille, the German Admiral's Cup yacht *Saudade II* had to contend with it (Figs. 131, 132, 133), struggling in a choppy sea.

The boat is glistening wet from her bow to the tip of her mast. The howling wind tears at the sails that reach up into the cloudy sky. The cold seeps through raingear that can never be waterproof enough (Fig. 130). Breakers thunder down on the ship from astern and rush past, roaring and hissing. Among these mountainous waves that set the horizon jumping (Fig. 134), we sense the magic of the earth and the rhythm of life.

The sea was completely erratic: huge waves, small waves, steep waves, shallow waves, cross waves, waves on the backs of other waves (Fig. 137). The helmsman had to sense the wave and bring the stern into it with a sure touch on the tiller before coming back onto his course. But even with a wind of Force 8, things are uncomfortable (Fig. 135), and the crew is kept busy, especially if the waves follow closely on each other. On *Superstar of Hamble*, battling heavy seas in the English Channel, every crewman's last ounce of strength is needed to cope with the chaos that the combined forces of wind and spray create (Fig. 138). The crews of the yachts that took part in the Round-the-World Races of 1973-74 and 1977-78 had to deal with all kinds of weather. The most difficult lap of the journey, however, was the Cape Town-Auckland run. The grim balance for 1974 was two men drowned, many injured, and immense damage to boats. Whether or not to set a spinnaker is a critical question in winds of Force 7 and 8 in the long, rolling swells of the Indian Ocean. A high wave or a gust can make the yacht broach. This is what the crew of *Gauloises II* feared most (Fig. 136).

IX
APPENDIX

THE BIRTH OF A YACHT

Designing and building *Flyer* was an unusually interesting and rewarding experience for all of us who had a part in it. It all started when Cornelius van Rietschoten asked us to design a boat that could compete—and win—in the Whitbread Around the World Race of 1977-78.

In designing her, we drew on our experience in building the Swan 65, *Sayula*, winner of the first Whitbread Race. And because of *Sayula*'s success, we decided on a ketch-rigged boat of similar length. We made *Flyer* somewhat longer at the waterline than *Sayula* and reduced displacement to increase her speed when running before the wind. To achieve the necessary hull strength while keeping the weight as low as possible, we decided on aluminum construction.

The contract was opened for bids from qualified boatyards in the United States and Europe, and was awarded to Hulsman Overijsselse Jachtwerft in The Netherlands. A wonderful, productive spirit of cooperation developed among the owner, the

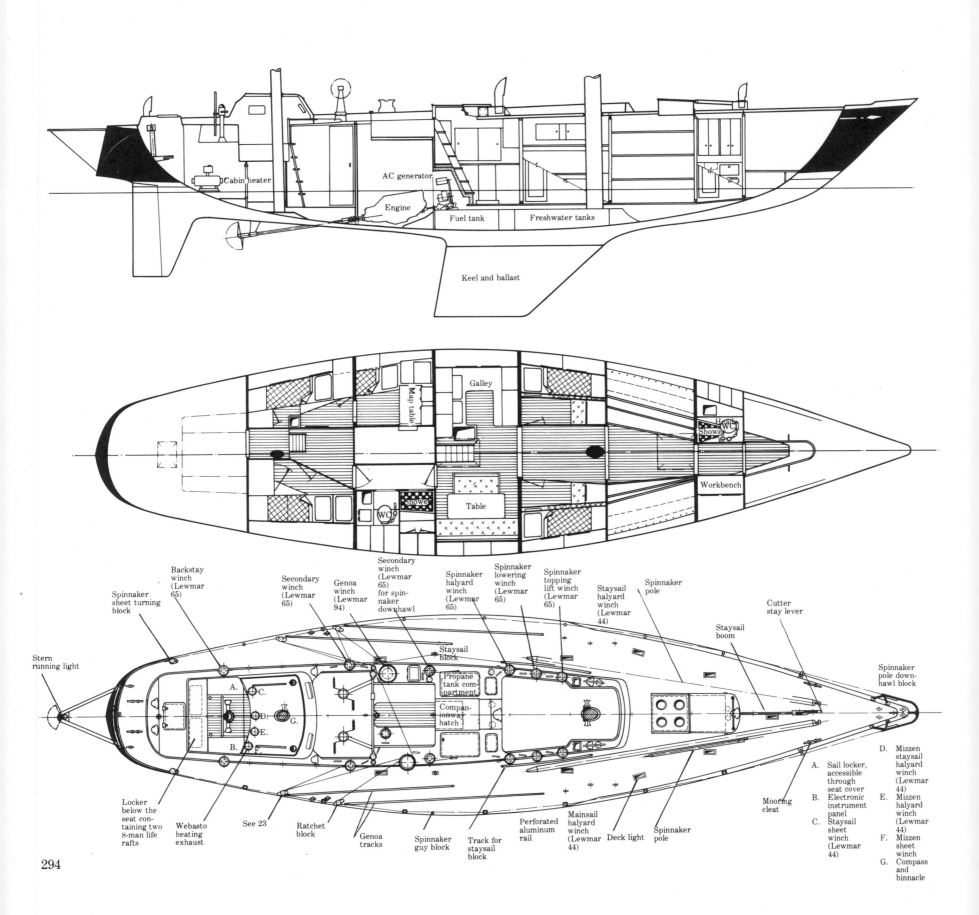

Cabin heater
AC generator
Engine
Fuel tank
Freshwater tanks
Keel and ballast

Galley
Map table
WC Head Shower
Shower
Table
Workbench
WC

Backstay winch (Lewmar 65)
Spinnaker sheet turning block
Secondary winch (Lewmar 65)
Genoa winch (Lewmar 94)
Secondary winch (Lewmar 65) for spinnaker downhawl
Spinnaker halyard winch (Lewmar 65)
Spinnaker lowering winch (Lewmar 65)
Spinnaker topping lift winch (Lewmar 65)
Staysail halyard winch (Lewmar 44)
Spinnaker pole
Cutter stay lever
Staysail block
Staysail boom
Stern running light
Propane tank compartment
Companionway hatch
Spinnaker pole down-hawl block
Locker below the seat containing two 8-man life rafts
Webasto heating exhaust
See 23
Ratchet block
Genoa tracks
Spinnaker guy block
Track for staysail block
Perforated aluminum rail
Mainsail halyard winch (Lewmar 44)
Deck light
Spinnaker pole
Mooring cleat

A. Sail locker, accessible through seat cover
B. Electronic instrument panel
C. Staysail sheet winch (Lewmar 44)
D. Mizzen staysail halyard winch (Lewmar 44)
E. Mizzen halyard winch (Lewmar 44)
F. Mizzen sheet winch
G. Compass and binnacle

designer, and the builders. This boatyard has great experience and know-how, and *Flyer* profited from them. All equipment was carefully selected, and fortunately, we had set enough time to build the yacht well. Mr. van Rietschoten had conceived his timetable thoughtfully, and we had no problems meeting it. When she was finished, *Flyer* was a strongly built boat, with her weight well within specifications—and this has contributed greatly to her success.

Our first shake-down sail took place on Easter weekend, 1977. The weather was cold, but the wind was fine. All aboard were much impressed with the fit of the Hood sails, the good craftsmanship below, and the boat's responsiveness and performance on all headings.

Shortly after the final tests, *Flyer* crossed the Atlantic to Marblehead, Massachusetts. We wanted to test both boat and gear offshore and to have a full set of sails fitted in the Hood loft there. Finally, she was to participate in a Transatlantic race back to Plymouth, England. And we would have time in England before the start of the World Race for final preparations.

Flyer was successful from her first race. She was first to finish and won on corrected time in the race to Plymouth. In the first leg of the World Race, from England to Cape Town, South Africa, she was again the first across the finish line, far enough ahead of all the other boats to overcome her handicap even against the smaller contestants. At the end of the race, in England, she led the second boat by two days, winning the Whitbread.

In her construction, *Flyer* does not deviate much from the guidelines we have long used in building boats, with athwartships and longitudinal reinforcements at such stress points as the externally mounted lead ballast keel. The interior, designed to Cornelius van Rietschoten's specifications, allows each crew member a maximum of privacy to guarantee rest between watches. There are twelve berths: four V berths above the sail bin forward, with another eight stacked two high in four cabins. The main cabin is located aft and can be reached from the cockpit hatch through a separate companionway. The main companionway is amidships, between the galley to port and the table to starboard. The engine room is directly behind the companionway. There are two heads, one forward, across from a workbench, the other by the starboard aft cabin. A large foul weather gear locker and a shower are located near the engine room. The navigator works from a chart table in the port cabin, where all the electronic instruments are mounted. The cockpit is easily accessible from this cabin, where, on long passages, smaller sails can be temporarily stowed. A sewing machine for repairing sails is stowed here, also.

Ventilation posed a major problem. We had to have effective air circulation in hot tropical climates and the capacity to conserve heat in icy polar waters. Dorade vents allowed us both, providing sufficient ventilation without admitting too much water. The rigging is conventional and uncomplicated, with spars and shrouds, of appropriate dimensions, supplied by Gibb, in England. The rigging and its equipment have withstood the rigors of two Atlantic crossings and the World Race with few problems. As the boat crossed the finish line in Plymouth, she looked as if she had come straight from the builder's.

The success of this boat, of course, was possible because of the fine collaboration of the entire crew, led by an unusually experienced and even-tempered skipper, who managed to maintain morale and drive the boat as hard as caution allowed throughout the Whitbread Race.

Roderick Stephens, Jr.

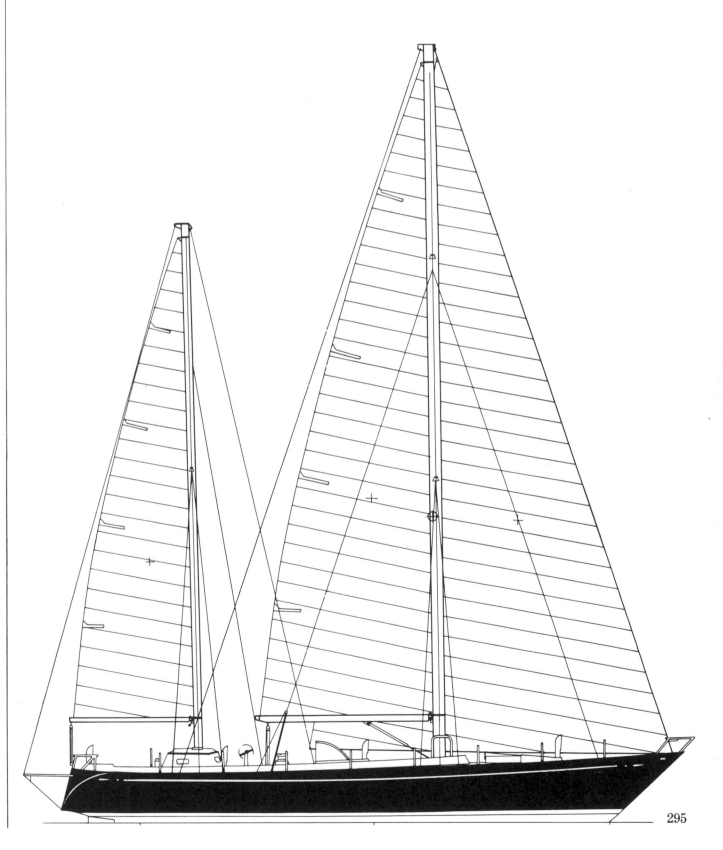

GLOSSARY OF SAILING TERMS

Aft
The back of a boat; behind the masts.

After Sails
Sails on masts back of the foremast.

Aground
When the hull or keel touches the bottom or the shore.

Ahead
The front of the boat; toward the front of the boat.

Ahull, Lying ahull
When all sails are lowered, usually in open water.

Aid to navigation
Mark that appears on charts—buoys, lights, etc.

Alee
Away from the direction of the wind.

Allowance
Handicap, in time, given to certain boats in races.

Aloft
In the rigging or up the mast.

Amidships
In the center of the boat.

Anemometer
An instrument that measures the velocity of the wind.

Angle of heel
The angle of a boat from the vertical, when sailing.

Apparent wind
The direction of the wind as it appears when the boat is moving. This varies with speed and direction of the boat.

Astern
To the rear of a boat.

Athwart
Across a boat; at right angles to the fore-and-aft line.

Auxiliary
An engine used as a secondary source of propulsion.

Aweather
To windward.

Aweigh
When the anchor is raised from the bottom.

Back
To force a sail out against the wind. The wind *backs* when it shifts in a counterclockwise direction.

Backstays
Wires that lead from the top of the mast to the stern of a boat.

Backwind
A wind that shifts in a counterclockwise direction.

Ballast
Heavy material placed in the bottom of a boat to give stability.

Balloon jib
Sail used on a reach; larger and fuller than a genoa.

Balloon sail
Any large lightweight sail used with working sails on a reach.

Bare poles
All sails lowered.

Bark
A three-masted boat, fore and mainmasts square-rigged, mizzenmast fore-and-aft rigged.

Barkentine
A three-masted boat, with main and mizzenmasts fore-and-aft rigged; foremast square-rigged.

Batten
A thin strip of wood or metal placed in a pocket on the leech of a sail.

Beacon
A light, or other navigation aid, usually on land, to warn boats of danger or obstruction.

Beam
The width of a boat at its widest point.

Beam sea
Waves running at right angles to the boat's course.

Beam wind
A wind that blows at right angles to a boat's course.

Bear
A direction word. *Bear down* is to approach from the windward. *Bear off* is to turn away from the wind. *Bear up* is to point the boat higher into the wind. *Bear in* is to approach shore.

Bearing
Direction. *To take bearings* is to pinpoint the position of a boat on a chart, or in relationship to points on land.

Beat
To sail in the direction from which the wind is blowing. This requires tacking.

Beaufort Scale
A table of wind velocity.

Before the wind
Sailing with the wind coming from behind.

Bell buoy
A buoy with a bell that sounds when the buoy is moved by the waves.

Below
Part of the boat that is under the deck.

Bend
To fasten by means of a knot.

Bermuda rigging
The use of triangular sails. Also called: Marconi and jib headed rigging.

Bight
A loop in a rope. Also a bend on a coastline.

Bilge
The lowest area in the hull, just above the keel.

Binnacle
The housing for a compass.

Bitter end
The end of a line or rope.

Block
A grooved wheel, housed in a frame. Lines are run through blocks to increase the force a person can apply to those lines.

Bobstays
Cables running from the bowsprit to the stem, near the waterline.

Bolt rope
The line sewn into the edge of a sail.

Boom
The bar to which the bottom, or foot, of the sail is attached. *Boom jack* is the tackle rigged to the boom to allow downward pressure.

Boot top
A stripe of paint applied to the hull at the waterline.

Bow
The front, or forward end, of a boat.

Bow line
A mooring line at the bow.

Bowline
A knot that forms a loop at the end of a rope.

Bowsprit
A spar, projecting from the bow, to which the jib stays are attached.

Breast line
Mooring line from the middle of the boat.

Bridge
Area of the deck where the helm and controls of the boat are located.

Brigantine
A two-masted boat. Foremast is square-rigged. Mainmast is fore-and-aft rigged.

Brightwork
Varnished wood on a boat.

Bring about
To come around, to reverse direction.

Bring to
To stop the forward motion of a boat by heading directly into the wind.

Broach
To swing broadside to the wind when sailing downwind.

Broad reach
Sailing with the wind between the quarter and the beam.

Bulkhead
A wall or partition below the decks, placed vertically along the centerline.

Bulwark
the partition formed where the hull rises over the deck.

Bumper
Any material placed on landings and piers to protect a boat from scraping.

Buoy
An anchored floating object marking a position. Some buoys are direction aids, some mark dangerous spots.

Burdened vessel
Any boat that must give way to another having the right of way.

By the lee
Running with the wind and the sails on the same side of the boat.

By the wind
Sailing as close to the wind as possible. Close-hauled.

Can
A buoy, shaped like a cylinder. It is painted black and used to mark the left side of a channel when entering port from open water.

Cardinal points
The four main directions on a compass.

Carvel
A smooth-planked hull construction.

Catamaran
A boat with twin hulls.

Catboat
A sailboat with a single mast placed well forward of amidships.

Centerboard
A device that acts as a keel in shallow-draft boats. It can be raised and lowered as necessary.

Chain plates
Metal plates attached to the side or the hull, to which the standing rigging is attached, stabilizing the mast.

Chart
A nautical map.

Chine
The line where the bottom of the boat joins the sides. When this line is an angle, the boat is said to be *hard chined*. When the point of juncture is rounded, the boat is said to be *soft chined*.

Chock
A guide for anchor and mooring lines.

Cleat
A fitting for securing a line.

Clew
The corner of the sail where the foot meets the leech.

Clinker
A lap-straked hull construction. The planks overlap one another.

Close-haul
To sail as close to the direction of the wind as possible.

Clove hitch
A knot used for mooring a boat.

Coaming
A sidepiece around an opening on the deck to keep water from coming in.

Colors
Flags identifying the boat by country, club, etc.

Come about
To bring the sail from one side of the boat to the other, when sailing into the wind. A maneuver in tacking.

Companionway
A stairway leading from deck to cabin.

Compass rose
A circle on a chart showing the points of the compass.

Compensate
To correct a compass reading to allow for magnetic attraction.

Corrected time
The actual time a boat takes to complete a race adjusted to the boat's handicap.

Crab
To move sideways in the water.

Craft
Any small boat.

Cutter
A sailboat with a single mast placed in the middle of the boat.

Daggerboard
A kind of centerboard that is raised and lowered in a trunk or housing.

Davits
A structure that projects over the side or rear of a boat used for raising and lowering a dinghy or small boat.

Day sailer
A boat that is not fitted for cruising over night. An open boat.

Dead ahead
A point directly in front of a moving boat. *Dead astern* is a point directly behind a moving boat.

Dead reckoning
Estimating a boat's position without using instruments, but applying to previous position and time.

Deviation
Compass error caused by local magnetic attraction.

Dinghy
A small boat fitted with oars and sometimes sails.

Dismast
To remove a mast or masts. To lose a mast or masts at sea.

Displacement
The weight, in tons, of the water displaced by the boat and its equipment.

Dory
A small seaworthy boat with a flat bottom and high sides.

Double-ender
a boat that is pointed at both bow and stern.

Downhaul
The line used to bring a sail down from the mast.

Downwind
Away from the direction the wind is coming from.

Draft
The depth of water required to float a boat. The depth of a boat from waterline to keel.

Ease
To loosen. To let out the line of a sail.

Ease off
To point slightly away from the wind.

Echo sounder
Depth finder.

Ensign
A flag identifying the nationality of a boat.

Fall off
To head a boat away from the direction of the wind.

Fathom
A unit of measurement for water depth. One fathom is six feet.

Fender
Any material attached to the side of a boat used to prevent scraping when tied up.

Fit out
To prepare a boat for a voyage.

Flashing light
A mark with a light that shows at regular intervals.

Following sea
Waves that approach from the rear of a moving boat.

Foot
The bottom edge of a sail.

Fore
Toward the front of a boat.

Fore-and-aft
From front to back of a boat.

Forecastle
The area under the deck of a boat that is toward the front.

Fore deck
The part of the deck of a boat that is toward the front.

Foremast
The mast of a two- or more masted boat that is closest to the front.

Forestay
A wire or cable that runs from the mast to the bow of a boat.

Forestaysail
A small triangular sail, used instead of a jib, attached to the forestay.

Foul
Tangled or twisted.

Freeboard
The vertical distance from the top of the hull to the water.

Furl
To roll a sail up and secure it to yard or boom.

Gaff
A spar that supports the head of a sail in a gaff-rigged boat.

Galley
A boat's kitchen.

Gear
All the equipment a boat carries.

Genoa
A large jib that overlaps the mainsail. It is controlled by sheets, or lines, that run outside the standing rigging. It is sometimes referred to as a *jenny*.

Gimbal
A device used to suspend equipment so that it remains level at all times.

Go about
To change tack to windward.

Ground tackle
Any equipment used to secure a boat to the bottom, or to a mooring.

Gunkholing
Taking short trips in a boat; shallow water cruising.

Gunwale
The railing along the deck of a boat; the bulwark along the upper side.

Guy
A wire used as a support for booms, davits, etc.

Half-hitch
A loop used to fasten a rope or line to a stationary object.

Halyard
Line used to raise or lower a sail.

Hatch
An opening in the deck that gives access to space below.

Hawser
A heavy rope or cable, used for towing or for mooring large vessels.

Head
A ship's toilet.

Heading
Direction in which a boat's bow is pointing.

Head down
To turn the boat away from the direction the wind is blowing.

Head into the wind
To point a boat in the direction the wind is blowing.

Head off
Head down.

Headsail
Any sail set forward of the foremast.

Head up
To turn the boat into the wind until the sails slacken.

Heave to
To turn the bow of the boat into the wind and keep it there, so that the boat lies almost still.

Heaving line
A line for throwing.

Heel
The lateral tilting of a boat in motion, due to wind, sometimes to waves.

Helm
The rudder and the tiller or wheel, used to steer a boat.

Hike
To lean out over the side of a small boat to counteract heeling.

Hoist
To haul up, to raise the sail.

Hold
The storage area below deck.

Hook
Anchor.

Housing
The section of a mast that is fitted below deck. Also called *step*.

Hull
The body of the boat.

Hull speed
A theoretical speed, computed by multiplying the length of the boat at waterline by 1.4, and taking the square root of that figure.

In irons
The nose of the boat is directly in the wind and all forward motion has stopped.

Inshore
Toward the shore.

International Code
A system of signals, using flags.

Jib
A triangular sail that is set before the foremast, that does not overlap the mainsail.

Jib boom
A spar to which the bottom, or foot, of the jib is attached.

Jibe
To change direction in a boat in such a way that the wind passes behind the boat. Also *Gybe*.

Jib halyard
The line that raises and lowers the jib.

Jib-headed rig
A boat that is fitted with all triangular sails.

Jib sheet
The line that controls the jib.

Jib stay
The forward standing stay to which the jib is attached.

Kedge
A kind of anchor.

Keel
A weighted, projecting fin on the bottom of a boat, for stability.

Ketch
A two-masted boat, the smaller of the masts placed behind the larger, and in front of the stern post.

Knot
A unit of speed. One knot is one nautical mile per hour.

Land breeze
A wind blowing from land to sea.

Landmark
A mark or object on shore used to aid navigation.

Lanyard
A line used to secure a small object on a boat, or on a person.

Lapstrake
Clinker. Construction of a boat with overlapping planks.

Lateral resistance
The capacity of a boat to resist being pushed sideways in the water.

Latitude
Position, in degrees, north and south of the Equator.

Lazarette
A small compartment for storing equipment.

Lazy guy
Rigging to prevent jibing in rough seas.

League
Three nautical miles.

Leeboards
Boards projecting from the hull to increase lateral resistance.

Leech
The after edge of a sail.

Lee helm
A tendency to bear off the wind.

Lee shore
The land toward which the wind is blowing. The *lee of a shore* is the side protected from the wind.

Leeward
Away from the wind.

Leeway
Movement away from the wind.

Lie to
To head into the wind and stop forward motion.

Lifeline
A safety device that consists of lines on posts or stanchions around the deck of a boat.

Lift
A line from a yardarm or boom to the top of the mast.

Line
Any rope used on a boat.

List
Leaning to one side because of improperly balanced loads.

LOA
Length of a boat at the longest measurement.

Locker
A storage compartment or closet.

Log
A device, mounted under the stern of a boat, that measures speed.

Logbook
A boat's record of activity.

Longitude
Position, in degrees, east and west of Greenwich, England.

Loose-footed
Describing a headsail that is not attached to a boom.

Loran
A system of radio navigation, requiring special charts and equipment.

Low
Low pressure system.

Luff
The leading, or forward, edge of a sail. When this edge shakes in the wind, the sail is *luffing*.

Luff rope
Rope sewn into the luff of a sail.

LWL
Length of a boat at the waterline.

Mainsail
The sail that is attached to main, or largest, mast of a boat.

Mainsheet
Line attached to the main boom that controls the mainsail.

Make fast
To secure a line or rope.

Marconi rig
A boat fitted with triangular sails.

Marline
A small tarred line or rope.

Marlinspike
A pointed instrument used in splicing.

Mast
The vertical spar or pole supporting boom and sails.

Mast step
The fitting on deck or the keelson to which the mast set. To *step the mast* is to put the mast into the boat in position.

Mayday
From the French *m'aidez*, a distress signal.

Mean high water
The depth of the water at average high tide.

Mean low water
The depth of the water at average low tide.

Measurement rule
A system of handicaps that permits small boats of similar but not exact size to race.

Mid-channel buoy
A marker placed in a channel. It may be passed on either side.

Midships
The widest point on a boat.

Mile
A nautical mile is 6,080 feet.

Mizzen
Mizzenmast. The shorter, after mast on a boat.

Mizzen sail
A sail set on the mizzen.

Motor sailer
A boat that uses both sail and engine. The engine in these boats is larger than an auxiliary.

Multihull
Any boat with more than one hull.

Navigation lights
At sundown all boats in open water are required to carry lights. The system of lighting differs for each kind of boat.

Neap tide
The lowest tide in the lunar month. The high tides are lower than mean high, and the low tides are lower than mean low.

Nose
Stem of a boat.

Nun
A cone shaped buoy, painted red, that is kept to the right side of a boat entering port.

Occulting light
A navigational light on a marker or buoy that has longer periods of light than of darkness in its signal. In flashing lights, this is reversed.

Offshore race
A race in open water, at sea.

Offshore wind
The wind blowing from the shore.

Oilskins
Waterproof clothing.

One-design boats
A boat built to class specifications for competition.

On the beam
At right angles to a boat. *On the bow* is the angle from the bow to 45 degrees on either side. *On the quarter* is midway from beam to stern.

Outboard
Off the boat's hull, over the water.

Outhaul
A line used to attach the end of a sail to the end of the boom, so that the sail can be adjusted.

Outpoint
To sail closer to the wind than a competing boat.

Over correcting
To swing the boat further than is needed to correct the course.

Overhang
Those parts of the boat that extend forward and back of the waterline.

Overhaul
Overtake. To catch up to a boat ahead and pass.

Overstand
To shoot past a mark, as a buoy or channel entrance.

Painter
A line at the bow of a small boat for mooring.

Parachute
Balloon spinnaker.

Parachute flare
A distress signal.

Parallel rules
Two rulers, hinged together, that can be adjusted in distance while remaining parallel.

Parallels
Lines of latitude, north and south of the Equator.

Passage
A route between points or ports.

Pay off
To turn a boat away from the wind.

Pay out
To let out line or rope.

Pelorus
A special compass card used for taking bearings.

Pennant
A small tapering flag.

Permanent backstay
Part of the standing rigging. A line or cable that runs from the stern to the top of the mast.

Pitch
The rhythmic bow-to-stern movement of the boat, due to waves.

Pitch-pole
To turn end over end.

Planing
Riding on top of the water, rather than plowing through it.

Planing hull
A hull that is constructed to plane.

Plot
To calculate a course.

Point
A thirty-second of a circle.

Point of sailing
Direction of a boat in relation to the wind.

Poop
To have a wave break over the stern of a boat.

Port
The left side of a boat, looking toward the bow.

Port tack
When the wind comes over the port side of a boat, and the sails are on the starboard side.

Pram
A small rectangular row boat.

Prevailing wind
Average wind direction for season and area.

Privileged vessel
Boat that has the right of way.

Pulpit
A guard rail at the bow of a boat.

Punt
A small, flatbottomed rowboat.

Quarter
The section of a boat between the stern and the beam, within 45 degrees of the stern.

Quartering
Sailing with the wind between the stern and the beam.

Race
A strong tide created by two currents meeting.

Radar
Electronic direction-finding equipment, used to locate marks and objects.

Raise
To sight an object from a boat.

Rake
Position of a mast backward from vertical.

Rating
Classification of a sailboat according to Measurement Rules.

Ratlines
Ladder used to climb the rigging.

Reach
Any point of sailing between close-hauled and running.

Reaching jib
A large, light sail used primarily in racing.

Ready about!
Warning cry before coming about.

Reckoning
Calculating the position of the boat in the water.

Reef
To reduce the working area of a sail by lowering it part way.

Reef knot
A square knot.

Reef point
Small rope used in reefing. These ropes are attached at intervals across the sail.

Regatta
A series of boat races.

Ride
To sit at anchor.

Rigging
All lines, shrouds, and stays on a boat that pertain to the sails and masts.

Right
To turn right side up.

Rip tide
A strong incoming tide.

Rode
Line that attaches to an anchor.

Roll
Side-to-side motion.

Rudder
A device attached to a boat for steering. It is controlled by tiller or wheel.

Rules of the Road
International regulations for boats.

Run
To sail with the wind astern.

Running lights
Lights required on all moving boats after sundown.

Running rigging
All lines, halyards and sheets used in controlling sails and spars.

Schooner
A boat with two or more masts, the mainmast set aft the smaller mast(s).

Scope
The length of anchor line while the anchor is down.

Scow
A rectangular, flat-bottomed boat.

Screw
Propeller.

Scud
To run before a stormwind.

Scull
A boat steered by a single oar at the stern.

Scupper
A drain hole in a rail or toe-rail or gunwale, allowing water to run off.

Seacock
A valve at a through-hull fitting, to allow intake or drainage of water.

Sea-kindly
Sea-worthy; handling well in rough seas or heavy winds.

Secure
To tie down; make fast.

Set sails
To hoist sails.

Sextant
An instrument that determines altitude of sun and stars.

Shackle
A metal fastener, shaped like a U with a moveable metal pin to close it.

Sheerline
A fore-and-aft curve of a boat's deck at the side.

Sheet
A line used to control the trim of a sail.

Shorten
To reef a sail, or drop a sail. To reduce sail area on a boat.

Shroud
A wire cable used as standing, or permanent, rigging to support the mast.

Sideslip
To move sideways through the water.

Single handed
To sail alone; without crew.

Sister ship
A boat built to the same design as another.

Skiff
A small, light rowboat or sailboat.

Skin
The outer covering of a boat. The planking or fiberglass.

Slack
To loosen, or ease, a line.

Slackwater
Period at the turning of the tide when the water is not moving.

Slide
A small device attached to the front edge and bottom of a sail to attach it to the mast and boom.

Slip
A mooring at dock.

Sloop
A boat with a single mast set forward of midships.

Sound
To measure the depth of water by means of a lead line or echo sounder.

Soundings
Depths as they appear on charts.

Spanker
A gaff-headed sail attached to the mizzenmast.

Spinnaker
A large, light triangular sail used in light airs.

Spinnaker pole
A spar or pole used to hold the spinnaker away from the mast.

Spitfire jib
A small strong storm jib.

Splice
To join two ropes or to make a permanent loop in a rope.

Spreader
A spar on the mast which holds the stays.

Spring lines
Mooring lines used to keep a boat from moving forward and back in a slip.

Squall
A sudden fast-moving storm.

Square-rigged
A boat with square sails.

Stanchion
A post or upright support for guard rail and lifelines.

Standing rigging
The shrouds and stays that support a mast; these are permanent fixtures while the mast is in place.

Starboard
The right side of a boat, facing the bow.

Starboard tack
Sailing with the wind coming from the starboard side, the sails on the port.

Stay
Cable or wire running from the mast to the bow or stern.

Staysail
A triangular sail set on a stay that runs behind the forestay.

Steerageway
Forward motion, allowing control of the tiller or wheel.

Stern
The after end of a boat.

Sternway
Moving backward in the water.

Stiff
Stable. Returning to even keel after heeling.

Storm jib
A small, strong jib.

Storm sails
Small, strong sails for use in heavy weather.

Storm trysail
A small, strong, loose-footed sail set in place of a mainsail to maintain a heading into the wind in a blow.

Stow
To put something in its place. To store.

Strake
Planks in a hull.

Strike
To lower on a line; to lower sails or flags.

Swab
To mop.

Swamp
To fill with water.

Swell
A series of large waves caused by heavy weather a distance away. *Ground swell* is the action of waves at sea.

Swivel
A device used to prevent lines or wires from twisting.

Tack
To sail to windward by alternating courses, staying as close to the wind as possible. To zigzag into the wind.

Tackle
A system of lines and blocks for hoisting and lowering sails, and for hauling.

Take in sail
To lower sail.

Telltale
Any lightweight device attached to mast or shrouds to indicate apparent wind.

Tender
Unstable. A boat that heels readily and does not return to even keel easily after heeling.

Tenon
The bottom or heel of the mast that fits into the step.

Tide
The regular movement of ocean water, caused by gravitational forces of moon and sun.

Tiller
A bar connected to the rudder for steering.

Top light
A signal light.

Topping lift
A line that attaches the boom to the mast and takes the strain off the mainsail while it is lowered or set. Also a device used with a spinnaker.

Topside
The deck.

Transom
The flat area of the hull, at the stern of a boat.

Trim
To adjust a sail by using the sheets to proper relationship with the wind.

Trimaran
A boat with three hulls.

Trough
The dip between two waves.

True course
The angle between the centerline of a boat and the true north-south line.

True wind
The actual direction of the wind, as observed from a stationary point. Opposed to apparent wind, which is affected by the movement of the boat.

Trunk
The centerboard housing.

Trysail
See storm trysail.

Turnbuckle
A device for adjusting the tension on the shrouds and stays.

Unbend
Untie.

Under bare poles
To have no sails up.

Under the lee
Out of the wind. Protected from the wind by land mass or another boat.

Under way
Moving.

Union Jack
A small flag representing the nationality of the boat.

Up
Into the wind.

Vane
A weathercock. A wind direction indicator.

Vang
A line used to stabilize the boom.

Variation
The degrees of difference between true north and magnetic north.

Veer
To change directions suddenly. To change direction clockwise.

Watch
The division of time on a boat.

Waterline
The theoretical line on the hull where the boat meets the water.

Way
Movement.

Weather helm
A tendency to head into the wind.

Weather side
The windward side, onto which the wind is blowing.

Well-found
Well equipped and fitted.

Wheel
Steering mechanism.

Whisker pole
A pole attached to the mast, booming out the jib.

Whistle buoy
A floating marker equipped with a whistle that sounds when the buoy moves in the water.

Winch
A device for hauling in lines.

Wing and wing
Having sails set on both sides of a boat.

Working sails
The sails used on a boat under ordinary conditions.

Yacht
Any boat used solely for pleasure.

Yaw
To swing off course in heavy seas.

Yawl
A two-masted boat, with the smaller, after mast stepped behind the stern post.

Zenith
The sky exactly overhead.

SINGLE-HANDED SAILORS, A CHRONOLOGY

* Circumnavigation
After 1965 only circumnavigations were recorded

1849–1876
J.M. Crenston (USA)
From New Bedford to San Francisco, 1849, by way of either Cape Horn or the Magellan Straits; 13,000 miles in 226 days. The first reliably confirmed single-hander.
Tocca, cutter, 40 ft. 4 in.

Alfred Johnson (USA)
From Shag Harbour (Canada) to Abercastle (Wales) in 46 days, from June 25 to Aug 10, 1876. First single-handed Atlantic crossing.
Centennial, a cutter rigged dory with squaresail, 20′ LOA.

1882–1883
Bernard Gilboy (USA)
Sailed August 18, 1892, from San Francisco for Queensland, Australia. Without making port en route, made 6500 miles in 162 days and was picked up January 29, 1883, with no provisions on board. First crossing of the Pacific from East to West.
Pacific, schooner, 19′ LOA.

1891—First Singlehanded Transatlantic Race
William A. Andrews (USA)
Started in Boston June 21, abandoned attempt 660 nautical miles from the European coast August 22.
Mermaid, sloop.

Josiah Lawlor (USA)
From Boston to Coverack (Lizards) from June 21 to August 5, 45 days.
Sea Serpent, double ender, 15′1″ LOA.

1892
William A. Andrews (USA)
From Atlantic City (USA) to Palos (Spain), July 20 to September 25.
Sapolio, sloop, 14′5″ LOA; own construction.

1894
A. Frietsch (Finland)
From New York to Queenstown (Ireland), August 5 to December 13.
Nina, schooner, hard chine, 39′4″ LOA; own construction.

1895–1898*
Joshua Slocum
(Canadian-born USA citizen)
From Yarmouth, Mass. to Newport in 3 years 4 days. First circumnavigation of the world through the Magellan Straits.
Spray, cutter (later, yawl), 36′7″ LOA; own construction.

1899
Howard Blackburn
(Canadian-born USA citizen)
From Gloucester (USA) to Gloucester (England), 60 days—June 18 to August 17; sailed without his fingers, which he had lost to frostbite.
Great Western, 30′ LOA; own construction.

1901
Howard Blackburn
(Canadian-born USA citizen)
From Gloucester (USA) to Lisbon; June 9 to July 17; 38 days.
Great Republic, cutter, 24′11″ LOA.

1903
Ludwig Eisenbraun
(German-born USA citizen)
From Halifax to Funchal; August 28 to October 23; 56 days. Continued to Gibraltar and Marseilles despite capsize.
Columbia II, cutter, 18′4″ LOA.

1920
Tommy Drake (USA)
Several world voyages, sailed a total of 130,000 nautical miles; shipwrecked several times.
Sir Francis I, *Sir Francis II*, *Pilgrim*, 34′11″ LOA; *Progress*, 37′ LOA.

1921–1925*
Harry Pidgeon (USA)
From Los Angeles to Los Angeles via the Torres Straits, Cape of Good Hope, and Panama, in 3 years, 11 months, 13 days. First circumnavigation through the Panama Canal. Winner of the Blue Water Medal of the Cruising Club of America.
Islander, yawl, 33′11″ LOA; own construction. 1909–1911

1923
Alain Gerbault (France)
Gibraltar to New York in 101 days, South Route; first Atlantic crossing from East to West; awarded Blue Water Medal for this achievement.
Firecrest, cutter, built 1892, 39′4″ LOA.

1924–1929*
Alain Gerbault (France)
From Cannes to Le Havre, via Panama and the Cape of Good Hope; November 1, 1924 to July 25, 1929.
Firecrest, cutter, 39′4″ LOA.

1927
Günther Plüschow (Germany)
From Germany to Bahia (Brazil).

1928
Teresio Fava (Italy)
From Italy to Newfoundland, May 16 to August 2, then lost at sea.
Cutter, 19′8″ LOA.

1928–1932*
Edward Miles (USA)
Via the Red Sea on an Eastern course, first to go through both the Suez and the Panama canals.
Sturdy, schooner, 37′ LOA; burned in Red Sea. *Sturdy II*, 36′8″ LOA; equipped with diesel engine, the first used by a singlehander.

1928–1929
Paul Müller (Germany)
From Hamburg, on July 6, 1928, via Spain and Barbados to Miami, on June 1, 1929. Boat lost off Cape Hatteras; swam to safety.
Aga, fishing sloop, 18′ LOA; own construction.

1931–1932
Vito Dumas (Argentina)
From Spain, in December, to Buenos Aires.
Legh, yawl.

1932
Alain Gerbault (France)
From Marseilles to the Pacific Islands.
Firecrest, sloop, 33′11″ LOA.

1932
A. Nardi (Italy)
From Australia via Panama to Italy.

1932–1933
Fred Rebell
(Latvia, living in Australia)
From Sydney, Australia, to San Pedro, Colombia, in 372 days. First over the Pacific from West to East.
Elaine, clinker sloop, 18′ LOA.

1932–1937*
Harry Pidgeon (USA)
From New London to New London; June 8, 1932 to June 15, 1937, via Guinea. The first to circumnavigate the world twice, singlehanded.
Islander, yawl, 34′5″ LOA.

1932–1934
Alfon Hansen (Norway)
From Oslo by way of Las Palmas and Miami to Argentina; then the first around Cape Horn from East to West; disappeared off Chile.
Mary Jane, gaff sloop, 36′1″ LOA.

1933
Marin-Marie (France)
From Douranenez to Funchal in 14 days, from Funchal to Fort-de-France in 29 days, then to New York in 21 days.
Winnibelle, double-ender, 36′1″ LOA. Twin running jibs.

1933–1934
R.D. Graham (England)
From Bantry to St. John (Newfoundland) in 24½ days, sailed single-handed in Labrador waters, then to Bermuda and back. First across the Atlantic from East to West over the northern route.
Emanuel, cutter, 30′ LOA.

1933–1934
Lionel W.B. Rees (England)
From England to the Bahamas during winter; was awarded the Blue Water Medal.
May, Norwegian ketch, 32′ LOA.

1935
A.V. Kaariatta (Finland)
From Helsinfors to Rio de Janeiro.
Sport, cutter, 31′10″ LOA.

1936
Jean Gau (France)
From New York on June 15; ran aground and wrecked off Cadiz.
Onda, schooner, 39′4″ LOA.

1936
Marin-Marie (France)
From New York to Le Havre; July 23 to August 10; first and to this day only Atlantic crossing on engine power alone; awarded the Blue Water Medal.
Arielle, 42′8″ LOA; 4 cycle Baudoin Diesel engine, 1300 gallons fuel.

1936–1938*
Louis Bernicot (France)
From Crantec to Verdon via the Magellan Straits in one year, 9 months, and 22 days.
Anahita, sloop, 41′ LOA; engine.

1937
Ludwig Schlimbach (Germany)
Lisbon, the Azores, New York.
Störtebecker 3, yawl, 33′5″ LOA.

1938
Frank E. Clark (England)
From Portsmouth, August 23, then from Penzance to Charleston, November 10.
Girl Kathleen, fishing cutter, 31′ LOA.

1938
Hein Garbers (Germany)
From Hamburg, May 22 to Spain, July 9, and then to New York on August 28.
Windspiel III

1939
Guido Clifford Avery (USA)
From Tampa, Florida, to France.
Miss Tampa, ketch, 26′3″ LOA.

1939
Frank E. Clark (England)
From New York to Newlyn (Cornwall), June 13 to July 16; 33 days.
Girl Kathleen, fishing cutter, 31′ LOA.

1939
Harry Young (USA)
New York to the Azores in 39 days; second smallest boat to cross the Atlantic.
Open sloop, 13′9″ LOA; own construction.

1942–1943*
Vito Dumas (Argentina)
First circumnavigation from West to East on the southern route; was awarded the Blue Water Medal.
Legh II, 31′6″ LOA.

1946
Hans de Meiss-Teufen (Switzerland)
Non-stop from Casablanca to New York in 58 days.
Speranza, Bermuda yawl, aux. motor, 39′4″ LOA.

1947
Jean Gau (France)
On May 28 from New York via the Azores to Valras-Plage.
Atom, ketch, 30′ LOA.

1948
Joseph F. Pettersen (USA)
From Estramadura, Portugal to Northest Harbour, Nova Scotia in 55 days.
Seven Seas, yawl, 37′9″ LOA.

1948–1952
Alfred Peterson (USA)
From Oxford, Maryland, in June 1948 to New York; awarded the Blue Water Medal. The first to use the Panama and Suez canals on the western route.
Stornoway, double-ender, 33′ LOA; engine.

1949
Jean Gau (France)
From Valras-Plage to Funchal, from there to Montauk (via New York) in 55 days.
Atom, ketch, 30′ LOA.

1949–1951
Edward Allcard (England)
From Helford, Cornwall, to Gibraltar; from there to New York in 80 days, back from New York on August 5, 1950; returned to Plymouth on July 17, 1951.
Temptress, yawl, 42′8″ LOA.

1949–1952*
Jacques-Yves le Toumelin (France)
Sailed with crew to Papeete, then single-handed, from Le Croisic to Le Croisic via Panama, the Torres Straits, and the Cape in 2 years, 9 months and 18 days. Aged 28 at departure.
Kurun, double-ender, 32′10″ LOA.

1950–1953
Adrian Hayter (England)
First singlehanded sailor from England to New Zealand by way of Port Said, Aden, and Bombay.
Sheila II, double-ended yawl, 32′ LOA; engine.

1950–1958*
Marcel Bardiaux (France)
From Le Havre to Rio de Janeiro. Rounded Cape Horn on May 12, 1952. Via Papeete, Durban, and New York to Le Havre; awarded the Blue Water Medal.
Les Quatre Vents, sloop, 30′9″ LOA; own construction.

1951
Clyde Deal (USA)
From Mandal, Norway, on June 25, 1950 to Gibraltar; then the Canary Islands, April 29, to New York in 55 days.
Ram, double-ender, 33′ LOA.

1951
Lee (first name not known) (USA)
From the USA to the Marquesas Islands.
Manzanita, 40′ LOA.

1951–1952
Dick Tober (the Netherlands)
From Ijmuiden, Netherlands, on August 21, 1951 to Auckland in 15 months. Crossed Atlantic in 25 days. Panama to Galapagos in 9 days. Aged 26 when voyage began.
Onrust, steel ketch, 37′1″ LOA.

1952–1953
Ann Davison (England)
From Plymouth via Casablanca, Las Palmas and Miami to New York. First woman to cross the Atlantic single-handed.
Felicity-Ann, sloop, 22′11″ LOA.

1953
Olavi Kivikosky (Finland)
From America to Wilhelmshaven in 66 days.
Turquoise, 32′10″ LOA.

1954
Sven Toffs (USA)
From New York to Ireland.
Latea, cutter, 34′5″ LOA.

1955
George Boston (USA)
35 years of age. From America to Gibraltar in 21 days. Tahitian pirogue, ketch, 29′6″ LOA; own construction; engine.

1955
Bernard Moitessier (France)
From the Mauritius Islands to Durban.
Marie-Therese II

1955
Jacques-Yves le Toumelin (France)
From Croisic by way of Grand Canary Island, January 9; and Guadeloupe to Le Croisic, July 27.
Kurun, double-ender, 32′10″ LOA.

1955–1956
Jean Lacombe (France)
From Marseille by way of the Canary Islands, Puerto Rico, and Atlantic City to New York.
Hippocampe, cutter, 18′ LOA; own construction.

1955–1957*
Jean Gau (France)
From America to Durban, December 1955, in 87 days. Ascension Island, May 1956, then Azores to Gibraltar; Valras-Plage, October 1956. Arrived in New York on July 17, 1957.
Atom, ketch, 30′ LOA.

1955–1959*
John Guzzwell (England)
Departure from Victoria, Canada, on September 10, 1955. San Francisco-Honolulu in 29 days, then Samoa, New Zealand. Two-year layover. Sydney, Torres Strait, Panama, Galapagos, Hawaii, and finally arrived in Vancouver, Canada, September 10, 1959; awarded the Blue Water Medal. Aged 25 years at beginning of voyage.
Trekka, yawl, 20′6″ LOA; own construction.

1955–1959
Hannes Lindeman (Germany)
Crossed the Atlantic in 1955-56, 1956-57 and 1959; three times aboard three different boats.

1956
Bill Geering
From Freemantle to the Mauritius Islands.
Kate, 20′8″ LOA.

1956
John Goodwin (England)
From Las Palmas to Barbados in 26 days.
Speedwell of Hong-Kong, sloop, 25′1″ LOA.

1956
Peter Hamilton (Great Britain)
From August 1 from Clyde, Scotland, to Quebec, Canada, September 10.
Salmo, sloop, 24′8″ LOA.

1956
Joseph Havkins (Israel)
The Pacific from Mexico to Israel.
Lamerhak II, yawl, 22′11″ LOA.

1956
Harold Jacobsen (Norway)
Atlantic crossing, East to West.
Nengo, cutter, 22′11″ LOA.

1956
Donald Shave
From Plymouth to Rio de Janeiro.
Colin Archer, cutter, 34′5″ LOA.

1956–1957
Pierre Guillaume (France)
From Singapore to Cape Guardafui via Chagos and the Seychelles. Ran aground in the Red Sea.
Monahora, ketch, 28′10″ LOA.

1957
Joseph Cunningham (Canada)
From southern Ireland to the West Indies via Las Palmas.
Icebird, sloop, 24′7″ LOA.

1957
Richard Doran
Atlantic crossing from East to West.
Verity, 37′9″ LOA.

1957
Bernard Kohler (Switzerland)
Concarneau, the Canary Islands, Fort-de-France in 38 days.
Va danser, cutter, 21′ LOA.

1957
Peter Tangvald (Norwegian-born USA citizen)
Las Palmas to Antigua in 31 days.
Windflower, yawl, 45′ LOA.

1957–1973*
Edward Allcard (England)
From East to West around Cape Horn.
Sea Wanderer, ketch, 36′ LOA.

1958
George Ballas (Canada)
Sailed, January 6 from Las Palmas; in Barbados at the beginning of February, then to New York.
Fei Lin, sloop, 30′ LOA.

1958–1960
Gui Clabaud (France)
From Las Palmas, October 23, 1958, to Panama, Tahiti, the Loyalty Islands, June 1959. Died of jaundice during his world voyage.
Eole, ketch, 32′ LOA; own design.

1959
Tom Dower
Wrecked off the Canaries coming from Newfoundland; built a new boat and sailed it to Africa.
Newfoundlander, sloop, 36′1″ LOA.

1959
Cristopher de Grabowski (Poland)
From Tangiers, April 12, 1959 to New York, July 5, 1959; 84 days.
Thetys, cutter, 25′1″ LOA.

1959
Mervyn Liappiat (Great Britain)
From the Cape Verde Islands to Carlisle Bay in 18 days.
Fingal, cutter, 32′10″ LOA.

1959
Axel Pederson (Denmark)
From Auckland to San Francisco; then to Denmark. Pacific crossing from West to East.
Marco Polo, ketch, 27′10″ LOA.

1959
Peter Phillips
Atlantic crossing from East to West.
Morna, ketch, 48′8″ LOA.

1959
Briant Platt (USA)
Hong Kong, Okinawa, Midway (dismasted). Arrived in San Francisco on December 25, 1959, after 2 months and 3 days.
High Tea, three masted junk, 32′ LOA; diesel.

1959
Lars Roedhal
Atlantic crossing from East to West.
Serene, schooner, 50′10″ LOA.

1959–1960
Colin L. Fox
Las Palmas, December 24, 1959, to St.Croix, February 12, 1960; then to New York.
Vaiger, cutter, 33′1″ LOA.

1959–1960*
Patrik Moore (New Zealand)
From Rarotonga, August 16, 1959 to Auckland, March 6, 1960; missing at sea on the Pacific for 7 months.
Drifter, cutter, 29′6″ LOA.

1959–1964*
Peter Tangvald (Norwegian-born USA citizen)
From Brixham to Las Palmas. To Antigua in 29 days, then Los Angeles to Tahiti; reached Mediterranean in 1963, returned to Brixham by August 1964.
Dorothea, cutter, 32′ LOA.

1960
Sir Francis Chichester (England)
Winner of the Plymouth–New York Transatlantic Race in 40 days; awarded the Blue Water Medal.
Gipsy Moth III, cutter, 39′8″ LOA.

Daniel Gautier (France)
From Le Croisic, May 31, 1960, to New York, November 6, 1960; 159 days.
Isis, sloop, 24′7″ LOA; Couach engine

Blondie Hasler (England)
Second in the Transatlantic Race from Plymouth to New York, in 48 days.
Yester, folk boat with fully battened sail, 25′1″ LOA.

Valentine Howells (England)
Fourth in the New York–Plymouth Transatlantic Race in 63 days
Eira, folk boat.

Claude E. Johnson (USA)
From Norway to San Diego.
Farida, ketch, 40′8″ LOA; engine.

Jean Lacombe (France)
Fifth in the Transatlantic Race, in 74 days.
Cap Horn, sloop, 21′4″ LOA.

David Lewis (England)
Third in the Plymouth–New York Transatlantic Race, in 54 days.
Cardinal Vertue, sloop, 25'1" LOA.

1961–1962
Edward Allcard (England)
From Antigua to Montevideo in 100 days.
Sea Wanderer, ketch, 36' LOA.

1961–1966*
Michel Mermod (Switzerland)
World cruise via the China Sea from December 4, 1961 to February 7, 1966.
Geneva, sloop, 25'1" LOA.

1962
Sir Francis Chichester (England)
Across the Atlantic in 33 days.
Gipsy Moth III, cutter, 39'8" LOA.

1962
Kenichi Horie (Japan)
From Osaka on May 12, 1962, to San Francisco, August 12; 5300 miles.
Mermaid, sloop, 19' LOA.

1962
Bill Howell (Australia)
From Las Palmas on July 12, arrived in Barbados on August 5.
Stardrift, 8-ton cutter, 30' LOA.

1962–1963
Jim Stephenson
From England to Florida.
Le Reve, sloop, 26'3" LOA.

1962–1965*
William E. Nance (Australia)
From England via Buenos Aires and Cape Town to Melbourne.
Cardinal Vertue, sloop, 25'1" LOA.

1963
Tom Dower
Newfoundland to Senegal by way of the Antilles.
Newfoundlander, sloop, 36'1" LOA.

Stanley Jablonski (Poland)
From Poland to USA.
Amethyst, sloop, 28'3" LOA.

Ron Russel (England)
Atlantic crossing from East to West.
Gannet, Hillyard sloop, 21' LOA.

1963–1968*
Jean Gau (France)
From Valras, May 26, 1963. Tahiti, Auckland, New Guinea, Durban, until capsized and dismasted; managed to reach Mossel Bay. Without stopping at the Cape, sailed to Puerto Rico in 123 days. Miami to New York on June 10, 1967; Valras on October 9, 1968.
Atom, ketch, 30' LOA.

1964
Rene Blondeau (France)
From Corsica on October 23, to Las Palmas and Mindelo (Cape Verde Islands). Arrived November 18 in Fort-de-France.
Aigle de Mer, Diable double keel, 265'3" LOA.

1964
Sir Francis Chichester (England)
Second in the Transatlantic Race, in 29 days.
Gipsy Moth III, cutter, 39'8" LOA.

1964
Valentine Howells (England)
Third in the Transatlantic Race, in 32 days.
Akka, sloop, 35' LOA.

1964
Jean de Kat (France)
From La Rochelle, April 1, 1964, via the Canaries, to New York on June 22.
Ombrine, 32'8" LOA.

Arthur Piver (England)
Bermuda to Plymouth, first transatlantic crossing in a trimaran; lost at sea 1968.
Seabird, trimaran.

Phillipe Puiais (France)
From Las Palmas, February 8, to Fort-de-France, March 14.
Mahina

Sir Alex Rose (England)
Fourth in the Transatlantic Race.
Lively Lady, yawl, 36' LOA.

Oliver Stern-Veyrin
From Martinique to Tangiers.
Smile, ketch.

Eric Tabarly (France)
Winner of the Transatlantic Race, in 27 days; awarded the Blue Water Medal for this achievement.
Pen Duick II, ketch, 44' LOA.

1964–1966*
Pierre Auboiroux (France)
From La-Trinté-sur-Mer, September 2, 1964, via the Torres Straits, Red Sea, Genova, to Hyères, August 29, 1966.
Néo-Vent, sloop, 27' LOA.

1964–1967*
Frank Casper (Germany)
From Florida through the Panama Canal around South Africa and back to Germany; received the Blue Water Medal in 1970.
Elsie, cutter, 29'5" LOA.

1964–1967
John Riding (England)
England, Azores, Bermuda, Rhode Island; boat lost in the Tasmanian Sea.
Sjo-Ag, sloop, 12' LOA.

1964–1969*
Walter Koenig (Germany)
Third German single-handed circumnavigator; Hamburg, Panama, New Zealand, Suez, Germany.
Zarathustra, sloop, 27' LOA.

1965–1966
John Goetzcke (USA)
From Brisbane through the South China Sea to Malaya; across the Indian Ocean to Durban.
Valkyrie, ketch, 32' LOA.

1965–1966
Alex Carozzo (Italy)
Pacific crossing, West to East, 6000 miles.
Golden Lion, sloop, 32'8" LOA; own construction.

1965
Robert Manry (USA)
In 78 days, from Falmouth (USA) to Falmouth (England).
Tinkerbelle, sloop, 13'5" LOA.

1965–1968*
Wilfried Erdman (Germany)
First German single-handed circumnavigator; in 420 days at sea, made port only six times and covered approx. 30,000 miles.
Kathena, centerboarder, 25' LOA.

1965–1968*
Rusty Webb (Great Britain)
From East to West through the Panama Canal, covered 84,000 miles with his boat, in seven years.
Flyd, Bermuda sloop, 29'2" LOA.

1965–1969*
Alan Eddy (USA)
New York, Panama, Tasmanian Sea, Cape Horn, Antilles.
Apogée, fiberglass ketch, 39'7" LOA.

1965–1969*
Robin Lee Graham (USA)
At 16 years, the youngest circumnavigator. Left July 27, 1965 from California to the New Hebrides, Indonesia, South Africa. Subject of 1964 film, "The Dove."
Dove, fiberglass sloop, 23'11" LOA.

1965–1969*
Alfred Kallies (Germany)
Second German circumnavigator; on the Trade Wind route, from East to West.
Pru, double-ended, 25'1" LOA.

1966–1967*
Sir Francis Chichester (England)
Plymouth to Sydney in 107 days. Sydney to Plymouth in 118 days, rounding Cape Horn. Awarded Blue Water Medal, at age 65.
Gipsy Moth IV, 54' LOA.

1966–1969*
Leonid Teliga (Poland)
Casablanca, Panama, Fiji; return voyage non-stop to Dakar in 165 days. Casablanca on April 29, 1969.
Opty, yawl, 32'4" LOA; own construction.

1966–1970*
John Sowden (USA)
From East to West route through the Panama Canal.
Tarmin, Bermuda sloop, 24'7" LOA.

1966–1973*
Nicholas Clifton (Great Britain)
From East to West through the Panama Canal, at times with crew.
Stardrift, Bermuda cutter, 30'6" LOA.

1966–1974*
Wolfgang Hausner (Austria)
From East to West through the Panama Canal. First with a catamaran and first Austrian.
Taboo, catamaran rigged as a Bermuda sloop, 31'10" LOA.

1967–1968*
Roger Plisson (France)
Despite a broken mast, the fastest classical circumnavigation, in 18 months.
François-Virginie, sloop, 24' LOA; own construction.

1967–1968*
Sir Alec Rose (England)
Sailed July 18, 1967, at age 60, from Portsmouth, to Melbourne, December 17, 1967; Portsmouth July 4, 1968. Awarded Blue Water Medal.
Lively Lady, yawl, 36' LOA.

1967–1970*
Rollo Gebhard (Germany)
Fourth German to circumnavigate the world; departed December 12, 1967 from the Canary Islands, then to Barbados, Panama, Galapagos, Tahiti, Port Moresby, Thursday Island, Durban.
Solveig III, fiberglass sloop, 24'3" LOA.

1968–1969*
Robin Knox-Johnston (England)
The first to circumnavigate the world non-stop in 313 days.
Suhaili, ketch, 32'6" LOA.

1968–1969*
Bernard Moitessier (France)
Longest non-stop voyage in seafaring history, over 38,000 miles.
Joshua, ketch, 39'7" LOA.

1968–1969*
Nigel Tetley (Great Britain)
First circumnavigation in a trimaran. His boat sank in a storm off the Azores.
Victress, trimaran, 33'5" LOA.

1968–1971*
Tom Blackwell (Great Britain)
Largest yacht to sail around the world by way of the Panama Canal.
Islander, ketch, 58'7" LOA.

1970–1971*
Chay Blyth (Great Britain)
Non-stop circumnavigation from East to West, through the "roaring forties," in 292 days.
British Steel, ketch, 59' LOA.

1970–1971*
Bill King (Great Britain)
First Irish single-handed circumnavigator.
Galway Blazer II, junk-rigged schooner, 42' LOA.

1971–1972*
Jörgen Meyer (Germany)
Fifth German single-handed circumnavigator; fastest circumnavigation on the Equator route, only three stops; sailed over 30,000 miles in 349 days.
Paloma, sloop, 34'7" LOA.

1971–1973*
Göran Cederström (Sweden)
First Swedish single-handed circumnavigator.
Tua Tua, sloop, 27'5" LOA.

1971–1974*
Hiroshi Aoki (Japan)
Smallest boat around Cape Horn and second smallest to sail around the world.
Ahodori II, yawl, 21'1" LOA.

1971–1974*
Graeme Dillon (Great Britain)
From East to West through the Panama Canal, at times with crew.
Mayfly, gaff cutter, 29'11" LOA.

1972–1973*
Krystof Baranowsky (Poland)
From Hobart (Tasmania) to Cape Horn in 45 days.
Polonez, ketch, 45'3" LOA.

1972–1975*
Richard Konkolski (Czechoslovakia)
From East to West route through the Panama Canal.
Nike, yawl, 24'4" LOA.

1972–1975*
John Struchinsky (France)
From East to West route through the Panama Canal.
Bonaventure de Lys, 25'3" LOA.

1973–1974*
Alain Colas (France)
Fastest single-handed voyage, in 167 days.
Manureva, ketch rigged trimaran, 70' LOA.

Ambrogio Fogar (Italy)
First Italian circumnavigator.
Surprise, sloop, 38'9" LOA.

Kenichi Horie (Japan)
Fastest voyage from East to West, in 275 days.
Mermaid III, sloop, 28'1" LOA.

Ryusuke Ushijima (Japan)
West to East around Cape Horn.
Gingitsune, ketch, 31' LOA.

1973–1976*
Paul Graute (Germany)
From Cuxhaven, via the Panama Canal, Cape Town, Azores, to Leboe; covered a total of 35,000 miles.
Albatros, sloop, 28'8" LOA.

1974–1975*
Julius Heinrich Henze (Germany)
From East to West through the Panama Canal, at times with crew.
Leda II, Bermuda sloop, 24'7" LOA.

1974–1976*
Utz Müller-Treu (Germany)
From Bremen, August 10, 1975, via Falmouth, Las Palmas, Barbados, Panama Canal, Durban, Cape Town to Helgoland July 7, 1976.
Frauken, cutter, 39'4" LOA.

1976–1977*
Krystyna Chojnowska-Liekiewicz (Poland)
From East to West through the Panama Canal. Starting and finishing point Las Palmas. 723 days. First woman to accomplish a single-handed circumnavigation.
Mazurek

1977–1978*
Naomi James (New Zealand)
First woman to sail single-handed on the Cape Horn route. 272 days. Stopped only in Cape Town and Port Stanley.
Express Crusader, 53'4" LOA.

AMERICA'S CUP

The America's Cup Races are among the most important sailing events in the world. In the history of this sailing sport, no equivalent races have required such an investment of time and effort, research and money — from defender and challenger alike. This race is associated with the longest uninterrupted winning streak for a single nation and yacht club.

1851:
Sixteen British yachts and the *America*, a pilot schooner-type yacht hailing from New York, race around the Isle of Wight for the 100 Guinea Cup. The trophy, a silver cup, is won by the *America*, put up by the New York Yacht Club for international competition in 1850. The race has been called the America's Cup ever since.

1870:
The British attempt for the first time to win back the America's Cup. Their *Cambria* races alone against 23 American yachts off New York and finishes in tenth place. *Magic* wins. The old *America* comes in fourth.

1871:
The British *Livonia* loses four of five races against the Cup defenders, *Columbia* and *Sappho*. The Americans race the lighter or the heavier of the two yachts, according to weather conditions in each race.

1876:
Madeline defeats the Canadian *Countess of Dufferin* in two races.

1881:
Mischief defeats the Canadian *Atalanta* in two races.

1885:
The British return. Their *Genesta* loses in two races to *Puritan*.

1886:
Mayflower defeats British *Galatea* in two races.

1887:
Volunteer wins in two races against the British *Thistle*. *Thistle* is later sold to Kaiser Wilhelm and renamed *Meteor*.

1893:
The number of races necessary to win is raised to three. *Vigilant* beats the British *Valkyrie II* three times straight.

1895:
Defender beats *Valkyrie III* in three races.

1899:
Sir Thomas Lipton commences his challenges for the America's Cup on behalf of Great Britain. His *Shamrock* loses to *Columbia* in three straight races.

1901:
Columbia, already a winner in 1899, beats *Shamrock II* in three races.

1903:
Reliance, 143 feet long, beats *Shamrock III* in three straight races.

1920:
The contest planned for 1914, and canceled because of World War I, is revived. *Resolute* defeats *Shamrock IV* in three out of five races — the closest series yet.

1930:
From now on the best four out of seven races are held off Newport in a new class: the 130-foot J-boats. *Enterprise* wins in four straight races against *Shamrock V*, Lipton's last challenger.

1934:
Rainbow wins four of six races against *Endeavor*, owned by British aircraft manufacturer T.O.M. Sopwith.

1937:
Ranger beats *Endeavor II* in four races.

1958:
12-Meter yachts, about 675 feet long, are raced from now on. *Columbia*, with Briggs Cunningham, of automobile racing fame, at the helm defeats the British *Sceptre*.

1962:
The Australians pick up the fight for the America's Cup. Their *Gretel* is defeated by *Weatherly*, Bus Mosbacher at the helm, in four of five races.

1964:
Constellation, skippered by R. Bavier, wins in four races over the British *Sovereign*.

1967:
Intrepid, with Mosbacher at the helm, beats Australian *Dame Pattie* in four straight.

1970:
The French join the contest. Their *France*, property of ballpoint pen manufacturer Baron Marcel Bich, loses in the trials to Australia's *Gretel II*. In the finals, *Gretel II* is defeated by the reconstructed *Intrepid*, winner of 1967, this time with Bill Ficker at the helm, four of five races.

1974:
In the trials, *France* is defeated by *Southern Cross*, owned by Australian real estate dealer Alan Bond. The finals against the Australian yacht are won by *Courageous*, belonging to an American syndicate and skippered alternately by Dennis Conner and Ted Hood, in four races.

1977:
The Swedes challenge the America's Cup for the first time, with the Australians and the French. Their *Sverige*, financed by Swedish industry, skippered by Pelle Petterson, loses in the qualification series against *Australia*, owned by Alan Bond. The finals are won by *Courageous*, the 1974 winner, with Ted Turner at the helm, against *Australia*, in four straight races.

Handicap or Class	Year	Cup Defender/ Name of the Yacht	Skipper	Challenger/ Name of Yacht	Country	Skipper or owner	Number of races possible	Races sailed	Average Course Distance
Waterline area	1870	Magic	A. Comstock	Cambria	Great Britain	J. Linnock	1	1	35,1 nm
Displacement formula	1871	Columbia	N. Comstock	Livonia	Great Britain	J. R. Woods	5	3	36,6 nm
Displacement formula		Sappho	S. Greenwood	Livonia	Great Britain	J. R. Woods		2	37,5 nm
Volume Formula	1876	Madeleine	J. Williams	Countess of Dufferin	Canada	J. Ellsworth	3	2	36,3 nm
Volume Formula	1881	Mischief	N. Clock	Atalanta	Canada	A. Cuthbert	3	2	32,3 nm
Length and sail area	1885	Puritan	A. Crocker	Genesta	Great Britain	J. Carter	3	2	36,3 nm
Length and sail area	1886	Mayflower	M. B. V. Stone	Galatea	Great Britain	D. Bradford	3	2	36,3 nm
Length and sail area	1887	Volunteer	H. C. Haff	Thistle	Scotland	J. Barr	3	2	36,3 nm
Length and sail area	1893	Vigilant	W. Hansen	Valkyrie II	Great Britain	W. Cranfield	5	3	30,0 nm
Length and sail area	1895	Defender	H. C. Haff	Valkyrie III	Great Britain	W. Cranfield	5	3	30,0 nm
Length and sail area	1899	Columbia	C. Barr	Shamrock	Great Britain	A. Hogarth	5	3	30,0 nm
Length and sail area	1901	Columbia	C. Barr	Shamrock II	Great Britain	E. A. Sycamore	5	3	30,0 nm
Length and sail area	1903	Reliance	C. Barr	Shamrock III	Great Britain	R. Ringe	5	3	30,0 nm
Universal rule	1920	Resolute	C. F. Adams	Shamrock IV	Great Britain	W. T. Burton	5	5	30,0 nm
Universal rule, J class	1930	Enterprise	H. S. Vanderbilt	Shamrock V	Great Britain	T. Heard	7	4	30,0 nm
Universal rule, J class	1934	Rainbow	H. S. Vanderbilt	Endeavour	Great Britain	T. O. M. Sopwith	7	6	30,0 nm
Universal rule, J class	1937	Ranger	H. S. Vanderbilt	Endeavour II	Great Britain	T. O. M. Sopwith	7	4	30,0 nm
International Rule, 12-Meter class	1958	Columbia	B. S. Cunningham	Sceptre	Great Britain	G. Mann	7	5	24,0 nm
International Rule, 12-Meter class	1962	Weatherly	E. Mosbacher jr.	Gretel	Australia	J. Sturrock	7	5	24,0 nm
International Rule, 12-Meter class	1964	Constellation	R. Bavier jr.	Sovereign	Great Britain	P. Scott	7	4	24,3 nm
International Rule, 12-Meter class	1967	Intrepid	E. Mosbacher jr.	Dame Pattie	Australia	J. Sturrock	7	4	24,3 nm
International Rule, 12-Meter class	1970	Intrepid	W. Ficker	Gretel II	Australia	J. Hardy	7	5	24,3 nm
International Rule, 12-Meter class	1974	Courageous	T. Hood	Southern Cross	Australia	J. Hardy	7	4	24,3 nm
International Rule, 12-Meter class	1977	Courageous	T. Turner	Australia	Australia	A. Bond	7	4	24,3 nm

THE FASTNET RACE

The oldest regularly held distance race in European waters is the Fastnet Race. From 1925 to 1931 the race was held yearly, and then every two years, starting in 1933. Only one yacht ever succeeded in winning the Fastnet Race three times: *Jolie Brise*, 1925, 1929 and 1930. The field sometimes consisted of fewer than ten boats. Then, in 1975, 288 yachts started. The race is open to all seagoing yachts, which are handicapped by The International Offshore Rule, and is sailed on corrected time. The fastest time on the 605-mile course was clocked in 1971 by *American Eagle*, a converted 12-Meter racing yacht. Skippered by Ted Turner, she took 3 days, 7 hours, 11 minutes, and 58 seconds — an average speed of 8.05 knots.

Year	Winning Yacht	Country	Owner
1925	*Jolie Brise*	Great Britain	E. G. Martin
1926	*Ilex*	Great Britain	Royal Engineer Yacht Club
1927	*Tally Ho*	Great Britain	Lord Stalbrigde
1928	*Nina*	USA	Paul Hammond
1929	*Jolie Brise*	Great Britain	Robert Somerset
1930	*Jolie Brise*	Great Britain	Robert Somerset
1931	*Dorade*	USA	R. Stephens
1933	*Dorade*	USA	R. and O. J. Stephens
1935	*Stormy Weather*	USA	P. Le Boutillier
1937	*Zeearend*	The Netherlands	C. Bruynzeel
1939	*Bloodhound*	Great Britain	Isaac Bell
1947	*Myth of Malham*	Great Britain	J. H. Illingworth
1949	*Myth of Malham*	Great Britain	J. H. Illingworth
1951	*Yeoman*	Great Britain	O. A. Aisher
1953	*Favona*	Great Britain	Sir Michael Newton
1955	*Carina*	USA	Richard S. Nye
1957	*Carina*	USA	Richard S. Nye
1959	*Anitra*	Sweden	S. Hansen
1961	*Zwerver*	The Netherlands	W. N. H. van der Vorm
1963	*Clarion of Wight*	Great Britain	D. Boyer and D. Miller
1965	*Rabbit*	USA	R. E. Carter
1967	*Pen Duick III*	France	Eric Tabarly
1969	*Red Rooster*	USA	R. E. Carter
1971	*Ragamuffin*	Australia	S. Fischer
1973	*Saga*	Brazil	E. Lorentzen
1975	*Golden Delicious*	Great Britain	P. Nicholson
1977	*Imp*	USA	D. Allen

THE ADMIRAL'S CUP

In 1957, five members of the Royal Ocean Racing Club (R.O.R.C.), among them Admiral Sir Myles Wyatt, originated the Admiral's Cup. They thus created the most important international offshore series. Each participating country can enter up to three yachts, with an I.O.R. rating of between 30 and 44 feet. The competition consists of five races: the Channel Race (220 miles), three inshore day races, and the Fastnet Race (605 miles).

Year	Top Yacht	Skipper	Winning Country
1957	*Myth of Malham*	John Illingworth/ Peter Green	Great Britain
	Uomie	Selwyn Slater	
	Jocasta	Geoff Pattinson	
1959	*Myth of Malham*	John Illingworth/ Peter Green	Great Britain
	Griffin II	Gerald Potter	
	Ramrod	Selwyn Slater	
1961	*Windrose*	Jakob Isbrandtsen	USA
	Figaro	Richard Nye	
	Cyane	Henry B. du Pont	
1963	*Noryema III*	Ron Amey	Great Britain
	Clarion of Wight	Dennis Miller/ Derek Boyer	
	Outlaw	Max Aitken	
1965	*Firebrand*	Dennis Miller	Great Britain
	Quiver IV	Ren Clarke	
	Noryema IV	Ron Amey	
1967	*Mercedes III*	Ted Kaufmann	Australia
	Balandra	Robert Creighton-Brown	
	Caprice du Huon	Gordon Ingate/ Gordon Reynolds	
1969	*Red Rooster*	Dick Carter	USA
	Carina	Dick Nye	
	Palawan	Thomas J. Watson, jun.	
1971	*Cervantes IV*	Bob Watson	Great Britain
	Morning Cloud	Edward Heath	
	Prospect of Whitby	Arthur Slater	
1973	*Saudade*	Albert Büll	Germany
	Rubin	Hans-Otto Schümann	
	Carina III	Dieter Monheim	
1975	*Battlecry*	I. O. Prentice	Great Britain
	Noryema	Ron Amey	
	Yeoman XX	R. Aisher	
1977	*Marionette*	C. A. F. Dunning	Great Britain
	Moonshine	J. Rogers	
	Yeoman XX	R. Aisher	

SOUTHERN CROSS CUP

The Southern Cross series is the Australian counterpart of the Admiral's Cup. Several inshore and offshore races of varying distances take place. It is held every second year.

Year	Winning Yacht	Skipper	Country
1967	Mercedes III	Ted Kaufman	Australia
	Moonbird	Norm Brooker	
	Calliope	Charlie Middleton	
1969	Ragamuffin	Syd Fisher	Australia
	Mercedes III	Ted Kaufman	
	Boambillee	Vince Walsh	
1971	Pathfinder	Brin Wilson	New Zealand
	Runaway	John Lidgard	
	Wai-Aniwa	Ray Walker/ Chris Bouzaid	
1973	Prospect of Whitby	Arthur Slater	Great Britain
	Quailo III	Donald Parr	
	Superstar	Alan Graham/ Dave Johnson	
1975	Prospect of Ponsonby		New Zealand
	Quick Silver	Brin Wilson	
	Tempo		
1977	Jenny H	Ray Hasler	New Zealand
	Smir-Noff-Agen	Don Lidgard	
	Swuzzle Buddle	Jan Gibbs	

THE ONION PATCH RACES

The series for the Onion Patch Trophy is comparable to the Admiral's Cup. National teams of three boats each sail several triangle and offshore races on Long Island Sound and off Newport, R.I. The longest race of the series is the Newport — Bermuda race. This series is held in even numbered years.

Year	Winning Yachts	Skipper	Country
1964	Reindeer	E. Newbold Smith	USA
	Prim	Sonny Neff	
	Shearwater	Thomas Young	
1966	Firebrand	Dennis Miller	Great Britain
	Noryema IV	Ron Amey	
	Assegai	Mike Vernon	
1968	Thunderbird	Vince Learson	USA
	Robin	Ted Hood	
	Inverness	Bob McCullough	
1970	Carina	Dick Nye	USA
	Equation	Jack Potter	
	Bay Bea	Pat Haggerty	
1972	Charisma	Jesse Philips	USA
	Yankee Girl	David Steere	
	Aura	Wally Stenhouse	
1974	Scaramouche	Charles Kirsch	USA
	Dynamite	Llywd Ecclestone	
	Harpoon	Mark Ewing	
1976	Williwaw	Lowell North	USA
	Rattler	Robin Doyle	
	Tenacious	Ted Turner	

SOUTHERN OCEAN RACING CONFERENCE (S.O.R.C.)

The S.O.R.C. consists of a total of six races varying in length from 70 to 405 miles and held every February off Florida and the Bahamas.

Year	Winning Yachts	Skipper	Country
1947	Ciclon	Gomez-Mena/ Bustamante	Cuba
1948	Stormy Weather	Fred Temple	USA
1949	Tiny Teal	Langdon/Bertram	USA
1950	Windigo	Walter Gubelmann	USA
1951	Belle of the West	Will Erwin	USA
1952	Caribbee	Carleton Mitchell	USA
1953	Caribbee	Carleton Mitchell	USA
1954	Hoot Mon	Brown/Ulmer/Pirie	USA
1955	Hoot Mon	Brown/Ulmer/Pirie	USA
1956	Finisterre	Carleton Mitchell	USA
1957	Criollo	Luis Vidana	Cuba
1958	Ca Va	Hershey/Mosbacher, Jr.	USA
1959	Callooh	Brown/Mosbacher, Jr.	USA
1960	Solution	Thor H. Ramsing	USA
1961	Paper Tiger	Jack Powell	USA
1962	Paper Tiger	Jack Powell	USA
1963	Doubloon	Joe Byars	USA
1964	Conquistador	Fuller E. Callaway	USA
1965	Figaro IV	Bill Snaith	USA
1966	Vamp X	Ted Turner	USA
1967	Guinevere	George Moffett	USA
1968	Red Jacket	Perry Connolly	USA
1969	Salty Tiger	Powell/Frank	USA
1970	American Eagle	Ted Turner	USA
1971	Running Tide	Jakob Isbrandtsen	USA
1972	Condor	Hill Blackett	USA
1973	Munequita	Valley/Schreck	USA
1974	Robin Too II	Ted Hood	USA
1975	Stinger	Dennis Conner	USA

LEVEL-RATING CHAMPIONSHIPS

The first race for the One-Ton Cup was sailed by the French yacht *Belouga* on the Seine, off Paris, in 1899. The challenger was *Vectis*, hailing from Cowes. They were small open keelboats, whose rating was exactly one ton or below under current rules. The cup is now sailed for by ocean-racing boats of the same handicap rating and about 35 feet long. The value of these international invitational races lies in the fact that they are sailed with similar yachts and without time handicaps.

Spin-offs of the One Ton Cup are the Two Ton Cup, the Threequarter Ton Cup, The Half-Ton Cup, the Quarter-Ton Cup, and the Mini Ton Cup. The designations of "half," "quarter," or "three quarter" only mean that the yachts participating are respectively larger or smaller. The Two-Tonners are 40-footers. The Three Quarter Tonners are about 33 feet long. The Half-Tonners are about 30 feet, The Quarter Tonners about 25 feet, and Mini Tonners about 22 feet. Each class has its own rating.

Winner of the One–Ton Cup

Year	Sailed at	Winning Yacht	Country
1965	Le Havre	*Diana*	Denmark
1966	Kopenhagen	*Tina*	USA
1967	Le Havre	*Optimist*	Germany
1968	Helgoland	*Optimist*	Germany
1969	Helgoland	*Rainbow*	New Zealand
1971	Auckland	*Stormy Petrel*	Australia
1972	Sydney	*Wai-Aniwa*	New Zealand
1973	Porto Cervo	*Ydra*	Italy
1974	Torquay	*Gumboots*	Great Britain
1975	Newport	*Pied Piper*	USA
1976	Marseille	*Resolute Salmon*	USA
1977	Auckland	*The Red Lion*	New Zealand

Winners of the Two-Ton Cup

Year	Sailed at	Winning Yacht	Country
1967	—	*Airela*	Italy
1968	—	*La Meloria*	Italy
1971	—	*Villanella*	Italy
1972	—	*Locura*	Italy
1974	San Remo	*Aggressive*	USA
1975	Lake St. Claire	*Ricochet*	USA
1976	Kieler Förde	*Williwaw*	USA
1977		not raced	

Winners of the Three Quarter-Ton Cup

Year	Sailed at	Winning Yacht	Country
1974	Miami	*Swampfire*	USA
1975	Hanko	*Solent Saracen*	Great Britain
1976	Plymouth	*Finn Fire*	Finland
1977	La Rochelle	*Joe Louis*	France

Winners of the Half-Ton Cup

Year	Sailed at	Winning Yacht	Country
1966	La Rochelle	*Raki*	France
1967	La Rochelle	*Safari*	France
1968	La Rochelle	*Dame d'Iroise*	France
1969	Sandhamn	*Scampi*	Sweden
1970	Sandhamn	*Scampi*	Sweden
1971	Portsmouth	*Scampi III*	Sweden
1972	Marstrand	*Bes*	Denmark
1973	Hundested	*Impensable*	France
1974	La Rochelle	*North Star*	Germany
1975	Michigansee	*Foxy Lady*	Australia
1976	Triest	*Silver Shamrock*	Ireland
1977	Sydney	*Gunboat Rangiriri*	New Zealand

Winners of the Quarter-Ton Cup

Year	Sailed at	Winning Yacht	Country
1967	Breskens	*Defender*	Belgium
1968	Breskens	*Pirhana*	The Netherlands
1969	Breskens	*Listang*	Germany
1970	Travemünde	*Fleur d'Ecume*	France
1971	La Rochelle	*Ecume de Mer*	France
1972	La Rochelle	*Petite Fleur*	France
1973	Weymouth	*Eygthene*	USA
1974	Malmö	*Accent*	Sweden
1975	Le Havre	*45 Degrees South*	New Zealand
1976	Corpus Christi	*Magic Bus*	New Zealand
1977	Helsinki	*Manzanita*	Spain

THE AUTHORS

Joseph Conrad
Born Josef Konrad Korzeniowski, 1857, in the Ukraine, died 1924 in Bishoppsburne (Kent); went to sea at age 17, sailed on French and English sailing ships; became English citizen in 1889; began writing in 1894. Main works: *Mirror of the Sea, Lord Jim, The Heart of Darkness.*

Vito Dumas
Born 1900 in Argentina, died 1965; first singlehanded circumnavigation from West to East in 272 days during 1942–1943 on *Legh II*; received Blue Water Medal for his singlehanded voyages aboard *Legh I* (1931–32), *Legh II* and later *Sirio* (1955); published: *Towards the Southern Cross, On Impossible Course.*

Edward Heath
Born 1916; studied philosophy, and political and economic sciences at Oxford; leader of the (British) Conservative Party 1965–1975, Prime Minister 1970–1974; winner of the 1969 Sydney–Hobart Race as skipper of *Morning Cloud;* team captain of the British Admiral's Cup team in 1971; published *Old World, New Horizons; Sailing: A Course of My Life.*

Hans Domizlaff
Born 1892 in Frankfurt/Main, died 1971 in Hamburg; after studies in art and painting became active in the advertising business and as a consultant for heavy industry, wrote several books on mass- and advertising psychology; extensive sailing voyages; published *Dirk II, Dirk III, Passat.*

Alain Gerbault
Born 1893 in Laval, died 1941 on the Island of Timor; bridge and highway engineer pilot in the French Army, 1924 Davis Cup (tennis) winner; sailing on *Firecrest* in 1924, the first European to cross the Atlantic singlehanded in 101 days from East to West; first receiver of the Blue Water Medal; published *The Fight of the Firecrest, In Quest of the Sun.*

Neil Hollander
Born 1939 in New York; studied communications research at the University of Washington, where he taught after graduation; extended sailing voyages in the Atlantic, Pacific, and Caribbean 1973–1977; writes for various American publications and wrote *The Cook is Captain* with H. Mertes.

Svante Domizlaff
Born 1950 in Hamburg; after studying at the Staatlichen Internatsgymnasium at Castle Plöhn, became editor of *Yacht* magazine, 1972–1976; extensive offshore sailing since 1967; many journalistic contributions to domestic and foreign sailing magazines, translation of technical books, presently editor at the *Hamburger Abendblatt.*

Patrick van God
Born 1941 in Belgium, missing at sea since October 1977; dentist; won in numerous international sailing races; 1972, first to round Cape Horn in winter from East to West on board *Trismus I;* 1976, voyages to the Antarctic and South America on *Trismus II;* published *Trismus.*

Jack Knights
Born 1929 in England; lives on the Isle of Wight as a cattle farmer; participated in many sailing championships in *Finn, Dragon* and *Tempest;* winner of the German Open Tempest Championships; crew and skipper in the One-, Half- and Quarter Ton Cups; numerous contributions to international yachting magazines; author of: *Sailing Step by Step, Sail Racer.*

Robin Knox–Johnston
Born 1939 in London; entered the merchant navy 1957 and received his captain's license in 1965; built his yacht, *Suhaili* between 1963 and 1965; sailed *Suhaili* around the world in the first nonstop singlehanded circumnavigation in 312 days in 1968–69; won the Round Britain Race in 1970 and 1971, the RORC Class 1 championships in 1976; participated as a skipper in the Whitbread Around the World Race.

Georg Lauritzen
Born 1895 in Flensburg, trained on the sailing vessels *Oceana*, *R.C. Rickmers* and *Kurt* starting 1911; four Cape Horn roundings; 1914–1917, cruises on American steamers; pilot's license in 1920; promoted 1925 after studying political sciences; retired 1946 after 30 years of service with the Hamburg-America line; freelance journalist and writer since 1954.

Jochen Orgelmann
Born 1946 in Bremen; after high school, pilot training with the Lufthansa; later studied political science and law; presently active as a law clerk; member of "The Arms Seal of Bremen" (Das Wappen von Bremen); sailing fellowship since 1962; skipper since 1968; sailed to Surinam, Iceland and Spitzbergen, the Caribbean.

Hans Otto Schuman
Born 1916; son of a Hamburg merchant; apprenticed before the mast on his father's ship; since 1951, the most successful German ocean racer aboard *Rubin I* to *Rubin V*; member of numerous national and international committees on sailing; German representative of the offshore Racing Council; as vice-president of the German National Sailing Authority, responsible for the mass- and recreational aspects of the sport.

Roderick Stephens, Jr.
Born 1909 in New York; since 1933, designer for Sparkman & Stephens; now their vice president; took part in several Atlantic crossings, America's Cups, Fastnet, and Bermuda races; designer and co-designer of the America's Cup yachts *Ranger*, *Columbia*, *Constellation*, *Intrepid*, and *Courageous*.

Rudolf Koppenhagen
Born 1908 in Berlin; sailing experience from early childhood; four years of sailing ships training after attending school in Angerburg (E. Prussia); four Cape Horn roundings; attended Naval School in Bremen, later Navy officer, corvette captain, and squadron commander; participant in transatlantic Bermuda and Aguilhas races; 1963–1975, director of the Hanseatic yacht School in Germany.

David Lewis
Born 1919 in England; doctor; participant in the first singlehanded transatlantic race, 1960; abandoned his medical practice in 1964 and initiated a three-year world circumnavigation with his family, in a catamaran; 1972–74 singlehanded on the steel sloop *Ice Bird* from Sydney to Cape Town; presently living on an island in the vicinity of Sydney; published *Daughters of the Wind*, *Ice Bird*.

Hans Rudolf Rösing
Born 1905 in Wilhelmshaven; entered the Imperial navy in 1924; squadron commander and staff duty with U-boats; starting 1952, active at Amt Blank, elaborating the first shipbuilding programs there; commanding officer of Defense sector 1 until 1965; 1967–1972, involved in the creation of the Olympic exhibition at Kiel, "The World of Sailing" translated technical books; consultant to German Shipping Museum.

Ludwig Schlimbach
Born 1876 in Munich, died 1949 in Hamburg; after seven years aboard foreign square-riggers; officer for the Hamburg-America Line starting 1900; captain of the passenger steamer *Oceana*; singlehanded from Hamburg to New York in 35 days on *Stortebecker I*, 1935; participant in the 1935 Newport-Bergen and the 1936 Bermuda-Cuxhaven races.

Erling Tambs
Born 1888 in Larvig, Norway, died 1967 in Nevlungshaven; spent his youth in Flensburg; many years of voyaging on sailing ships; captain's license; first extended cruise with wife and children on the 37-ft. pilot cutter *Teddy* from Oslo to the south Pacific; Atlantic crossing from East to West with the ketch *Sandfjord* in 1935; published *Wedding Trip–And How*, *Cruises of Terror*.

Kai Krüger
Born 1934 in Hamburg; after receiving a business education, spent five years in South America, then business manager and editor-in-chief of *Yacht*; later free-lance writer for *Die Zeit*, *"stern," GEO*; reporter for *"stern"* since 1977; participant in numerous international championships on *Stars* and *Finns*.

Harald Mertes
Born 1943 in Trier; studied journalism and ethnology at the University of Mainz; after concluding his studies, engaged in a three-year sail of approximately 25,000 nautical miles through the Atlantic and Pacific; presently a freelance journalist for sail and travel publications at home and abroad; author with N. Hollander, of *The Cook is Captain*.

Alexander Rost
Born 1924 in Konigswusterhausen; education as a ships officer (sailing vessel experience) until in 1947, he became a captain in the International Mine Sweeper Service; journalist, after studies in Kiel; winner of the Theodor Wolf Award 1964; wrote technical books on seafaring and sailing under the pseudonym Peder Pedersen; presently an editor, living in Hamburg.

Joshua Slocum
Born 1844 in Wilmont, Canada, lost at sea 1909; at 25, captain of the barque *Washington*; lost his ship *Aquidneck* at Rio de Janeiro 1887; built yacht *Liberdade* from the wreckage; he sailed *Liberdade* to the States; first singlehanded world circumnavigation on the yawl *Spray*; published: *The Voyage of the Liberdade*, *Sailing Alone Around the World*.

NAME INDEX

SHIP INDEX

CREDITS

PHOTOS

Cover photo: Bob Fisher, London

Agence cedri, Paris
Facque: 146, 147; Quéméré: 140, 140, 140/141; Rubinstein: 144/145

Agence TOP, Paris
Czap: 36

Beken of Cowes, Isle of Wight/
England
21, 62/63, 64, 65, 66/67, 68, 69, 70, 71, 72/73, 74/75, 76, 85, 86, 86/87, 90, 92/93, 94/95, 96/97, 129, 138, 139, 151, Vor-und Nachsatz

Alastair Black, Lee-on-Solent/
England
102

Camera Press, London
216/217

Gerry Cranham, Coulsdon
Surrey/
England
170/171

J. Eastland, Southsea/England
168/169, 218, 218

Bob Fisher, London
177

Daniel Forster, Murten/Schweiz
104, 104/105, 150, 175, 241, 284, 284, 284/285, 288/289

Ambrose Greenway/Popperfoto,
London
172/173, 242/243, 292

Guy Gurney, London
104, 150/151, 174, 176/177

Rudolf Koppenhagen, Glücksburg
132/133

Georg Lauritzen, Hamburg
130, 130, 131, 215

Robin Leach, London
25

Harald Mertes, Koblenz
244/245

Mertes-Archiv, Koblenz
213, 214, 214, 214

Carl Emil Petersen, Oslo
21, 22/23, 26/27, 30/31, 32/33, 33, 34/35, 252/253, 254, 255, 255, 256

Revue Neptune Nautisme/foto-
loisirs, Paris
216, 216, 220
Black: 152; de Constantin: 24/25; Deguy: 148/149, 286/287; van God: 250/251; de Greef: 25, 175, 218; Loizeau: 28/29, 144, 282/283, 289; Moitessier: 219; Rubinstein: 142/143

Morris Rosenfeld & Sons, Inc.
New York
68, 86, 88/89, 90, 91, 95, 98, 98/99, 100, 100, 101, 102, 103, 106/107, 108, 152/153, 273, 274, 275, 280, 281

Roger M. Smith of Cowes, Isle of
Wight/England
156, 180, 290/291

stern/Baumann, Hamburg
154/155

Ulf Vagt, Bremen
249

Hans-Georg Will, Düsseldorf
246, 246, 247, 248/249, 249

Yacht Photo Service, Hamburg
134, 135, 136/137, 165, 166/167, 170, 177, 178, 178/179, 276/277, 278/279, 281

ILLUSTRA-
TIONS

The drawings in this book were assembled and edited by Christel Hudemann-Schwartz. They were prepared by or reprinted courtesy of the following sources:

For the article by Hans-Rudolf Rosing:
Figs. 1-4: Seglers Handbuch 1897.
Fig. 5: Ludwig Dinklage, Ozean-Wettfahrten, Bremen 1936.
Fig. 6: Reprinted courtesy of Horst E. Glacer, Garlstedt.
Fig. 7: Rerinted courtesy of Carsten Wagner, Hamburg-Schenfeld.
Fig. 8: Reprinted courtesy of Christel Hudemann-Schwartz, Hamburg.

For the article by Jack Knights:
Figs. 1-4: Carlo Sciarelli, Die Yacht, Bielefeld/Berlin 1973, S. 207, 214, 369. With courtesy of Verlags Delius, Klasing & Co., Bielefeld.

For the article by Ludwig Schlimbach:
Artwork reprinted courtesy of Georg Lauritzen, Hamburg.

For the article by Roderick Stephens, Jr.:
Figs. 1-3: Reprinted courtesy of Overijsselse Jachtwerf W. Huisman BV, Vollenhove/Holland und Sparkman & Stephens, Inc., New York.

ACKNOWL-
EDGMENTS

The publisher acknowleges permission to reprint the following articles.

Macmillan Publishing Co., Inc., for permission to reprint "Sea Fever" by John Masefield. Copyright 1913 by *Harper's* Magazine, copyright 1949, 1951 by John Masefield. Reprinted with permission of Macmillan Publishing Co., Inc.

W:W. Norton & Company, Inc., for selections from *Ice Bird* by David Lewis. Copyright 1975 by David Lewis. Reprinted with permission of the publisher.

Granada Publishing Limited, for selections from *Dead Man's Road* by Vito Dumas, translated by Captain Raymond Johnes. Reprinted with permission of the publisher.

TRANS-
LATORS

The articles in this book were translated by the following persons: Andrei Campeanu, Robert Kimber, and Mary Selo-Fralin. The publisher also acknowledges the help of John Rousmaniere for his comments and suggestions.

PRODUC-
TION

Designed by Jan Buchholz and Reni Hinsch.
Printed by Graphic Litho Corp., Lawrence, Massachusetts